MW01595038

The Giver...
and His Gifts

An In-Depth Study of the
25 Gifts of the Holy Spirit

By:

Pastor Ernie Gruen

The Giver... and His Gifts

An In-Depth Study of the 25 Gifts of the Holy Spirit
© Copyright 2000 by Pastor Ernie Gruen
7819 Twilight Lane
Lenexa, KS 66217-9405

ISBN: 0-9701629-1-X

Published by:
GRACE PUBLICATIONS
8948 SW Barbur Blvd., #86
Portland, OR 97219

First Printing 2000

PRINTED IN THE UNITED STATES OF AMERICA

DEDICATION

When the prodigal son returned to his home, the Father ran down the path to meet him. "When he was still a great way off, his father saw him and had compassion, and ran and fell on his neck and kissed him."

God is like that! God forgave the son who failed easily, quickly, and totally.

Not only so, the Father gave him:

- The best robe (the robe of righteousness i.e. justification);
- The signet right (the restoration of authority and the right to use His name);
- Sandals on his feet (the restoration of his walk in the Spirit);
- And finally, the fatted calf was slain for a huge party of celebration thrown by Father God (the restoration of joy) — "Let us eat and be merry; for this my son was dead and is alive again; he was lost and is found." And they began to be merry!

My wife, Delores has loved me in the same manner as Father-God: easily, quickly, totally, and with full joy.

I dedicate this book about the "grace gifts" of God to her. Of all the gifts of God's grace – Delores my wife of 43 years is the choicest!

Dee, I dedicate this book to you with all gratefulness and thankfulness!

A VERY SPECIAL THANKS TO . . .

the faithful saints at Faith Fellowship of Love in Osawatomie, Kansas who allowed me to write this book while being their pastor:

Tex and Margie Thompson;

Forest and Eula Wollard;

Vickie Arnold;

Richard, Mary, and B. J. Botteron;

Ron and Martha Brotheron;

Jim, Diana, Isaac, Lauren, Risa,

Jessalyn, Emily and Libby Conard;

Geoff and Liz D'Urso;

Keith and Peggy Duensing;

Mike and Vicki Eastwood;

Patsy Gladfelder;

Vernon and Carol Kauffman;

Vince and Joy King;

Patty Ogden;

David and Marlene O'Neal;

Francis, Donna and Cris Richert;

Mike, Carol and Rebecca Richey;

Rhonda Ryan;

Randy and Bonnie Ward;

Gloria Weaver;

Don White;

Linda Wilkerson;

and George and Glenda Williams.

FOREWORD

Over twenty-five years ago our family moved to the community where we live. Not long after our arrival I began to hear of a Spirit-filled church that was large and growing. The pastor was Ernie Gruen. He was a visionary; he was overseeing the care of a large congregation; he was known for his thorough, Biblical teaching. For the last fifteen or so years Ernie has become my dearly loved friend. I respect his life-style before God and man.

I have a natural skepticism for those I don't know. However, when I read his first book several years before we became friends I found myself relaxing. It was just excellent, sound, spiritual food. Ernie was especially astute when the Holy Spirit was flowing through him and those around him with the Gifts of the Spirit. For instance he had managed to provide freedom for the speaking gifts in a congregation of several thousand people. No small feat.

The main quality that commends this book to you is the humility, earnestness, and intensity with which Ernie approaches the scripture. He is a very gifted Bible student and researcher. When all these traits are joined, the result is the thorough, well-balanced treatment of the subject that you have in your hand.

Rev. Bill Newby, M. Min.

Pastor of Central Assembly of God

Raytown, MO 64133

Assistant Superintendent

Southern Missouri District of the Assemblies of God

ACKNOWLEDGMENTS

Without the encouragement, support, and generosity of Leonard and Shay Hoffman of Addison Texas, this book would literally, have not come into existence.

Leonard and Shay love to minister, holding meetings a little bit everywhere, but especially in the prison ministry. Jesus said, "For where your treasure is, there your heart will be also!" Both their heart and treasure are in "ministry" and "service" to others. They truly lay their treasures up in heaven, rather than storing up wealth for this temporal existence. They are rich towards God.

Their help in getting this book printed and published is only the latest example of their faithfulness. Much gratitude to you Leonard and Shay for being "good and faithful servants" of the Lord Jesus!

A special note of gratefulness is expressed to Jim Conard, who spent many hours editing and proof reading this manuscript. Mere words are not adequate to communicate my thanks to you, Jim, for taking valuable time away from your law practice to assist me.

In addition, I would like to recognize and convey my appreciation to John and Virginia Conard who joined their son in providing invaluable editing. Mr. and Mrs. Conard at one time owned and published three newspapers in Kansas. I was blessed of the Lord to have access to their professionalism and expertise.

PREFACE

"For God so loved the world that He gave..." (John 3:16)

What is it about God's great love that compels Him to give so much to mankind? What does His abundance of gifts tell us about the matchless love and grace of the Giver of every good and perfect gift? There is an old hymn that goes something like this:

"For out of His infinite riches in Jesus,

> He giveth...
>> and giveth...
>>> and giveth again!"

No matter what we have received from God or what our level of growth is, He is offering us far more than we have ever dreamed of.

> *"But God, who is rich in mercy, because of His great love with which He loved us, even when we were dead in trespasses, made us alive together with Christ (by grace you have been saved), and raised us up together, and made us sit together in the heavenly places in Christ Jesus, that in the ages to come He might show the exceeding riches of His grace in His kindness toward us in Christ Jesus. For by grace you have been saved through faith, and that not of yourselves; it is the gift of God,"* (Ephesians 2:4-8).

God wants to express His great love towards each and every one of us in each and every thing we do, starting from before the foundation of the Earth and extending into eternity future.

Congratulations on choosing to receive every gift His matchless grace offers. It is an eternal journey that begins with but one step of faith - each and every moment!

It will be the most rewarding journey you'll ever take.

TABLE OF CONTENTS

CHAPTER 1

THE NEW BIRTH AND BAPTISM –
TWO DEFINITE EXPERIENCES

When I was nine years old, at a little Baptist church in Abilene, Kansas, I can still remember hearing the people sing, *"Into my heart! Into my heart! Come into my heart Lord Jesus. Come in today, come in to stay. Come into my heart Lord Jesus!"*

I don't remember exactly what the preacher said that day, but my heart felt the message of that hymn. When the preacher gave the invitation to receive Christ, I raised my hand. My brother Richard raised his hand too. Together we rose to our feet, walked to the front of the tiny sanctuary and received Jesus into our hearts. That is what happened the day my brother and I were saved.

It was not until the age of 19, a decade after my initial salvation experience, that God called me to preach. I heard His voice compelling me into His service. I had wisely refused the urging of others for me to enter the ministry, until God spoke to me personally, telling me to do just that.

It was yet another ten years, at the tender age of 29, after having pastored diligently in a Baptist church, that I began to hunger and thirst after God in a new and exciting way.

It was the night of Christmas, 1966, that I began to cry out in my need to God, saying, "I will not let You go until You bless me!"

I began to wrestle with God like Jacob did of old, and I pressed on in prayer for hours. It was during the darkest hours of that blessed night that I was baptized in the Holy Spirit. It was a distinctly different and definite experience from that night 20 years earlier, when I had first raised my hand and called on the name of the Lord, asking Him to save me. It had taken nearly two decades for me to reach that place of filling in my life and ministry. But, my intense hunger had finally been filled. Yet, I questioned in my heart, "Why did it take me so long?"

As a younger man, I had found the difference between the New Birth and the Baptism in the Holy Spirit to be very vague, and somewhat confusing. People further muddied the issues involved, because they used religious terms to explain their convictions. The words they used were vague and imprecise. To me, and indeed to most honest people, accuracy, facts and the truth are the foundational building blocks for understanding and belief.

Over the years, I have found that there is a great distinction between the Baptism in the Holy Spirit and the New Birth. Using the right words to explain what I have discovered over the years is the key to helping others understand.

You could accurately word the difference between the New Birth and the Baptism in the Holy Spirit by asking the simple question: "Do you have the Holy Spirit, or Does the Holy Spirit have you?"

You see, it is one thing to <u>have</u> Him, and quite another for Him to <u>have</u> you!

The "New Birth" is that blessed experience God designed for sinners that turns them into Christians. They are born anew, into the Kingdom of God. The New Birth turns a sinner into a Christian, whereas the Baptism in the Holy Spirit brings God's power to the Christian for God's higher purposes.

The "Baptism in the Holy Spirit" is an experience designed for Christians, to anoint them with power to live a holy life as a testimony to God, thereby enabling them to serve God and mankind out of a pure and powerful resource, God Himself.

EVERY TRUE CHRISTIAN HAS THE HOLY SPIRIT

"But you are not in the flesh but in the Spirit, if indeed the Spirit of God dwells in you. Now if anyone does not have the Spirit of Christ, he is not His" (Romans 8:9).

Christianity is not about collecting Sunday School attendance pins and scripture memorization awards. It is not learning to enunciate the correct wording of high, theological concepts or repeating a collection of sayings, verses and old stories. Becoming a "believer" in Christ through the "New Birth" is not a mental or intellectual assent to the historical proofs of Christ's existence.

Indeed we are told in Scripture, *"You believe that there is one God. You do well. Even the demons believe; and tremble!"* (James 2:19).

Christianity is actually about the blessed event when Someone Who was not within you comes to live forever on the inside of you. You are a Christian when you can honestly say, "The Spirit of God is dwelling within me." This is why the Apostle Paul declared in no uncertain terms, "If any man has not the Spirit of Christ, he does not belong to God." When Paul said this, he was speaking specifically of the NEW BIRTH.

Paul was saying that the Holy Spirit is instrumental in making each sinner into a legitimate child of Almighty God. In Paul's letter to Titus, in chapter three and verse five, he says this about Salvation, Regeneration and the Renewing Birth of a Christian: *"Not by works of righteousness which we have done, but according to His mercy He saved us, through the washing of regeneration and renewing of the Holy Spirit."* Paul said that the Holy Spirit brings about the entire process... of becoming a new life, in Christ!

It was in the Garden of Eden that Adam and Eve originally lost mankind's access to the Holy Spirit! While they managed to stay alive physically at the time, they lost their spiritual relationship with God. But, when you become a Christian there is a washing of regeneration, where you are washed by the blood of Jesus and the Holy Spirit is renewed to you.

THE EPHESUS EXPERIENCE

"And it happened, while Apollos was at Corinth, that Paul, having passed through the upper regions, came to Ephesus. And finding some disciples he said to them, 'Did you receive the Holy Spirit when you believed?' So they said to him, 'We have not so much as heard whether there is a Holy Spirit.' And he said to them, 'Into what then were you baptized?' So they said, 'Into John's baptism.' Then Paul said, 'John indeed baptized with a baptism of repentance, saying to the people that they should believe on Him who would come after him, that is, on Christ Jesus.' When they heard this, they were baptized in the name of the Lord Jesus. And when Paul had laid hands on them, the Holy Spirit came upon them, and they spoke with tongues and prophesied" (Acts 19:1-6).

It was in the course of looking at this historical account in Acts 19:1-6, that I began to realize that my journey of twenty years was not totally unique. Few people take note of the fact that these Ephesian Christians ended up waiting 23 years after Pentecost to get their filling. Talk about God's remedial training program!

When Paul first arrived he knew there was something "rotten in Denmark" because something vital was missing. Not being one to mince words, Paul directly asked them, "Did you receive the Holy Spirit when you believed?" What he heard in their reply must have been more than a little amazing!

They, the Ephesian believers, answered saying, "We haven't even heard that there is a Holy Spirit!" Paul knew they were disciples, for scripture tells us they had already "believed;" so Paul went logically to the next issue at hand in order to fill them with what was missing.

So Paul asked, perhaps incredulously, "Into what then were you baptized?"

They answered, "Into John's Baptism."

Paul, knowing they were believers, decided it was time to bring them up to speed. And like the good teacher he was, he did it quickly and clearly, with maximum impact:

"John indeed baptized with a baptism of repentance, saying to the people that they should believe on Him who would come after him, that is, on Christ Jesus. When they heard this, they were baptized in the name of the Lord Jesus" (Acts 19:4-5).

The first thing Paul did was "rebaptize" the Ephesian believers with Christian baptism in water. We can rest assured that Paul would never have baptized them if they were not already saved at this point. But Paul did not stop there. Then we see in Acts,

"...when Paul had laid hands on them, the Holy Spirit came upon them, and they spoke with tongues and prophesied. Now the men were about twelve in all" (Acts 19:6-7).

Once Paul made sure they were actually believers in Christ and had water-baptized them, he didn't simply hand them a towel and say "Praise God, brother. You're done now." Paul did something else: He laid his hands on them so that they would receive the Baptism in the Holy Spirit.

This was the first time in their life as believers that the Spirit came upon them and they spoke with other tongues and prophesied. These Ephesian believers had two distinct experiences, much like me. They were definitely born again at the time of their water baptism, if not long before. Now, two decades later, the Baptism in the Holy Spirit marked the founding of the Church and all ministry at Ephesus. Thank

God, there were twelve men to form the leadership of the Ephesus church—the strongest New Testament church. (When I was a Baptist pastor I always explained away the Baptism in the Holy Spirit as being emotional and for women.)

In Galatians 4:6-7, Paul had some more to say on the subject, *"...because you are sons, God has sent forth the Spirit of His son into your hearts, crying out, 'Abba Father!' Therefore you are no longer a slave but a son."* If you're a son, then you're also an heir of God through Christ. God has already sent the Spirit of His Son into your heart, crying, "Abba Father."

So what does it mean to be saved?

Salvation is about becoming a son of God and terminating the role of slavery to sin and death, once and for all. But the core of the issue is about the "Spirit of HIS SON" taking up residence within, forever changing the paradigm from slavery to sonship. The new life as a son comes only by receiving the Spirit of Jesus inside the heart, to live forever.

That is what is meant when we say, "Jesus comes in to your heart!" We don't mean that a miniature, physical *body* of Jesus comes mysteriously into *your* physical body. We mean that His *Spirit* comes to live inside of you. His Spirit within your heart calls out "Daddy!" to Almighty God, because it is literally just so. God really becomes the "Daddy" to all who receive the Spirit of His Precious Son. Have *you* had that experience?

In I John 5:10 we see,

> *"He who believes in the Son of God has the witness in Himself. He who does not believe, makes God a liar, because he has not believed the testimony that God has given him. This is the testimony that God has given us eternal life in His Son."*

Do you have that inside witness yourself today that you are saved? Does your heart call out to "Daddy?" It's very important that God tells you that you're saved, instead of some preacher. That's what it means to become a Christian. This is not about Church membership, Sunday School pins, religious confessions or advanced theological degrees.

PHARISEES

Nicodemus was a Pharisee. That means he was far more religious than you or I. He not only kept the ten commandments, he also followed the 613 Jewish laws. He kept *all* of them.

What an enormous pile of rules he carried around in his life! No work was to be done on God's ordained "day of rest."

Jewish law insisted you could not even carry a chair on the Sabbath, because if you did you might drop it and one leg hit the ground and that would be considered *plowing*.

And that was just *one* interpretation, on one application of the ridiculous roster of rules = the 613 laws. There were laws stipulating what type of knots you could not tie or untie on the Sabbath. You could tie a knot on a girdle, but definitely not on any kind of thing deemed to be "a rope." Ropes were used for "WORK!"

How far would *you* go to obey that law? What if your children needed water to drink, drawn from a well in your own back yard? How would you get around that one? Imaginative Pharisees tied a girdle (clothing item) to the water bucket and then tied the girdle to the rope (not the rope to the girdle) and lowered the entire mess down to get their water.

Religion still makes people crazy today! It makes them strictly *religious*, but sadly lost. "The more things change," they say, "the more they stay the same!"

Now, Nicodemus was one of this kind of guys. He was sincere, he was totally committed to God, and he was lost in the knotted insanity of religion. He interpreted, taught and likely enforced "the rules" that others had to live by. With an advanced degree in the law of the land, it is clear he was gifted, intelligent and wanted to understand the God he truly loved. He was called in scripture, "The Ruler" of the Jews and was a member of the Sanhedren, a Jewish governing council of 70.

This is the man in John 3:2-3, who,

> *"...came to Jesus by night and said to Him, 'Rabbi, we know You are a teacher come from God; for no one can do these signs that You do unless God is with Him.' Jesus answered..."*

Notice how Nicodemus never even completed a question before Jesus started feeding him the answers? Nicodemus probably didn't even know how to ask what he needed to know anyway. Religion does that to folks!

But, Jesus knew the man's heart and gave him the answer he sought, even before he could get the question out, *"...Most assuredly, I say unto you, unless one is born again, he cannot see the kingdom of God."*

A little bit later Jesus asked him incredulously, "Are you the teacher of Israel?", and Jesus used the definite article there. "Are you THE teacher of Israel and you still do not understand these things?"

You see, Nicodemus was not just a teacher, but the teacher of Israel. We can gather pretty clearly from this that Nicodemus was the *key* rabbi in Jerusalem.

Jesus said to him, "Except you are born-again, you can never see these things. They will not make sense to you."

Nicodemus wanted to know the same things that are on the hearts of men and women today: "What does it mean to be born-again? Do I have to climb into my mother's womb twice?" Jesus explained, "No... there is a physical birth and there is also a spiritual birth." This spiritual birth comes about on the specific day that a person gets saved. It is *then* that the Spirit of God comes inside to dwell.

Nicodemus was also a rich man. Prior to the resurrection story found in Matthew 28, he provided a year's worth of wages in spices just to bury Jesus. Jewish tradition tells us that he was one of the three richest people in all of Israel. Strictly religious, a member of the Sanhedrin, a political power broker, THE teacher, and yet Nicodemus was *lost*.

Jesus told Nicodemus, "you must be born-again." Jesus didn't say salvation would be nice. He didn't say it would be advantageous. He simply said, "Nicodemus, **you must** be born-again."

THE DIFFERENCE BETWEEN THE NEW BIRTH AND THE BAPTISM IN THE HOLY SPIRIT

The New Birth is the initial experience for a sinner that makes "him or her," a Christian. This is where our dealing with the Holy Spirit starts. We have an experience where someone who is not "us" comes inside of us. The very Spirit of Jesus comes to live in us. At that point we are born–again. It happens *once*, at a very definite point in time. No one is a Christian because their *parents* are Christians. Jesus said, "You must, you must be born-again."

On the other hand, the Baptism in the Holy Spirit is an experience only for the *Christian*. It is an experience that anoints a believer in Christ with power to live a holy life and witness.

We are to be baptized, immersed, covered up and dunked into the Holy Spirit. There are three possible Greek prepositions: ("meta" = with), ("sun" = with), and ("en" = in"). In the Bible, whenever it speaks of Baptism in the Holy Spirit, it always uses the preposition, "en," which means "in" the Holy Spirit. It is incorrect to say, "Baptism of the Holy Spirit" or "Baptism with the Holy Spirit," – incorrect and confusing!

Now, when I was taking a Greek class at Friends University, we had a Methodist student who tried to tell us that the Greek word "baptidzo" meant to sprinkle. Our professor said, "well, let's translate it that way in this verse."

He opened to Matthew 3:11, and paraphrased, "I sprinkle you with water and He who comes after me, who is mightier than I, He is going to sprinkle you with the Holy Spirit."

May I suggest that much of what is wrong with the Church today is that it has been only sprinkled. Many people have never had true water baptism which includes sanctification. They've never been dunked, burying the old nature. They've also never had the Baptism in the Holy Spirit, where they were held under, immersed, dunked into the Holy Spirit. Derek Prince, who taught Greek and Hebrew at Cambridge University in Britain, said that he went through every classical book, including Aristotle, Socrates, Plato, and looked at every single occurrence of the word "baptidzo" in the Greek. Never *once* was it translated in any other way than "immersed."

If you're going to have a baptism, you always have to have three things: You need a candidate, a minister and an element to be baptized into. If you were baptized in water, you were the candidate, the preacher was the minister, and the element he lowered you down into was water.

John the Baptist says, *"He who comes after me shall baptize you in the Holy Spirit."* You are the candidate, this time the minister is Jesus, and what He lowers you down into and covers you up with is the Holy Spirit.

To say that the Baptism IN the Holy Spirit is the Baptism OF the Holy Spirit is absolutely unscriptural. Jesus is the one doing the baptizing. What He's lowering you down into is the Holy Spirit. It's the "Baptism of Jesus in the Holy Spirit." It helps to remember this when reading any passage in the Bible where the word "baptize" occurs; always ask these three questions: "Who is the candidate?", "Who is the minister?" and "Into what are they being baptized?"

For example, I Corinthians 12 says the Holy Spirit baptizes us into the Body of Christ. Here, the Holy Spirit is the minister, we are the candidates and what He puts us into is the Body of Christ. Every single Christian is part of the Body of Christ. Here, the Holy Spirit is the One who has baptized us or placed us into the Body of Christ.

LAST WILL AND TESTAMENT

Jesus, prior to ascending into Heaven, commanded us to be baptized into the Holy Spirit.

"And these signs will follow those who believe: In My name they will cast out demons; they will speak with new tongues; they will take up serpents; and if they drink anything deadly, it will by no means hurt them; they will lay hands on the sick, and they will recover" (Mark 16:17-18).

Jesus did not say the signs will follow *Apostles*. He did not say they would follow *preachers*. He said these signs will follow *those who believe.*

That was Jesus talking and He wasn't confused when He said it, either! This is part of the great commission and if you're a believer these signs will follow you. Believers will cast out demons and speak in new tongues.

In the context of the great commission, the two major challenges faced by the early church when carrying the Gospel were: bad water and deadly snakes. In carrying out the great commission, Jesus said if you drink any deadly thing, it won't hurt you. If a snake bites you, it won't hurt you either. Nothing will by any means hurt you. Paul, on the island of Malta, was bitten by a poisonous viper and the natives expected him to die immediately. Instead, Paul just shook the viper off into the fire. The natives started thinking, "Well, he must be a god because he didn't die."

Today, that promise would apply to airplane crashes and car accidents. It is about divine protection.

The healing issue Jesus raised here will be dealt with later. For now, I want to continue building an understanding of the baptism into the Holy Spirit.

"Behold I send the Promise of My Father upon you; but tarry in the city of Jerusalem until you are endued (or clothed) *with power from on high"* (Luke 24:49).

Consider the point: these disciples went to the best seminary anyone could ever go to: 3½ years with Jesus Himself. They had not only "head knowledge" of God and ministry, they also had experience and living examples on a daily basis. Eating with Him. Walking with Him. Living with Him. Talking with Him. They saw the miracles. They heard His voice. They heard His teachings. But after all that training, Jesus still said, "Tarry ye until ye be endued with power from on High." If they weren't ready to go after 3½ years of training by God Himself, how much less are you and I ready to go without being endued with power. Jesus said, "Don't go anywhere. Sit down. Don't leave until..."

"And being assembled together with Jesus, He <u>*commanded*</u> *them not to depart from Jerusalem but to wait for the promise of the Father. For John truly baptized in water, but you shall be baptized with the Holy Spirit not many days from now"* (Acts 1:4-5).

When Jesus gives a command, it is always something we should take very, very seriously.

Realize this point is a fact. If they were *going* to be baptized in the Holy Spirit, that means they didn't have it yet. But, Jesus had already breathed on them and said, *"Receive the Holy Spirit,"* in John 20:22.

So here sit the disciples. They have the Holy Spirit and yet Jesus said that they were going to be *baptized* in the Holy Spirit not many days from now.

"But you shall receive power when the Holy Spirit has come upon you; and you shall be witnesses to Me

in Jerusalem, and in all Judea and Samaria, and to the end of the earth" (Acts 1:8).

Power to witness, power to live a Christian life. You need to receive this! It's a command from Jesus Himself.

Have you had these two experiences: being born OF the Spirit of God and being baptized IN the Spirit of God? They are two *separate* experiences.

In John 14:15-17, Jesus said,

> *"If you love Me, keep My commandments. And I will pray the Father, and He will give you another Helper, that He may abide with you forever; the Spirit of truth, whom the world cannot receive, because it neither sees Him nor knows Him; but you know Him, for He dwells with you and will be in you."*

This is a great verse because Jesus said He was going to give us another Helper. And He says that Helper is the Holy Spirit. The Helper is the third person of the Trinity.

And Jesus said that, *"He will abide with you forever."* We do not have a "come and go" Holy Spirit. The Holy Spirit doesn't leave when you sin. The Holy Spirit doesn't leave when you fail. The Holy Spirit doesn't leave when you fall short. The reason we feel so miserable is not that the Holy Spirit left, but that He stayed inside us and is mourning. *"And do not grieve the Holy Spirit of God, by whom you were sealed for the day of redemption"* (Ephesians 4:30).

Now every phrase in these verses is important. First of all, Jesus said, "The world can't receive the Holy Spirit." They neither recognize Him, nor can they know Him. But Jesus said, "You know Him, because He dwells with you and He shall be in you."

Now let's take a quick look at John 20:21-22. This is the post-resurrection appearance of Jesus where He came through the doors that were closed.

"So Jesus said to them again, 'Peace to you! As the Father has sent Me, I also send you.' And when He had said this, He <u>breathed</u> on them, and said, 'Receive the Holy Spirit.'"

Now, this verse proves the deity of Jesus. A pastor or preacher may breathe on you and the most you will get is his halitosis. The Greek word used for "breathed" in verse 22 is "infusao." It literally means, "to blow or breathe upon." We get words such as "infusing" and "infused" from it. This word was only used once in the Septuagint (that's the Greek translation of the Old Testament). That one time it was used in the Old Testament was when God breathed into Adam and he became a living man. As the original creation of man was completed by an act of infusion of life by God, so the "new creation" was completed by an infusive act from the living Head of the Church, Jesus Christ.

Jesus had already said to His disciples, before His death at Calvary, "The Holy Spirit was with you, but He will soon be in you." Now, after the resurrection He breathed on them and said, "Receive ye the Holy Spirit." Obviously, at that point they received the Holy Spirit and were definitely born again of the Spirit of God! This is important to note because this event was before Pentecost.

This upsets some people's theology, but the truth is the disciples had the Holy Spirit in them <u>before</u> Acts chapter 2.

This also proves that the Day of Pentecost event recorded in scripture was a second distinct experience for the disciples.

The obvious conclusion is this: if these disciples, hand-picked, hand-chosen and hand-trained by Jesus at the best seminary in this world needed something more than just the New Birth, how much more do we need it today?

Look again at what Jesus said in Luke 24:49,

"Behold, I send the Promise of My Father upon you; but tarry in the city of Jerusalem until you be endued with power from on high."

Have you ever been with someone as they passed on? If you have been, you would know that their last words to you would have special importance to you. Similarly, Luke 24 is the last thing our Savior said before He ascended into Heaven. He said, "Tarry until you be endued or clothed with power from on high."

If you have never experienced the Baptism in the Holy Spirit, don't be so audacious, so presumptuous, as to say, "I got it all when I was saved."

The Apostles didn't get it all, and they already had the Holy Spirit.

The issue is not, do we have *Him*, but rather, does He have *us*! As God breathed on Adam and Eve, thus infusing them with His life, they became living souls. The Son of God breathed on His disciples in John 20 and we see they were spiritually born-again.

Isn't it interesting that after all of that, Jesus told them twice to wait for the promise of power from on high? In Luke 24 and again in Acts 1:4, Jesus insists that they stay put in that upper room waiting.

Let's look at Acts 1:4-5 again. It says,

> *"And being assembled together with them, Jesus commanded them not to depart from Jerusalem, but to wait for the Promise of the Father, 'which,' He said, 'you have heard from Me; for John truly baptized with water, but you shall be baptized with the Holy Spirit not many days from now.'"*

IN THE TONGUE!

So, here we have the disciples and other believers waiting in the upper room, in Acts 2. We know by reading on that there were "the twelve," Jesus' brothers, Mary (His mother) with the women, totaling 120 men and women.

> *"When the Day of Pentecost had fully come, they were all with one accord in one place. And suddenly*

there came a sound from heaven, as of a rushing
mighty wind, and it filled the whole house where they
were sitting. Then there appeared to them divided
tongues, as of fire, and one sat upon each of them.
And they were all filled with the Holy Spirit and began
to speak with other tongues, as the Spirit gave them
utterance" (Acts 2:1-4).

This is a very important passage of scripture. The last
mention of Mary, His mother, is as she is praying in tongues
in the upper room. Acts 1:14, *"These all continued with one*
accord in prayer and supplication, with the women and Mary
the mother of Jesus, and with His brothers." That is
astounding. Notice all of Jesus' natural brothers were there as
well, which would include the authors of the New Testament
books of James and Jude. All of Jesus' brothers received the
Baptism! There were 120 key people in the upper room who
experienced receiving the Baptism in the Holy Spirit.

The Bible tells us that first of all there came a sound from
heaven of a mighty, rushing wind. I always think of a Kansas
wind storm or Texas tornadoes as I read that. I've lived my
whole life in the state of Kansas. I know what real wind is
like.

I can almost hear John say to Peter, "Shut the window,
Peter." And chagrined, Peter would reply, "It's already shut
John!" The manifest presence of God was moving in on them.
Then they saw something that stunned them, *"Then there*
appeared to them divided tongues, as of fire, and one sat upon
each of them" (Acts 2:3).

One day I was reading this passage and the Lord spoke to
me and He said, "Fire is in the tongue," (James said so in
James 3:6).

The gift of tongues is not the least of the gifts, because
tongues is prayer! When you pray in the Spirit, it will loose a
word of wisdom, a word of knowledge or the discerning of

spirits. It will loose healings and miracles. Tongues can be thought of as the <u>gateway</u> to operating in all the other gifts.

Tongues is most powerful in private, in our prayer closet or while driving to work. When you pray in tongues, many times the English interpretation will come right back to you. You gain astounding insights as you flow with God in prayer.

At the risk of making a point, if God didn't do something with our tongue when He filled us with the Holy Spirit, God would risk becoming an utter failure. The tongue is the unruly member of our body. With the tongue we criticize and run people down. With our tongue we backbite, complain and whine, gossip and slander.

We can cut people to pieces with our tongue like a sword. It is only after receiving the power from above and God's saving grace that our tongue can be used to praise God perfectly with our Holy Spirit-given language.

POWER OVER EMOTIONS

When we start to get angry, if we'll quietly turn on the prayer language of the Spirit within us, our whole Spirit will sweeten up.

One day, I was in the parking lot of a grocery store. A guy almost ran into my car as my wife and I were pulling out. I said, "Where did he get his driver's license? In the cereal box?" I was starting to heat up inside, when I suddenly felt peace. I asked, "Dear, are you praying in tongues?" My wife answered, "How did you know?" I said, "I just couldn't stay upset any longer."

Tongues bring a divine flow of God's love and peace. In Jude 1:20-21 it says, "*...praying in the Holy Spirit, keep yourselves in the love of God.*"

The gift of tongues is a supernatural way to directly connect with God. We will explore praying in tongues during a church assembly and supernatural interpretation of tongues in a little bit.

IN THE PRESENCE OF OTHERS

Notice also that when those in the upper room received, they were sitting. We read, *"...as of a rushing mighty wind, and it filled the whole house where* <u>*they were sitting*</u>*."* They were not doing something stupid. They were not even standing, just sitting calmly. And, as they did, the Holy Spirit fell upon them.

It is quite normal to receive the baptism of the Holy Spirit while sitting in a church meeting as someone is teaching and explaining the Holy Spirit to you. Receiving very calmly and sweetly is the normal experience of most believers.

SAMARITANS

In Acts 8, we see where Philip went on an evangelistic mission to a city called Samaria. Verse 6 confirms that the multitudes heeded what he was preaching. He did miracles and cast out demons, which came out of the possessed, screaming with loud voices. Quite a revival seemed to be going on there!

The paralyzed and lame were healed. These were not "curing-of-headache" types of miracles, but visible, indisputable feats of divine power taking place. Even the town sorcerer named Simon, who practiced witchcraft, was supposedly converted. The entire city opened up to Philip as he preached concerning the Kingdom of God and the name of Jesus Christ. His message was not an Old Testament message!

The end of verse 12 reveals that the new believers were also being water-baptized.

Now, would you be satisfied with such a revival? It says the multitude "with one accord gave heed." The <u>whole city</u> was converted to Christ, but the Apostles were emphatically dissatisfied with this revival. This Samaritan group was the equivalent of a typical evangelical church. At this point, the

Samaritans were like the Baptists. They had been converted and they had been water-baptized.

I myself was raised and ordained as a Baptist. But when the Apostles, who were in Jerusalem, heard that Samaria had received the Word of God, they sent Peter and John, who were two Holy Ghost heavyweights, who came down and prayed for them that they might receive the Holy Spirit.

The Samaritans had already received the Holy Spirit at the time of their salvation. Philip wouldn't have baptized them if they hadn't yet accepted Jesus. The Bible says, however, that the Apostles came and prayed that they might receive the Holy Spirit. *"For as yet He had fallen upon none of them"* (Acts 8:16).

Until that point, the believers had been born again and baptized in the name of the Lord. Then, when Peter and John laid hands on them, they received the Holy Spirit. Philip got them saved, but they were not Baptized in the Holy Spirit yet. So Peter and John, the writers of seven books in the New Testament went up and said, "We're going to lay hands on you so that you can receive the Holy Spirit."

The Samaritans are yet another scriptural example of believers in Christ receiving a second definite experience at the hands of the apostles. They were baptized in the Holy Spirit.

GREEK WORD LOGOS

It appears that even Philip was for some reason unable to do what the apostles did. Now, Simon the sorcerer, a recent convert, also wanted the power to give this gift. He wanted to be in control of God's power. In Acts 8:19 Simon asked, *"Give me this power also, that anyone on whom I lay hands may receive the Holy Spirit,"* offering the apostles cash for the privilege. Verses 20-21 report,

"But Peter said to him, 'Your money perish with you, because you thought the gift of God could be

purchased with money! You have neither part nor portion in this matter, for your heart is not right in the sight of God."

The Greek word used for "matter" here is "logos." "You have neither part nor lot in these words."

What had Simon seen previously? He had seen demons scream as they were cast out. He'd seen cripples walk. And yet, when the Holy Spirit fell, he got so excited, because to his view, the Baptism in the Holy Spirit was greater to him than all the miracles, healings and even an entire town accepting Christ! He saw and heard the Samaritans speaking in tongues!

Pat Robertson, a tremendous Greek Scholar (a Southern Baptist by denomination) indicates that there is no doubt that the use of the Greek word, "logos," here refers to the fact that these Samaritans were speaking in tongues. So, the Samaritans were saved and water baptized, and then they received a definite experience of the Baptism in the Holy Spirit that was accompanied by speaking in other tongues.

PERSONAL TESTIMONY

I was preaching a revival one day in a Baptist church in Kansas.

A Pentecostal couple attending that church came to me and asked, "Ernie, have you ever received the Baptism in the Holy Spirit and spoken in tongues?"

I replied, "No, because I don't believe in it."

After one particular service, they said, "If we show you an indisputable passage of scripture that shows there is a second, definite experience ordained by God for each believer, will you believe it?"

I quite audaciously said, "If you can show it to me in the Bible, I will always believe it."

Then they turned to this passage about the Samaritans and asked me if they were saved after accepting Jesus as their Savior and being water baptized.

I replied, "Yes, of course they were!"

Then they asked, "What was going on when Peter went down to lay hands on them that they might receive the Holy Spirit?" I didn't know. I grew very quiet.

They questioned, "Is this scripture?"

Because of Acts, chapter 8, I began to seek the Baptism in the Holy Spirit because I had been "nailed." There was no way I could explain it away. In my heart of hearts, I didn't even want to try.

They proved it to me in scripture, very gently and yet emphatically, that the Baptism in the Holy Spirit was a second definite experience occurring after salvation.

THE HOUSE OF CORNELIUS – GENTILES ALSO

Now, in Acts 10 we see a similar story where Cornelius was praying and an angel appeared to him.

The angel said, *"Now send men to Joppa, and send... for Peter"* (Acts 10:5).

Can you imagine what it would be like to be praying, as a Roman soldier, and then suddenly a real angel of God appears in the room with you. After his season of prayer, Cornelius said, in effect, "An angel told me to send for Peter who would tell me, 'Words whereby I might be saved'" (see Acts 11:13-14).

Cornelius' men left on a mission!

At the critical time of his men's arrival, Peter "just happened" to be up on his roof top praying. As he was praying he had a vision of a sheet being let down. He heard God say, "Rise, Peter, kill and eat!"

Peter was a practicing Jew so he refused God, saying, essentially, "I'll never eat any unclean animal, Lord" (Acts 11:8).

This happened three times. Then, right after Peter's vision Cornelius' men arrived asking, "Is there a man here named Peter. We need him to come with us."

The Spirit of God told Peter, "...go with them, doubting nothing" (Acts 11:11). We must be very wary of imposing our interpretation of "the rules" on God. He makes the rules!

When Peter arrived in Caesarea where Cornelius was, his whole house was already full. As Peter entered, Cornelius announced, "We are all here." They couldn't have known the exact day, or the particular hour that Peter was going to arrive. It stands to reason that all of the folks must have been camped out in Cornelius' house for a week or so waiting.

Now, I want to show you what Peter preached:

> *"And He* [Jesus] *commanded us to preach to the people and to testify that it is He who was ordained by God to be Judge of the living and the dead. To Him all the prophets witness that, through His name, whoever believes in Him will receive remission of sins"* (Acts 10:42).

Now, that was the end of his sermon. "If you believe in Jesus, you will receive remission of your sins." "Remission" literally means to send away. It is a much stronger word than merely "forgive."

While Peter was still speaking these words, the words of salvation, the Holy Spirit fell upon all those who heard the Word. So, they believed that their sins had been forgiven and experienced salvation. These people were born again and then received the Baptism into the Holy Spirit a few seconds later. They had two experiences, but only a few moments occurred between their salvation and their Baptism into the Holy Spirit.

Those of the circumcision (the Jewish believers), the ones who came with Peter, were astonished because the gift of the Holy Spirit had never (to their knowledge) been poured out on the Gentiles. How did these folks with Peter know the

Holy Spirit had been poured out? *"For they heard them speak with tongues and magnify God."* Then after their Holy Ghost Baptism, it says that Peter commanded them to be baptized in the Name of the Lord, using water.

Allow me to summarize what we have found:

Number one, the apostles accepted tongues as the evidence that they themselves had received the Holy Spirit baptism.

Number two, the apostles accepted tongues as the evidence that the Samaritans had received the Holy Spirit.

Number three, the apostles required no other evidence.

It is astounding that today, in the mission field, when someone gets saved and filled with the Holy Spirit, some denominational leaders suggest that new converts must prove their salvation for six months, before going through baptismal classes. Peter and John just showed up to a group of total strangers, who were definitely Gentiles. God interrupted Peter's sermon by pouring out the Holy Ghost on them, and then Peter baptized them!

Do you think Peter went home that night and said, "God, I am really angry. I was really getting into my sermon. I had my notes. I had it all outlined, and You interrupted me. I didn't even get to finish preaching!"

It is my desire that God would interrupt every church service, and every evangelistic crusade with an outpouring of the Holy Spirit and His Gifts.

CHAPTER 2

RECEIVING YOUR BAPTISM IN THE HOLY SPIRIT

*"So I say to you, ask, and it will be given to you;
seek, and you will find; knock, and it will be opened
to you. For everyone who asks receives, and he who
seeks finds, and to him who knocks it will be opened.
If a son asks for bread from any father among you,
will he give him a stone? Or if he asks for a fish, will
he give him a serpent instead of a fish? Or if he asks
for an egg, will he offer him a scorpion? If you then,
being evil, know how to give good gifts to your
children, how much more will your heavenly Father
give the Holy Spirit to those who ask Him!"* (Luke
11:9-13).

THREE FEARS

These five verses from scripture, relate in a parable, the
basic fears that people face when it comes to receiving the
Baptism in the Holy Spirit. As Jesus tells the story, he describes
the three common fears as: a rock, a snake and a scorpion.

The "rock" relates to the fear we have that our supposedly
supernatural experiences may have their origin from within
ourselves. Jesus was saying that many people fear that when they
start to move in the Holy Spirit, it is really just their own thoughts
or emotions – their own being that creates the experience instead
of God.

If one of my three daughters or my son were to ever come
to me and say, "Dad, I want some bread," do you honestly
think I would grab a handful of gravel or a rock and put it on
their plate? Absolutely not! We, as believers, are hungry for

God, and are expected to be filled with a desire to be filled with Him. No father or mother in their right mind would give a rock to their hungry child.

But, God is our Father! Such an attitude is a stinging slap in the face of our Father, Who stands with open arms ready to give us everything we need.

The "snake" that Jesus mentioned relates to the fear that we will receive something from the enemy – something demonic or Satanic (Satan is often, since the Garden of Eden, represented by a "snake" in scripture). Let me share this with you, to clear up whatever confusion you might have: it is impossible to receive something from the devil, when you are praying to the Father, in the Name of Jesus, to receive the Baptism in the Holy Spirit. The _entire_ _Trinity_ is involved, folks!

In the Middle East, during the time of Christ's earthly ministry, they ate fish much more than we do today. In that historical context, if your son or daughter came and said, "Can I have something to eat? Some fish, Daddy?" Would you pull your hand from behind your back with a snake in it, saying, "Ha, ha, ha, it's snake time for you Junior!"

Jesus said that even though we see ourselves as evil or fallen, we still know how to give good gifts to our children! Not only that, but we _desire_ to give them _good_ gifts. Now, if we being evil know how to do good, certainly our Father in Heaven does even more. We don't pull dirty tricks like that on _our_ hungry kids, and neither does God!

The third illustration that Jesus gives is about the egg, versus the scorpion. This is the fear that we will be stung socially, emotionally or mentally. After all, "a person can get too much religion" we may reason. However, you will never get too much of Jesus. Once again, if your child came to you and said, "Daddy, I want an egg," would you instead put a poisonous and deadly scorpion in your little 3-year-old's hand?

My wife and I were visiting some friends in Southern Missouri. The family there had a nice cabin and they said that we could use it while we were there. Well, one night I was asleep and I felt something crawling on the back of my left leg. So, I reached over to knock it off.

When I hit it, it felt big. So, in my half-asleep state of awareness, I figured that I should look and see what it was. I flipped on the light and crossing the floor was this scorpion. I reached over and got my shoe and went, "wham!" The scorpion put his tail up looking for someone to sting! It was a frightening experience! I had never been awakened to a scorpion crawling on my leg before. None of us would place a scorpion in our child's hand!

So, in this parable, Jesus was saying that when we ask for the Baptism in the Holy Spirit, that is exactly what we are going to receive. It won't be us, it won't be the devil, and we will not get stung by it. Obviously, Jesus knew that there were fears involved.

Looking at verse 10 in this chapter, there is something else of interest to note. Jesus said that all who ask WILL receive. But you do have to ask. Everyone who asks receives the gift of the Holy Spirit. If you've asked for the Baptism in the Holy Spirit, in the Name of Jesus, to God the Father, you have received it. I have noticed in leading people to the baptism that there is always someone who will say, "I want to be filled with the Holy Spirit, but I don't want the tongues. Do I have to speak in tongues?" The answer is, you "get to" have the tongues, not that you "have to." It is just like a pair of shoes. The tongues are part of the package. Tongues are the prayer language part of the Baptism in the Holy Spirit.

DIVINE-HUMAN COOPERATION

Often there are people who say, "I want God to do it all." They pray for the Baptism in the Holy Spirit, then they cross their arms and say, "I'm ready. I'm not going to say anything, because I want it to be real." These people do not understand the principle of divine-human cooperation.

Do you remember the story of Peter walking on the water with Jesus? If he had pulled that boat up on the shore, he would have used the exact same muscles to stand up, lift up his leg, step over the edge of the boat and start *walking* on the sand. There was no miracle in Peter *walking* when he was out on the sea of Galilee. That was his own natural physical act. The miracle was that he didn't sink.

What if Peter had said, "I'm not going to get out of this boat. I want You to do it all, Jesus? I want You to stand me up. I want you to lift my leg over the side of the boat." Ridiculous! Peter did the natural act of walking. God did the supernatural act of not letting him sink. So it is with tongues.

When a person speaks in tongues, they must do the natural act of speaking.

The Holy Spirit gives you the syllables. You have to have enough confidence in Him to begin to speak. Speaking is not a miracle. It's a natural physical act. The syllables are the miraculous part. Your part is to begin speaking and God's part is to supply the language.

One of my favorite examples of divine-human cooperation took place when Jesus healed a blind man. This blind man in John, chapter 9, came to Jesus and said, "I want to be healed." Jesus spat in the mud, made him a mud mixture and smeared it on.

Now, if you were the blind man, you might have thought. "Jesus, I don't need a divine spit bath or a divine mud ball." Jesus said, "Go wash in the pool of Siloam." It was a natural act.

When you tell a blind person to go across the city of Jerusalem, it isn't a matter of just going! They have to take someone's arm and be led. There was no special miracle water floating in the pool of Siloam, but the blind man went. He splashed the water in his eyes and he could see. That is divine-human cooperation. His part was to "go, wash." God's part was to heal. God will make you act on your faith before He completes the miracle.

Another similar example took place in the synagogue. Jesus said to the man, *"Stretch forth your withered hand."* The guy could have said, "Yeah, right. If I could have stretched forth my hand, I would have done it a long time ago, Jesus." But instead, he reached out as best he could, and was healed. Jesus required the man to take the natural, physical act of stretching forth. God then did the supernatural by healing the man's arm.

There was a big wedding party at Cana once (John 2). At this party they ran out of wine and Jesus said, *"Fill these six jugs full of water"* (and these jugs held between 25 and 30 gallons each). The scripture says they filled them to the brim. So there were at least 150 gallons of water.

It must have taken them an hour to get the water, bring it back and fill these jugs. That was a natural, physical act. "Why didn't Jesus just create the wine; He was going to perform a miracle anyway?" He required that in order for Him to do something, they had to do their part in the miracle.

Whenever I pray for someone's healing, I always ask the individual to do something they couldn't do before. I tell them to exercise something or do something to demonstrate their faith. I saw a little girl in a Kathryn Kuhlman meeting once who was completely crippled. She acted by throwing her crutches down and attempting to take a step. Her eyes opened wide with excitement as tears started streaming down her little face, and then she began to run!

You can say, "I want God to do it all," but He will not do it all. Your salvation is another example. Jesus did His part on the cross when He shed His blood for you. Your sin was put upon Him. He was judged, He was damned for your sins, He died, He was buried, He rose again. God did His part.

Now it is your turn to act. You have to say, as an act of your will, "I want to be saved. I want Jesus." That decision and that faith to receive Jesus is your part. God won't do your part and you certainly can't do God's part.

The Holy Spirit and receiving the prayer language of tongues invoke the same principles of divine-human cooperation. You cannot speak in another language with your mouth clamped shut. You must have enough faith to begin exercising your vocal chords.

The Lord will give you the right syllables. You won't get a rock, and you won't get a snake, and you won't get a scorpion either. Jesus said so!

IT'S YOU

In every instance in the Bible where the prayer language of tongues is mentioned, it is always the person doing the talking. You speak in tongues by faith. In I Cor. 14:18 Paul said, "*I thank my God **I speak** in tongues more than you all.*" The Holy Spirit was not doing the speaking! If it was that way, you would have no control over it. Acts 2:4 says, "And **they** *were all filled with the Holy Spirit and* **began to speak** *with other tongues.*" "**They** all" began to speak with other tongues!

I remember a lady who was in a meeting where Derek Prince was ministering. She came forward to receive the baptism with 50 or 60 other people and she began praying in tongues. As soon as she quit, a look of discouragement came over her face. Brother Prince went to her and said, "What's the matter?"

She said, "Well, I know I'm just making this up. It isn't real for me."

She thought "If I am doing the speaking, this cannot be God speaking through me."

He replied, "Lady, you were speaking in perfect Aramaic, praising the Lord." "Aramaic is the language that Jesus spoke in," Derek continued, "Isn't that good enough for you?"

The lady said, "Oh, I see," and began speaking in tongues again, this time in perfect peace.

WHO IS IN CONTROL?

Whenever you speak in tongues you remain in control of yourself. The Bible says the fruit of the Holy Spirit is self-control.

> *"If anyone speaks in a tongue, let there be two or at the most three, each in turn, and let one interpret. But if there is no interpreter, let him keep silent in church, and let him speak to himself and to God"* (I Corinthians 14:27-28).

If scripture says here that you can keep silent, then you must have control over the gift. And again, scripture says, *"And the spirits of the prophets are subject to the prophets"* (I Corinthians 14:32).

When I received the baptism, I had been a Baptist preacher for ten years. God acquiesced to my denominational viewpoint at the time and sent me a spirit-filled Baptist, because I could never have received the Baptism in the Holy Spirit from Pentecostals. I believe I had to receive it from a Baptist. So, I visited a pretty good size church called the Evangelistic Center in Kansas City. They were having a revival, and when I got there; there were no seats left except on the front row. So, I went down and sat in the front row.

The man sitting to my right was a Northern Baptist preacher. On my left was a Southern Baptist Preacher. As I sat next to the Northern Baptist preacher, I started talking to him. He said, "Yeah, I'm from Ohio. I pastor a church there." He said, "All my deacons have the Baptism in the Holy Spirit and they cast out demons."

"Hmm? Kind of scary!" I thought. "I think I'll try the Southern Baptist." I didn't want to learn anything more about casting out demons. So, I turned and talked to the other guy. His name was Ralph Powell, pastor of a church in Kansas

City. He asked, "Well, Brother Gruen, do you have the Baptism in the Holy Spirit?"

I said, "Yes I do."

He said, "Do you speak in other tongues."

I said, "No I don't, but I do have the Baptism in the Holy Spirit."

His response was, "If you didn't get it the Bible way, you don't have it!"

I knew the Bible, so I said, "You show me one verse in the Bible where it says you have to speak in tongues!"

He said, "Brother Ernie, do you believe in water Baptism?"

I said, "Of course."

He said, "Do you believe in water Baptism by immersion?"

Again I said, "Of course."

He replied, "You show me one verse in the Bible where it says you have to be baptized in water by immersion."

"Well," I said, "the Ethiopian Eunuch went down in the water. John the Baptist took them down to the water. There is no verse that actually says you have to baptized by immersion in water, but it is the biblical pattern."

His answer was, "All the Apostles spoke in tongues, Mary the Mother of Jesus spoke in tongues. All 120 in the upper room spoke in tongues. Paul, author of 13 New Testament books, spoke in tongues. The Ephesians spoke in tongues. The Corinthians spoke in tongues. They spoke in tongues at Samaria. It is the biblical pattern." He continued, "You will never know that you have what they got, until you get it the way they got it. If you don't get it the way they got it, you'll always wonder if you ever really got it at all!"

With my thinking thus shocked into a sense of scriptural reality, I went home and dropped to my knees saying, "Lord, give me what they got, the way they got it, so I'll know I have it." Well, a couple syllables came out of my mouth. Of course, I was new and a little apprehensive, but I wasn't afraid.

I went back over to the revival the next day and the Southern Baptist preacher was there and he said, "Don't listen to the words, put your mind on Jesus. Don't think about the language, think about the Lord. You just talk to Jesus and say those words to Him.

When I got in my car to leave, I put the key in the switch and the Lord spoke to me. Not audibly, but it was a louder than an audible voice inside my mind. He said, "Neglect not the gift that is within thee!" Of course I knew that was scripture. I was driving down I-70 speaking in tongues and it just gushed out of me. The first interpretation I received regarding my prayer in tongues was that the denomination I belonged to was "tried in the balance and found wanting." That really shook me up! The second interpretation I received was, "Today is the day of salvation for Gary."

At the time, I pastored a church of about 110 people. I had only one Gary in my Church and I headed straight for his house! I knocked on his door and his father answered the door saying, "Well, why are you here, Brother?"

I said, "I've come to talk to Gary."

Gary had just gotten home from High School and when he saw me he said, "Why did you come talk to me, pastor?"

I did not tell him where I got it. I simply said, "Gary, today is the day of salvation for you!"

He instantly began to weep. I took out my Bible and showed him God's plan of salvation. He knelt down by the divan and I led him to Jesus. I was sent to his house supernaturally, by a tongue and its interpretation.

Incidentally, this answers the question I have heard so often, "What good is the gift of tongues—who needs it?"

This precious young man was converted because of the gift of tongues, together with the interpretation. To this day, Gary doesn't know how or why I came to his house. But there was someone saved and going to heaven because I got an interpretation of my prayer in tongues. When you pray in your prayer language, you will always want to flip back and forth between the language you understand and languages unknown to you. As you do this, you'll gain insights and words of wisdom about business, family problems, relationships, problems at work, and situations you didn't even know were in existence.

HAVE IT ALL

Many Christians say things like, "Well, we want the fruit of the Holy Spirit, not the gifts."

Thank God, Christians don't have to choose between them. Every gift of God is a dispensation of His grace and love. It is God imparting His love, mercy and grace. Never say, I don't need God's gifts. Remember, salvation is God's gift too.

Do you know the difference between the gifts and the fruit of the Spirit? A gift is like Christmas day when you open up a present and explain, "Hey. That's mine." Fruit is character development and it takes years to develop. A person can receive a gift instantly, while still being deficient in fruit.

Never exalt the gifts above character development; we need both.

"The fruit of the Holy Spirit is love, joy, peace, patience, gentleness, goodness, faith, meekness and self-control."

A fruit tree requires several years of growth before we can harvest fruit from it. If we want love, joy, peace, patience, gentleness, goodness, faith, meekness and self control, we must always focus patiently on issues of character development. It should be our desire to have the fruit of the Holy Spirit operating in conjunction with the gifts of the Holy Spirit. But, we don't want to choose between the two.

IT WILL HAPPEN TO YOU

When my wife received the baptism, it wasn't in Church. She was laying in bed beside me and she woke me up praying in tongues!

I asked, "What are you doing?"

She acted really embarrassed and said, "Well honey, I was praying in tongues." The Spirit had come upon her as she was praying. It woke me up. What a wonderful way to wake up, hearing your wife receive the baptism.

There are people who receive the Baptism in the Holy Spirit, seemingly without their prayer language. They go home and dream that they are speaking in tongues. When they wake up, they are speaking in tongues. Others, while driving down the road just start speaking in tongues. Suddenly it's released. I know a little about that.

There was a Catholic nun that my wife and I prayed with to receive the baptism, but she didn't seem to immediately receive the prayer language. She wrote us a letter a week later, telling us how she had been brushing her hair the morning following our prayer session with her, when suddenly she received the gift of tongues.

She said, "I'm a German. I was too stubborn. I wasn't about to say just anything." She continued, "As I was brushing my hair, my mind was turned off and, suddenly the tongues came flowing out of me." It came while she was brushing her hair, but her brain had to be in neutral!

We cannot dictate to God how to give us His gifts!

ASK, SEEK, KNOCK

I want us to look back to the key scripture for this chapter.

"Ask, and it will be given to you, seek, and you will find; knock, and it will be opened to you. For everyone who asks receives, and he who seeks finds, and to him who knocks it will be opened" (Matthew 7:7-8).

Jesus was specifically talking here about the Holy Spirit. He said in Luke 11:13, "*...how much more will your Heavenly Father give the Holy Spirit to those who ask Him!*"

Here Jesus spoke of the three different levels of receiving.

He says if you ask then you receive.

Seek and you will find!

Seekers will find things that askers didn't even know existed!

"*Knock, and it will be opened to you,*" tells us that a knocker has things opened to them that seekers do not know are available.

There are three New Testament levels of having the Holy Spirit—asking, seeking and knocking.

In the Old Testament you had three as well. In the temple, you had the Outer Court, the Inner Court and the Holy of Holies. And in the New Testament parable of the sower, we see some seed brought forth 30 fold, some 60 fold, and some 100 fold.

None of us should ever think that we have finally reached the pinnacle. You may be an asker and a receiver, but God wants you to be a seeker who finds, because we need to discover some new things in God.

BARRIERS AND OBJECTIONS

When it comes to receiving the Baptism in the Holy Spirit, there are several objections and barriers that hold people back from receiving. A barrier is anything that keeps people from receiving, while an objection is an argument against receiving the Baptism in the Holy Spirit.

A common barrier is, "I don't want to speak in tongues. I want God to do it all, so that I am not the one making it up." These people are sincere, but they are also sincerely wrong. They don't understand that they have a part to play as an act of their free will. God will not violate your free will! Human-divine cooperation is a very necessary aspect of receiving the prayer language, as previously explained.

A second barrier is, "I sought the Baptism of the Holy Spirit for years; why won't God give it to me?" Actually, the first time you asked in faith, you received. The Bible says, everyone who asks receives and he who seeks finds. You received it the very first time.

The prayer language of the Holy Spirit in other tongues is already within you, but lies dormant waiting for you to release it. Many times, people want to know they have it through some kind of emotional experience. But emotions are not trustworthy! Sometimes God gives the Baptism with very little emotional release, because our faith is to be in Him and His Word – not our feelings! If your faith is in your emotions, your faith is in yourself, because your emotions are part of you. Emotions vacillate, changing with our body chemistry of the moment, while God's Word remains constant. *self control*

Another one of the barriers to receiving is the fear of losing control. The fruit of the Spirit is self-control. This is why God always requires human-divine cooperation. Your will has to be active. There are people who do foolish or dumb things, and then blame the Holy Spirit. But, the Holy Spirit does not do foolish or dumb things! It is individuals who get out of control, not the Spirit of God!

I Corinthians 14:32 says, *"And the spirit of the prophets are subject to the prophets."* That means that in spiritual matters, you can control yourself. Spiritual things should increase "self-control" or enhance it, but never diminish it.

I have a Southern Baptist friend who pastors a church. He had a woman in his congregation who would get going, take off, spin around and perform all kinds of weird, out-of-control behavior. One day, he took her aside and said, "You're disrupting the service. You're going to have to quit that."

She said, "Bless God, when God puts it on me, I'm going to turn it loose."

He said, "Well, next time go out in the parking lot and turn it loose." I couldn't agree more!

"AM I GOOD ENOUGH TO BE BAPTIZED IN THE HOLY SPIRIT,"

That's another barrier people have to receiving God's best. They forget that the <u>only</u> thing that can make anyone good enough is the blood of Jesus. I was invited by a group of nuns once to explain the Baptism in the Holy Spirit to them. I said to these dear sisters, "The only thing that can make you good enough to receive the Baptism in the Holy Spirit is the blood of Jesus." I asked, "Would you be willing to pray and ask the blood of Jesus to cleanse you of all sin?"

"Oh yes, yes, pastor. We'd be happy to pray about that." Catholics in particular, because of their special attention to the sacrament of communion, <u>love</u> the blood of Jesus.

So they all prayed and asked the blood of Jesus to cleanse them. Then I said to them, "Now we'll accept Him as our Lord and as our Baptizer in the Holy Ghost." I led them in that prayer, accepting Jesus in all those different aspects. Then, with no instruction from us, and having never heard of singing in tongues, all of them began singing in tongues. They didn't <u>speak</u> in tongues, they all <u>sang</u> in tongues simultaneously! Beautiful!

It was an awesome experience for every one of us there— very much like the Day of Pentecost!

If you ever wonder, "Why doesn't God just fall on people like He did in the New Testament?", He does. But, He meets most of us where we are. As a Baptist, I needed to receive it from a couple of Baptist preachers. God had to meet the level of my weakness. God's grace and goodness are so great! After all, had God not been willing to come down to our level by sending Jesus His Son, not a soul among us would even be saved!

"WHEN GOD IS READY, THEN I WILL RECEIVE THE BAPTISM IN THE HOLY SPIRIT"

I have heard that a lot – too much in fact. That is like calling a broadcast station, and saying, "When you're ready for me to listen, I'll turn on my radio." All along, there is nothing wrong with the signal that is being sent. It is your radio, just like it is your body and your voice. God sent the Holy Spirit on the Day of Pentecost. It has all been done for a very long time now! He has already been poured out.

Are you ready to ask, and believe, and go ahead and exercise your faith to speak? Alright then... just do it!

"DO I HAVE TO SPEAK IN TONGUES?"

This is a question I hear from people, asked in all sincerity. I always say, "No, you get to speak in tongues!" It's not like you are receiving something evil or bad, folks. Speaking in tongues is wonderful. It is not that you have to do it. It's that you get to.

I Corinthians 14:4 says, *"He who speaks in a tongue, edifies himself. He who prophecies edifies the church."* In verse 18, the Apostle Paul says, *"I thank God I speak in tongues more than you all."*

Paul was thrilled to have received the Baptism in the Holy Spirit — so read on to the next chapter!

CHAPTER 3

OBJECTIONS TO THE HOLY SPIRIT'S GIFTS

A thorough study of the Gifts of the Holy Spirit would never be complete without a study of the modern-day objections to these gifts. Over the last 2000 years, with the mixing and melding of cultures, many Christians have disregarded the truth of scripture for the temporary truths of the cultures in which they live. It is a real problem.

I want to cover the most common objections people have to the gifts of the Holy Spirit, giving a detailed and scriptural response to each. As I often ask, "If it is in the Bible, will you believe it is true, even before you read it?" Sometimes when I am preaching and I ask the people in my congregation to look up a particular passage of scripture, I ask, "How many of you believe this next scripture before you read it?" You see, some folks' belief in scripture is conditional, based on which particular verse that they are about to read. Does the verse I am about to read fit into my listener's particular doctrine? Does it fit into your or mine particular doctrine? Perhaps our doctrine should line up with the Word and not vice versa.

The Word is truth and life – all of it! But, sometimes having the courage to face and accept the truth takes a strong commitment to acknowledge, "God is always right; I could be wrong." With that in mind, will you make the commitment to believe the Word, instead of man's doctrines? Will you exercise the courage to examine the following "objections" in the light of what God has said? I thought so!

OBJECTION 1

Doesn't I Corinthians 13:8-9 teach that tongues ceased when the Bible was completed?

Let's look at I Corinthians 13:8-9:

> *"Love never fails. But whether there are prophecies, they will fail; whether there are tongues, they will cease; whether there is knowledge, it will vanish away. For we know in part and we prophesy in part."*

If you are going to say tongues have ceased, you would also have to say that knowledge has ceased as well. You would also have to say prophecy has ceased. Since neither of these have disappeared, the question we need to ask is, "When will this 'cessation' event take place?" Verse 12 explains it clearly. Compare the phrase containing the word "now" with the phrase containing "but then." Both of those phrases occur twice in verse 12:

> *"For <u>now</u> we see in a mirror, dimly, <u>but then</u> face to face. <u>Now</u> I know in part, <u>but then</u> I shall know just as I am also known."*

Taken in context, this passage teaches us that tongues, prophecy and knowledge will cease only <u>after</u> that blessed day when we see Jesus face to face; when we truly come to know Him by sight! This is talking about when we are literally <u>with</u> Jesus, face to face, for all eternity.

> *"But when that which is <u>perfect</u> has come, then that which is in part will be done away. When I was a child, I spoke as a child, I understood as a child, I thought as a child; but when I became a man, I put away childish things"* (I Corinthians 13:11).

The word "perfect," used in verse 10 is in the Greek in neuter form – meaning it is neither "male" or "female." In the original Greek, the word for "logos" is always in the masculine gender. In Greek, nouns are modified by adjectives and they must both be in the same gender (e.g. neuter, masculine, or feminine). Therefore "perfect," used here, cannot refer to the <u>Bible</u> (logos) because it doesn't agree in gender. To say that this passage refers to the Word of God (logos) would be adding significantly and destructively to scripture. God has some harsh warnings about those who do such things to His Word.

OBJECTION 2

Is there a Satanic counterfeit of tongues?

Many people say, "I want the fruit of the Spirit, not gifts, because there can be counterfeit gifts." Did you ever think about the fact that counterfeiters duplicate only items that have some great value?

There can be counterfeit fruits of the Spirit as well. For example, a person may say, "I love you." What they might mean is, "I lust for you, I want to possess you sexually for myself." That is not love at all!

The counterfeit of self-control is a religious practice called, "legalism." Have you ever seen the counterfeit for joy? Try looking at it in drug-induced euphoria and laughter. How about the counterfeit of peace? There are lots of counterfeit substitutes for true peace. The truth is that there is a counterfeit for each and every one of the gifts, as well as for all the fruit of the Spirit. But the truth is, when there is a counterfeit $50 dollar bill, it is because there must be a real one somewhere!

Not long ago, as one of my kids needed me to "kick in" a little money for something needed, I asked, "About how much do you need to take care of things?"

The reply, "Oh, about $150, should do."

Well, not being a stingy father, I took out my wallet and peeled off some $50 dollar bills, "One, two, three, and a fourth one, just for good measure. Go out to eat," I said. Do you honestly think that my child would say, "Sorry dad, I wouldn't want to take your $200. It's more than I needed and besides...

those $50 dollar bills could be counterfeit!" No way! My children would never respond that way to me because they know me and trust me. Would you really want to respond that way to your heavenly Father, God?

OBJECTION 3

Aren't "tongue talkers" actually immature, baby Christians?

Turn to Isaiah 28:9-10 which is a prophecy about tongues.

"Whom will he teach knowledge? Whom will he make to understand the message? Those just weaned from milk? Those just drawn from the breast? For precept must be upon precept, precept upon precept, Line upon line, line upon line, Here a little, there a little."

That's how people receive the baptism. It's line upon line. Precept upon precept. First they read the scripture and they say, "I didn't know this." Then they read another scripture and it begins to build up within them, so they visit another church, or listen to somebody else's testimony. Over time, it begins to add up.

When I received the baptism, my wife pretty well flipped out. She began to pray that God would take me home. She said, "He is always seeking God, and now he's got this baptism in the Holy Spirit. He's over praying at the church all the time. He's never going to be happy till he meets Jesus. So, just take him home Lord. Just take him home."

She was frustrated because she didn't understand. She was going to a seminary where we had both been in training to be Baptist missionaries. In seminary, she had been enrolled in a course that focused on I John. While reading in I John 2:20, she found where it says, *"But you have an anointing from the Holy One, and you know all things."*

She read that and thought, "You know, I don't really know all things. What can that possibly mean?" I know of no one else who ever got the baptism of the Holy Spirit off that verse. But Dee did!

She prayed, "I need this anointing God. I know I'm saved, but I don't understand all things. I do not have this anointing and I need it."

Laying in bed one night, shortly thereafter, she was praying because she couldn't go to sleep. It was then that the Spirit fell upon her and she began to speak a few syllables in an unknown language to the point that it woke me up! The Spirit of God had filled that bedroom.

I asked, "What are you doing?" She said, quite embarrassed, "I'm praying in tongues." I smiled, turned over, and fell into a glorious and peaceful rest.

Isaiah 28:10-12 says that we receive from God,

> *"For precept must be upon precept, precept upon precept, Line upon line, line upon line, Here a little, there a little. For with <u>stammering lips and another tongue</u> He will speak to this people, To whom He said, 'This is the rest with which You may cause the weary to rest,' And, 'This is the refreshing'; Yet they would not hear."*

This was an astounding prophecy for its time, <u>hundreds</u> of years before the events of Acts chapter 2. Yet, praying in tongues is a rest. It brings peace. Then the prophet added, *"Yet they wouldn't hear."*

Sadly if you go into many typical churches today, they won't hear the truth of this marvelous and peaceful gift from God.

OBJECTION 4

Did Jesus speak in tongues?

It is true: We have no scriptural record of Jesus ever speaking in tongues! We don't have chapter and verse for proving He got hot and sweaty either. We do however, have the Lord Jesus saying in Mark 16:17, *"And these signs will follow those who believe: In My name they will cast out demons; they will speak with new tongues..."* So the Lord tells us to do it and He poured out His Holy Spirit to make it possible for each one of us. What more do we need in the way of instruction?

OBJECTION 5

Isn't speaking in tongues simply preaching the gospel in foreign languages?

No, it isn't.

In I Corinthians 14:2 there are three phrases, all indicating that speaking in other tongues is usually not a foreign language. The first phrase, *"For he who speaks in a tongue does not speak to men but to God,"* pointedly states that the person is speaking to <u>God</u>, not to another created human being. The second phrase, *"For no one understands Him,"* indicates that it is not a <u>known</u> language. And the third phrase, *"However, in the spirit he speaks mysteries,"* states that the tongue being spoken is a mystery, that is why the gift of interpretation is needed.

And since you may have asked, there are actually five different manifestations of the gift of tongues in the Bible:

1. *Preaching in tongues*

This only occurred, according to scripture, on one occasion: on the Day of Pentecost. However, this remains one legitimate biblical use for tongues.

2. *Worship in tongues*

Another biblical usage of tongues is worship. Which occurred spontaneously at the end of Peter's sermon at Cornelius' house. In this incident, there was probably only one language group present. They weren't speaking to many different nations at that time.

It says in Acts 10:46, *"For they heard them speak with tongues and magnify God."* On this occasion the use of tongues was worship. There was apparently no message or interpretation.

3. *Intercessory prayer in tongues*

A primary use of tongues is for intercession.

Romans 8:26 says, *"But the Spirit Himself makes intercession for us with groanings which cannot be uttered."*

I Corinthians 14:14-15 tells us,

> *"For if I pray in a tongue, my spirit prays, but my understanding is unfruitful. What is the conclusion then? I will pray with the spirit, and I will pray with the understanding. I will sing with the spirit, and I will also sing with the understanding."*

I had a lady ask me once, "You mean tongues is prayer?"

I said, "Exactly."

"I thought it was all just gibberish!" she said.

"Exactly wrong!" I replied.

I guess most of us did think it was more gibberish at one time. But here, God says praying in other tongues by the Spirit is intercessory prayer that exceeds our capacity for understanding or speech. That changes our whole paradigm on the gift of tongues! If it is the way to pray beyond human wisdom, we must want it and need it today.

4. *Singing in tongues*

We just saw Paul say, "I'll pray with my understanding, and I will pray with my spirit. And I will sing with the spirit, and I'll sing with understanding." The fourth usage of tongues is singing in tongues like the Catholic nuns I mentioned before. That incident was a refreshing kind of worship and spontaneous praise!

5. *A Supernatural message in tongues for a particular group on a particular occasion*

A fifth use of supernatural tongues is to give a supernatural message for a particular group. It could also occur between two individuals, but I usually see it occur in a group, or at a church. When you speak out in tongues at church, the Bible says it <u>must</u> be interpreted. If it isn't interpreted, then things are out of order. It could be that the tongue was only personal worship and not a message for the group, or, on the other hand, perhaps the person with the interpretation did not speak it out. In I Corinthians 14:27-28, Paul also limits those who speak in tongues to two or three. There should not be more than three messages in tongues with their interpretations in any public meeting.

We must be careful not to be critical or judgmental; sometimes you might have four prophecies, and the second one was the one that was out of order. I don't want to be legalistic, but I do believe we must obey this scripture.

A man named Jim brought his girlfriend to church one Sunday night and she had never been to a charismatic church. A message came out in tongues and Jim got the interpretation, but he was afraid to speak it out. The Holy Spirit knocked him back into his chair. And out of his mouth came the interpretation, that went something like this:

"There is a woman here who must choose between me and another person. And you must make your choice today between the other person and me."

"I wonder who that was for!" I thought.

It was pretty dramatic. The next day, a Pastor's wife called me on the phone and asked, "Do you remember that tongue interpretation last night?"

Thinking the service over carefully, I replied, "Yes," and I waited to hear what she would say.

She said, "The lady from our church who came with us to your service was actually living with a man she was not married to. And as a result of that tongue and interpretation, she decided to choose Jesus and let that other man go."

The Holy Spirit can be very discreet. He would probably never say, "Yea, saith God, you are living in adultery." The Holy Spirit is usually gentle. We see that this is the case with many messages in tongues as they are interpreted.

Now, how many people have this ability to give a supernatural message in tongues for interpretation? It is not a rule, but my experience has been that it is less than 10%! Very few have that anointing, but everyone who has received the baptism in the Holy Spirit still can and should speak in tongues, asking God for interpretation and understanding. Since it is a supernatural way to pray, God wants us to use the prayer language continually to build ourselves, <u>and</u> His Kingdom!

OBJECTION 6

Everyone has different gifts; therefore God does not expect everyone to speak in tongues.

Many who raise this objection quote I Corinthians 12:28-31:

"And God has appointed these in the church: first apostles, second prophets, third teachers, after that miracles, then gifts of healings, helps, administrations, varieties of tongues. Are all apostles? Are all prophets? Are all teachers? Are all workers of miracles? Do all have gifts of healings? Do all speak with tongues? Do all interpret? But earnestly desire the best gifts. And yet I show you a more excellent way."

Of course not everyone speaks in tongues. I have known a lot of wonderful Christians who have never spoken in tongues. They love Jesus as much as you or I. But we must make this distinction between the prayer language, which every Spirit-filled believer has, and the gift of tongues which is the ability to speak out a message for interpretation in the church. Once again, the misunderstanding arises from taking the scripture out of its immediate and historical context! This gift of speaking out a message for interpretation is what this excerpt from the letter to the Corinthians is referring to.

OBJECTION 7

I want love and the fruit of the Holy Spirit; I neither want nor need tongues.

You don't have to choose between the two. Let's look at what is called the Love Chapter: I Corinthians 13, particularly verse 13, *"And now abideth faith, hope, love, these three; but the greatest of these is love."* In the next chapter, I Corinthians 14:1-2, in context it tells us to,

> *"Pursue love, and desire spiritual gifts, but especially that you may prophesy. For he who speaks in a tongue does not speak to men but to God, for no one understands him, however, in the spirit he speaks mysteries."*

If you pick up the context, right after the Love Chapter, Paul says, seek love <u>AND</u> desire spiritual gifts. We should all pursue love and desire spiritual gifts. We should desire to move in the gifts of the Holy Spirit powerfully and effectively to meet people's needs. This is the love of God in action! If we don't desire spiritual gifts, we are cheating people out of the power of God, cutting short the main function of His love in action, and we are disobeying this scripture passage in its context!

OBJECTION 8

The gifts all ended with the death of the apostles; they belong to a different dispensation and are not for us today.

Look at I Corinthians 1:7: "[You] *come short in no gift, eagerly waiting for the revelation of our Lord Jesus Christ."*

The Holy Scriptures would never warn us not to fall behind in any gift (spiritual or otherwise) while we are waiting for the second coming if the gifts had already passed away. Do you get that? We're to eagerly seek every gift the Spirit of

God has while we're waiting for the second coming of Jesus. This scripture passage proves that the gifts of the Holy Spirit will continue being poured out on us until the return of Jesus Christ, our Lord and Savior.

OBJECTION 9

Doesn't Paul strongly rebuke those who speak in tongues, saying, "...*I would rather speak five words with my understanding... than ten thousand words in an unknown tongue*" (I Corinthians 14:19).

No, he doesn't say that. Remember, context, context, context! The key phrase is "yet, in the church I would rather speak..." in the language of the group. I Corinthians 14:19.

First of all, the apostle said,

"I thank my God I speak in tongues more than you all" (I Corinthians 14:18). If he spoke in tongues more than ALL the Corinthians, then he must have done a powerful lot of "tongue talking." Paul did a lot of walking and he must have done a lot of talking in tongues as he walked along. History tells us that by the time he left one town and reached another, he was so full of God and the Holy Ghost that he either started a riot or a revival!

There is no doubt that the Corinthians abused the gifts, but I Corinthians 14 tells us how to use them correctly. **The correction of abuse is not a command to disuse but rather to practice proper use.** If something is abused, you don't disuse it; you use it <u>correctly</u>.

Verse 19 says, *"Yet, in the church, I would rather speak five words with my understanding."* Paul's point was that the prayer language is primarily a private gift to be used devotionally. Any preacher would prefer to preach or teach in the language of his audience. As a preacher, it is more beneficial for those listening that I speak words in English than 10,000 words in unknown languages. To edify others, it truly is better to speak in a known tongue!

When I teach others, English is my language of choice.

OBJECTION 10

If the gifts are for us today, why don't you go into all the hospitals and heal all the sick!

Why don't you go into the bars and save all the lost? Is salvation for us today? After all, isn't it God's will that everyone be saved, and not one be lost, and that all would go to heaven?

Yet, today we rarely go into bars, stand on the tables and preach the Gospel. Healing is not some sort of "hocus-pocus" magic act. There are conditions that must be met. For instance, forgiveness at times is required. Jesus said as much,

> *"Son, be of good cheer; your sins are forgiven you... Arise, take up your bed, and go to your house"* (Matthew 9:2, 6).

If someone isn't healed in one of my meetings, one of the very first things I ask them is, "Are you carrying resentment in your heart towards anyone?" Most people immediately come up with a mental list of between 40 and 400 people whom they need to forgive.

If we are not healed, it is we who need to change, not God or His gifts!

OBJECTION 11

Why do some "Charismatics" seem to manifest so little of the Fruit of the Holy Spirit?

For the same reason that some rich people fail to pay their bills on time! Not everyone lives up to their capacity physically or spiritually <u>all</u> the time; people are different! Some of the most wonderful Christians I've ever met have been those who are Spirit-filled. Sure there are always a few who fail to manifest the Fruit of the Holy Spirit, but I choose to focus on the positive.

When my wife and I first received the Baptism, we only had only $50 dollars to our name. We had wonderful Spirit-filled people come up to us, and shake our hand with a $20 dollar bill rolled up in theirs. We'd never seen them before; they just came to our church, seemingly from nowhere. They'd say, "Brother Gruen, I just want to bless you. God told me to give this to you."

One day my wife said to me, "I didn't even know these people were out there. I didn't even know these kind of people existed."

Christians, by and large, and especially those who are Spirit-filled, are quite wonderful, loving people. If someone is going to take pot-shots and say, "Well, I saw a Spirit-filled person of questionable character," I would have to say, "I've seen thousands who are just and honorable." You cannot measure a large group by a few individuals.

OBJECTION 12

Why doesn't anyone speak in a known foreign language, such as on the Day of Pentecost?

They do! A Catholic Priest, Robert Aerosmith, came to speak at my church. He was having supper in our home and the whole family was gathered around. I said, "Let's all hold hands and I'll bless the food. I'll just bless this food in tongues." So, I began praying and the Priest's eyes opened wide and his mouth hung open a little.

He asked, "Brother Gruen, have you ever been to Japan?"

I answered, "No, never been there."

He said, "After the war, I went as a Catholic Priest to Japan. You were just now praying in perfect formal Japanese."

It turns out that high classical Japanese is a kind of special and aristocratic form of the language.

He told me, "You were saying in Japanese, 'Lift us up into your heavenly prayer huts tonight as we worship you in the service.'"

That just blessed my socks off! Having an experience like that! And by the way, God did lift us up in the service that followed!

OBJECTION 13

The Baptism in the Holy Spirit brings division.

I was preaching a revival in a denominational church. The denominational leaders sent men in with tape recorders to record every word I spoke, in an effort to entrap me. They also refused to attend the meetings. They planted seeds of discord in the church by saying, "If you speak in tongues, you will have to leave this church." They were closed-minded leaders who planted seeds of division and then had the audacity to say that the Baptism in the Holy Spirit was responsible!

In fact, the very tender-hearted pastor stood before the congregation on the last Sunday of the series of meetings and said, "Honestly, a lot of us in this church have received and experienced the Baptism in the Holy Spirit and we speak in tongues, but you do not have to have that experience to be a member of this church or be in good standing with this church, be on a committee, or hold church office. We love all of you very much. We just want to receive all of God's people." Not long after this experience, the denominational leaders in town split that church wide open. The Charismatics, of course, got the blame, but the real opposition came from those who refused to receive or accept other Christians who were seeking to hear and obey the Word of God.

OBJECTION 14

If the Baptism in the Holy Spirit is of God, why do people have to be taught how to receive it?

My reply is: "We teach people how to get saved." It is true: we have piles upon piles of literature, tracts and brochures telling people how to get saved. We don't just say, "Salvation isn't real because somebody showed us how to pray and receive Jesus as Savior and Lord."

I have a question for you, "What have you that you did not receive from someone else and how can anybody hear if there isn't first a preacher?"

I would be offended if people weren't taught and shown scripture on how to receive the Baptism in the Holy Spirit. There is not enough good teaching in this area and that is why I am writing this book. I want to help provide adequate biblical teaching.

In fact, don't ever pray for the Baptism in the Holy Spirit unless you are fully convinced it's scriptural. God will not be offended if you say, "It seems to be real, but I am not sure and I want to search the scriptures for myself." When you get into a seeking position, your Heavenly Father is thrilled! God is not offended at your asking for scriptural understanding before you pray for the Baptism, or for that manner, anything.

OBJECTION 15

If you do not understand what you are saying, it is absolutely valueless.

Dr. Harold Bredenson was on a panel and the questioners asked him, "Dr. Bredenson, when you pray in tongues, do you understand what you are saying?" The question was intimidating, implying that what you don't understand is worthless. Dr. Harold Bredenson replied, "Praise God, no! Always before, my prayers were limited to my little tiny pea brain and just a few vocabulary words. I had to funnel my prayers through a few English words and phrases. But now, I can simply turn on the supernatural language of prayer, and exceed my limited understanding."

OBJECTION 16

Speaking in tongues is selfish.

While I was a Baptist minister, I probably would have said, "The Bible calls tongues selfish. After all, doesn't scripture say, '*He who speaks in a tongue, edifies, builds up himself?*'" But today, my perspective has changed. I would say that you are either an encourager or you need to be encouraged. You are either filled with the Holy Ghost, and your cup is running over with enough for others, or you are half-empty, hoarding what little you have.

That means you are either a missionary or you need one. It is not selfish to have yourself "built up." As a matter of fact, you cannot build up others when you, yourself, are falling to pieces. I want everybody who sees me to be happy, to be encouraged. One of the greatest compliments you can receive in this life is, "I like to be around him/her. He/she always seem to add something to my life that blesses me."

OBJECTION 17

"Spirit-filled people" act like they are a superior class of Christian.

I was on a live-radio broadcast once and the radio host interviewed me, trying to lay a snare. He said, "Now pastor Gruen, is the Baptism in the Holy Spirit for a special class of people?"

God spoke a word to my ear, and I said, "Yes!" He almost fainted. I continued, "It's for those who are desperate. It's for those who can't go on one more minute without more of God's grace. It's for those who are poor and needy. It is not for the better-off people; it seems to be targeted for a special class— the desperate!"

OBJECTION 18

Are all the strange things "Pentecostals" do true manifestations of the Holy Spirit?

Certainly not!

If you have ever seen an old steam locomotive in operation, you realize it can do two things with its energy. It can power itself along the track or it can go "whew woo, whew woo, whew woo," blowing its whistle. A fellow who is filled with the Holy Ghost, who is raised in a Pentecostal church, is "taught" certain manifestations by example. What he has is the Holy Spirit, but he lets it out in the human way he has learned. That's why some people always prophesy in King James language. They were taught that it isn't "Godly" if it doesn't sound "King James-ish."

Many manifestations seen in Pentecostal churches are learned religious practices. I know a man who was in a revival meeting once. The Spirit got on this guy and he went twirling around, dancing in the Spirit. He went clear around the whole auditorium with his eyes shut, his hands lifted, spinning like a top. When he came to a pillar he'd just go around it, not even opening his eyes.

So, what are you going to do about what you see as "weird stuff?" Leave it alone. If God doesn't tell you something is wrong, just leave it alone and stop worrying about it! On the other hand, don't preach that twirling or dancing in the Spirit like a top is what you must do when you get the Baptism in the Holy Spirit.

OBJECTION 19

Are there Christians who have been Baptized in the Holy Spirit, who have never spoken in tongues?

Every Christian who receives the Baptism in the Holy Spirit receives the gift of tongues—the prayer language. But some of them have never exercised it. My experience has been that it is in them, but it remains dormant, or latent. They could speak, God wants them to speak, they should speak, but because of their fear, or lack of knowledge, they haven't released it yet. This is why many people have their first experience with praying in tongues as they worship God. They had it all along, but it was released almost by accident through praise and worship.

Objection 20

Is "Sanctification" and the Baptism in the Holy Spirit, the same thing?

No way! There are people who have the Baptism in the Holy Spirit, but who have never experienced sanctification. On the other hand, there are people who have experienced sanctification who haven't experienced the Baptism in the Holy Spirit. Thank God, once again, we don't have to choose!

In the book of Acts, sanctification is always connected with water baptism, immersion and a burying of the old nature. That is the truth of the Romans 6 passage as well. Most people have not been taught the significance and the importance of water Baptism, of burying their old nature.

Both the Baptism in the Holy Spirit and sanctification are absolutely wonderful!

CHAPTER 4

REASONS FOR RECEIVING THE BAPTISM IN THE HOLY SPIRIT

"The poor and needy seek water, but there is none, Their tongues fail for thirst. I, the LORD, will hear them; I, the God of Israel, will not forsake them. I will open rivers in desolate heights, And fountains in the midst of the valleys; I will make the wilderness a pool of water, And the dry land springs of water. I will plant in the wilderness the cedar and the acacia tree, The myrtle and the oil tree; I will set in the desert the cypress tree and the pine And the box tree together, That they may see and know, And consider and understand together, That the hand of the LORD has done this, And the Holy One of Israel has created it" (Isaiah 41:17-20).

GRACE ALONE

Remember, I said earlier that there is a special class of people who can receive the Baptism. It is for those who are desperate, who can no longer go on without having more of God.

I had a dream not long ago, based on that familiar scripture where Jesus talked about "asking," "seeking" and "knocking." In this dream I was preaching to my congregation: "Some of you used to be seekers, and now you're only askers. Some of you used to be knockers, pounding on Heaven's door, saying, 'I've got to have more of God,' and you've gone back to just being a seeker. You ask for <u>some</u> things. You get <u>some</u> answers."

In the dream, as I was preaching, I posed this question, "Are you today an asker, or a seeker, or are you a knocker?"

I woke up at that point, and found myself praying and talking to the Lord about whether I was still a "knocker," or had become a "seeker," or whether I had backslidden into being a mere "asker." It was a sobering moment for me.

We need to be hungry for God's Word and presence. We need to hear His voice. Being a "seeker" or a "knocker" is not automatic. It is something that requires an effort on our part to maintain. This reminds me that when *"the poor and needy seek water, but there is none, their tongues fail for thirst. I the Lord will hear them. I the God of Israel will not forsake them"* (Isaiah 41:17). Notice God's promise to those who are hungry for Him.

Did you see all the "I's" in this passage: "**I**, the Lord will hear them." "**I**, the God of Israel will not forsake them." "**I**, will open up rivers in desolate places and fountains in the midst of valleys." "**I** will make the wilderness a pool of water." God says, "**I** will come through for you. **I** will heal you. **I** will make your desert a pool of water." Isn't our God <u>neat</u>? Isn't He <u>wonderful</u>? Thank God, we serve One Who says, "**I** will," without equivocation!

Then He says He's going to do some planting. God mentions a whole bunch of trees that horticulture experts tell us don't normally grow well together. These trees require different climates, and environments. This prophecy applies to us today. God is saying He is going to plant the Baptists, Catholics, Pentecostals, Presbyterians, Episcopalians, Lutherans, etc. all together. All these different denominations, with their different theologies and traditions, will be planted together, *"That they may see and know, And consider and understand together, That the hand of the Lord has done this,..."* (Isaiah 41:20). One example of this happening today is with the *Promise Keepers* organization.

What is going on? God is prophesying in this passage that poor and needy people are going to have their needs met.

They will not be forsaken. They will have a river, a fountain and a spring of water. Why?

The answer is in verse 20, *"That the hand of the LORD has done this, And the Holy One of Israel has created it."* This "last-day" move of God is rooted in what God wants to do. I will even make a road in the wilderness and a river in a desert!

Do you feel like you're in a desert place today or wandering in the wilderness all alone? Do you feel dry and withered up?

"The beast of the field will honor Me, The jackals and the ostriches, Because I give waters in the wilderness And rivers in the desert, To give drink to My people, My chosen. This people I have formed for Myself; They shall declare My praise" (Isaiah 43:20-21).

"Jackals" here represent people with demonic problems, while the "ostrich" represents those with their heads stuck in the sand and who are "clueless," spiritually speaking.

Look at verse 21: *"This people I have formed for Myself; They shall declare My praise."*

Isaiah 44:3 says, *"For I will pour water on him who is thirsty,..."*

Scripture doesn't say God is going to do something for the holy or righteous, but for the "thirsty." Our prayer should be that God will increase our thirst. His promise to us is:

"'I will pour My Spirit on your descendants, And My blessing on your offspring; They will spring up among the grass Like willows by the watercourses.' One will say, 'I am the Lord's;' Another will call himself by the name of Jacob; Another will write with his hand, 'The Lord's,' And name himself by the name of Israel" (Isaiah 44:3-5).

A GIFT

All we possess comes to us by God's grace, not by our own works or spirituality. All these "Isaiah" passages have God as their focus. It is never that you or I are so great; it is always our God who is. It is about how much He loves us.

The Baptism in the Holy Spirit is a gift of His grace received on the basis of our simply asking. As with any gift, if you must work to obtain it, it is no longer a gift. But the Baptism in the Holy Spirit is a gift given absolutely free.

Remember that since the basis for pleasing God is His grace, instead of our works, we can never claim to be spiritual because we have the Baptism. The only thing we can truthfully say is that God gave us His gracious gift wrapped in His love, and we opened the package.

NO PROOF OF HOLINESS

Romans 11:29 says the gifts and callings of God are irrevocable. Is that true? Of course it is. God will neither take away a person's gift nor will He take away a person's calling. The Baptism in the Holy Spirit does not indicate that someone has now become holy or excelled spiritually. Having the Baptism in the Holy Spirit is only what it is: a testimony of God's abundant grace and compelling love.

NOT CHRISTIAN MATURITY

Ephesians 5:18 says, *"And do not be drunk with wine, in which is dissipation; but be filled with the Spirit."* After verse 18, Paul becomes quite practical as to what being filled with the Spirit produces. He addresses relationships between wives and husbands, parents and their children, employers and their employees. Being full of the Holy Spirit must be worked out in getting along with people. Christianity that does not affect our people skills is largely irrelevant.

You can receive the Baptism in the Holy Spirit just a few moments after you are born-again, but it is no indication that you have become a mature Christian. You have to dig in and study the Word, develop a biblical value system and activate that value system in your lifestyle. Maturity is different from the Baptism. But, the Baptism in the Holy Spirit is a good starting point!

A NEW ROAD

Matthew 7:13-14 says,

"Enter by the narrow gate; for wide is the gate and broad is the way that leads to destruction, and there are many who go in by it. Because narrow is the gate and difficult is the way which leads to life, and there are few who find it."

Salvation is a process that begins with an experience called the New Birth. Being filled with the Holy Spirit is also a process that begins with an experience called the Baptism in the Holy Spirit! Any theology that over-emphasizes the initial experience, in place of the daily need to maintain holiness, will lead to our ultimate downfall. Regardless of our spiritual experiences, we remain free moral beings who must choose daily to be Christians in our actions and attitudes!

When I was in Jerusalem, I visited a very ornate gate called, "The Damascus Gate." This is where everyone gets their photograph taken. It is called the Damascus gate because it is the road which leads north to the city of Damascus. That gate has a distinction–not for what it is, but for where it leads! How stupid it would be to stay there, stuck at the gate, not realizing that it is the road leading to Damascus.

As Christians, we tend to elevate the New Birth, like that Damascus gate, and fail to emphasize the road of holiness that it begins. The Baptism in the Holy Spirit is like a second entrance ramp. Our goal is to get on the highway, not stall on the entrance ramp. It is vital to see the Christian life as a road or a path—and not just get our photograph taken at the Gate. Who would want to stop an exciting journey at the beginning!

Character development or maturity is indeed a continuing process.

IT IS A WAY TO PLEASE JESUS

The only legitimate objective for the Christian life is to be fully like Jesus. We are to honor Him with all of our words, attitudes, and actions.

"Therefore we make it our aim, whether present or absent, to be well pleasing to Him. For we must all appear before the judgment seat of Christ, that each one may receive the things done in the body, according to what he has done, whether good or bad" (II Corinthians 5:9-10).

Paul says, our ambition is to be well pleasing to Jesus and that we will stand before Jesus and give an account of what we have done – good or evil – with our lives. Romans 14:12 adds this, *"So then each of us shall give account of himself to God."*

You will not be giving an account to the Lord for your spouse, your children, your friends, or your enemies. You and Jesus are going to have a talk about you – and you alone!

TO WITNESS AND LIVE THE CHRISTIAN LIFE

The purpose of the Baptism in the Holy Spirit is to receive God's power to witness and also to live a Christian life. There are two Greek words for power: one is "dunamis" which means dynamite, and the other is "ekousia," which means power in the sense of having authority. Both of these words can be found throughout the New Testament. The word for "authority" is more powerful than the word for "dynamite." I want you to picture a semi-truck, an 18-wheeler tractor and trailer, traveling down the freeway at 75 miles per hour. It is really bookin' down the road! A 180-pound cop, with a whistle and a badge steps out, holds up his hand, and the semi comes to a screeching halt. The cop had the authority. The semi had the power. Authority prevailed. In spiritual warfare, we can blow the whistle on demonic activity and command it to come to a screeching halt, because Jesus has given us, *"authority (exousia)... over all the power (dunamis) of the enemy"* (Luke 10:19).

In the spiritual world, the real issue is always, "Who has the authority?" If you have the <u>authority</u>, you can control any <u>power</u>. That is why the name of "Jesus" is so important. It is not how <u>big</u> we are that matters most, but rather, who has the "exousia." The Baptism in the Holy Spirit is unique in the sense that it gives you both authority (exousia) and power (dunamis) at the same time.

As we examine issues concerning power and authority, we come up with the question: "We have been given power, but to do <u>what</u>?"

God gave me a list of 12 power-related areas that are for every Holy Spirit-filled believer.

POWER OVER THE WORLD

Power over the world includes witnessing. Unfortunately, with most Christians, the world has evangelized them. Instead of us being transformed into Christ's image, most Christians have been transformed into the world's image. So, power to evangelize would have to top the list of benefits of the Baptism in the Holy Spirit.

> *"But <u>you shall receive power</u> when the Holy Spirit is come upon you and <u>you shall be witnesses</u> to me in Jerusalem [your hometown], all Judea [your state], Samaria [your nation], and to the ends of the earth [the world]"* (Acts 1:8).

POWER OVER FEAR

This power comes along with our assurance of salvation. Let's look at Ephesians 1:13,

> *"In [Jesus] you also trusted after you heard the word of truth, the gospel of your salvation, in whom*

*also, having believed, you were sealed with the Holy
Spirit of promise, who is the guarantee of our
inheritance until the redemption of the purchased
possession, to the praise of His glory."*

The Holy Spirit is the guarantee. Many people have
doubted their salvation until they received the Baptism in the
Holy Spirit. When the Holy Spirit came upon them, they spoke
in tongues and knew instantly that they were forever sealed
with the Holy Spirit of promise. It was additional assurance
to them, validating their entire experience in Christ.

*"You did not receive the spirit of bondage again
to fear., but you received the Spirit of adoption by
whom we cry out, 'Abba Father'"* (Romans 8:15).

We didn't receive a spirit of fear; we received THE Spirit
of adoption! What could be more comforting than to know
that God adopted you? So this experience brings a wonderful
additional assurance of salvation and sonship.

POWER OVER SIN

*"But the anointing which you received from Him
abides in you, and you do not need that anyone teach
you; but as the same anointing teaches you concerning
all things, and is true, and is not a lie, and just as it
has taught you, you will abide in Him"* (I John 2:27).

John the Apostle did <u>not</u> say that we don't need teachers.
He couldn't have meant that because one of the five-fold
ministry gifts of the Holy Spirit is the "office" of being a
teacher. Instead, John is saying that the anointing of the Holy
Spirit teaches us as it flows in harmony with the particular
teacher who God sends our way. As Spirit-filled believers,
we have an internal response system that bears witness when
something is from God or isn't. For example, if someone
teaches something that condones sin, you would know
instantly that it is not right. If all is as it should be, the same
anointing is in both you and the person doing the teaching.

If they are in fact flowing in the same Spirit, those two anointings are going to flow and agree with one another, and you will know it. When they don't agree, somebody is out of the Spirit.

"...the same anointing...is true, and is not a lie,..." (I John 2:27). We can trust the Holy Spirit, just like we trust the Father and the Son. When the alarm bells of the Holy Spirit are going off, we need to pay close attention. People who have followed after false teaching and have recovered testify that God warned them over and over. They just kept turning it off, saying, "Perhaps, this is just me judging." Today many of them wish they had listened to the Holy Spirit.

The Holy Spirit is always going to vote for purity, holiness, truth, integrity and ethics. He is the Spirit of <u>truth</u> and the Spirit of <u>holiness</u>.

A girl who was traveling on a missions trip fell in love with a boy she met while she was in South Africa and became engaged to him. After she returned, she came into my office for pre-marital counseling and the Holy Spirit said to me, "Ask her if she has peace." So, I asked the girl, "Do you have peace?"

She said, "Yes." We spoke a while longer and then she left. Then, three days later, she called me back and said, "I was so shocked by your question that I blurted out 'yes,' but the truth is, I have no peace at all. I lied. I don't have peace." To make a short story out of it, she said, "I've suppressed this lack of peace I felt and kept rebuking the devil. It turned out that it was actually the Holy Spirit dealing with me." She broke off her engagement.

The young man had come all the way from Africa to live in the United States for the summer and was to marry the girl in the fall. She sent the young man home, back to South Africa. His heart was broken, of course, but she had learned to trust the Holy Spirit. It may have saved their lives!

The Holy Spirit will not go away. Thank God! You will not have peace if it is Him troubling your spirit. Getting back to the point, we should always respect and honor our spiritual leaders, but continue to listen for the confirming witness in our spirit.

<u>Never</u> turn off your Holy Spirit radar!

POWER OVER CIRCUMSTANCES

"...who by the mouth of Your servant David have said: 'Why did the nations rage, And the people plot vain things? The kings of the earth took their stand, And the rulers were gathered together Against the LORD and against His Christ. For truly against Your holy Servant Jesus, whom You anointed, both Herod and Pontius Pilate, with the Gentiles and the people of Israel, were gathered together to do whatever Your hand and Your purpose determined before to be done. Now, Lord, look on their threats, and grant to Your servants that with all boldness they may speak Your word, by stretching out Your hand to heal, and that signs and wonders may be done through the name of Your holy Servant Jesus.' And when they had prayed, the place where they were assembled together was shaken; and they were all filled with the Holy Spirit, and they spoke the word of God with boldness" (Acts 4:25-31).

Here Peter and John are threatened with summary execution. In response, they just had a big prayer meeting. And instead of being afraid, the Bible says that they were anointed with renewed boldness. The power made the whole building where the prayer meeting occurred to shake violently. Peter and John knew they were "on track" with their ministry and that they had God's anointing and protection. The Holy Spirit helps us to overcome difficult circumstances. This great passage demonstrates this principle!

POWER OVER IGNORANCE

The Baptism in the Holy Spirit will bring you revelation knowledge. Look at Proverbs 1:23: *"Turn at my rebuke; Surely I will pour out my spirit on you; I will make my words known to you."* This is a promise that if we repent, and turn at God's rebuke (reproof), He will pour out His Spirit on us. That outpouring will be demonstrated by a new understanding of God and His Word that overthrows ignorance. God says, *"I will make My words known to you!"*

POWER OVER CONFUSION

Clear and lucid decisions come about through the Holy Spirit's supernatural guidance. In Acts 16 we read that Paul wanted to go in one direction, and yet the Holy Spirit forbade him. He had a vision of Macedonia calling to him and went west instead. That is significant because it was the first time the Gospel was ever preached on European turf. We are undoubtedly saved because the Gospel went <u>west</u> that day instead of <u>east</u>. Thus, salvation and truth came to Europe and the western world!

It is interesting that the man in the Macedonian vision turned out to be a woman! The person, Paul discovered, was named Lydia. She was by a riverside having a prayer meeting. Paul joined that prayer meeting and led Lydia and her household to Christ. The Bible says the Lord opened her heart! She was a wonderful merchant woman; a seller of purple, who apparently used her business connections over the ensuing years to promote the Gospel of Christ. That's how the Gospel started in Europe.

Have you ever had the Holy Spirit forbid you to do something even though it wasn't a "sin?" Have you ever wanted to tell someone off and the Holy Spirit wouldn't let you?

"I'll give them a piece of my mind," you may have thought.

But, don't ever give someone a piece of your mind when it is under the influence of the devil. It will always lead to much difficulty and embarrassment. Stay under the Spirit's influence and imitate Him in such situations. You can always just "be quiet."

"However, when He, the Spirit of Truth has come, He will guide you into all truth; for He will not speak on His own authority, that is out of Himself, but whatever He hears He will speak, and He will tell you things to come. He will glorify Me, for He will take of what is Mine and declare it to you" (John 16:13-14).

Here we learn seven important things about the Holy Spirit:

- First of all, the Bible says He is the Spirit of truth.
- Second, He won't speak on His own authority.
- Third, He'll speak only what He hears God, the Father, speaking.
- Fourth, He will show you the future.
- Fifth, He will glorify the Father.
- Sixth, He will take what is of Jesus and make it known to you.
- Seventh, and finally, always remember: His name is the Spirit of Truth.

I would suggest that if you're facing a business or relationship decision, go to these verses of Scripture in John 16, and talk to God while keeping this passage in mind:

"Spirit of Truth, I need You to make known to me, what the future is. And make known to me what You want me to do. Take the things of God, the Father, and God, the Son, and make them known to me."

Remember, based on what this Scripture reveals, confusion always comes directly from a lack of prayer.

POWER OVER HUMANISM

Most people are led from without. We must be led from within, instead of by outside forces and voices. We must NEVER ask ourselves: "What is politically correct?" What people say, peer groups and opinion polls are all outside forces. A Christian is led from within – where God lives.

"Who has directed the Spirit of the Lord, or as His counselor has taught Him? With whom did he take counsel, and who instructed Him, And taught Him in the path of justice?" (Isaiah 40:13-14).

Who taught the Holy Spirit knowledge? Who showed the Holy Spirit the way of understanding things? When you pray, you should admit, "Holy Spirit, I am the one who needs counsel, teaching, instruction, knowledge and understanding. Who has ever directed You about what to do? I need Your counsel."

As you are praying, take the position of <u>hearing</u>, not <u>instructing</u> the Lord.

POWER OVER FLESHLY HABITS

"I say then: Walk in the Spirit, and you shall not fulfill the lust of the flesh. For the flesh lusts against the Spirit, and the Spirit against the flesh; and these are contrary to one another, so that you do not do the things that you wish. But if you are led by the Spirit, you are not under the law. Now the works of the flesh are evident, which are: adultery, fornication, uncleanness, lewdness, idolatry, sorcery, hatred, contentions, jealousies, outbursts of wrath, selfish ambitions, dissentions, heresies, envy, murders, drunkenness, revelries, and the like; of which I tell you beforehand, just as I also told you in time past, that those who practice such things will not inherit the kingdom of God. But the fruit of the Spirit is love,

joy, peace, longsuffering, kindness, goodness,
faithfulness, gentleness, self-control. Against such
there is no law. And those who are Christ's have
crucified the flesh with its passions and desires. If we
live in the Spirit, let us also walk in the Spirit"
(Galatians 5:16-25).

Being filled with the Holy Spirit causes our very nature
to change. We are, after all, the Temple of the Holy Spirit.
Over time, as the Holy Spirit goes through the process of
sanctification in our lives, we develop more and more authority
over fleshly habits.

Here is a mystery: some habits are broken instantly by
the power of the Holy Spirit, while others require a process. I
have known men and women who, after receiving the Holy
Spirit, just quit smoking, "cold turkey." Alcoholics have put
down their bottles, never to pick them up again. Drug addicts
have lost their craving for their former drug of choice.
However, these same people may continue to struggle in
another area of their life, such as with bitterness and
unforgiveness. God, in His wisdom, will deal with each of us
as individuals. In some areas He will make deliverance
instantaneous, while in others He will use a process that best
meets our truest needs and His ultimate goals, for eternity.

POWER OVER ROOTLESSNESS

"For I long to see you, that I may impart to you
some spiritual gift, so that you may be established..."
(Romans 1:11).

Again, we see God's desire to establish us, to plant us firmly
in our relationship with Him, with each other and with our
neighbors. Without the impartation of a spiritual gift of the Holy
Spirit, there is no foundation or anchor for the soul.

In this very unstable world of constant and unexpected
change, there is a stability available in the truth of God's Word
and His Holy Spirit. Stability is found in God's consistent love

and grace. Knowing that God is present within us via the Person of the Holy Spirit sustains the human spirit and keeps us from both falling and failing!

POWER OVER DISCOURAGEMENT

"To console those who mourn in Zion, To give them beauty for ashes, The oil of joy for mourning, The garment of praise for the spirit of heaviness; That they may be called trees of righteousness, The planting of the LORD, that He may be glorified" (Isaiah 61:3).

What a tremendous promise from God! He will comfort you and turn into beauty what has been burned up by your foolishness and sin. More importantly, He promises to give us an anointing of joy to replace our sadness.

Heaviness is a spirit, and on occasion it can actually be an evil spirit. As we begin to worship God, we can switch garments—from being clothed with heaviness to a cloak of praise. Whenever you are discouraged you can begin to worship, using your prayer language. God will dress you in a brand new garment—of praise.

POWER OVER PHYSICAL SICKNESS

"But if the Spirit of Him who raised Jesus from the dead dwells in you, He who raised Christ from the dead will also give life to your mortal bodies through His Spirit who dwells in you" (Romans 8:11).

Another translation says that *"He will also quicken"* your mortal bodies. Webster uses the words, "enliven," "revive" and the phrase "to move more rapidly," to define the word "quicken." That is what the Holy Spirit will do to your mortal body. He will make it work in ways it never did before. He will enliven even those old, dead cells. He will revive your body and make you move more rapidly. This goes well beyond the concept of healing, which I will discuss in greater detail shortly.

In the Holy Spirit, we have all of these wonderful things and yet there is so much more for us to rejoice about. For as scripture says: *"But he gives more grace"* (James 4:6).

CHAPTER 5

TWENTY-ONE SCRIPTURAL REASONS FOR SPEAKING IN TONGUES

When people ask us, "Who needs tongues?" or "What good is it?" we should not get angry because these are valid questions. Instead of getting upset, we should be prepared to give a clear, concise and biblical response.

A number of years ago I was on an extended fast, preaching a series of meetings in a Midwestern town. While I was waiting on the Lord, God said to me, "Open My Word and I will show you the scriptural values of praying in tongues." I opened my Bible and it all came to me in one afternoon. I didn't get it from any book; it's what the Lord gave to me that day.

1. A supernatural way that the deepest part of you— your spirit—can be released to worship God

I Corinthians 14:14 says, *"For if I pray in a tongue, my spirit prays, but my understanding is unfruitful."* The principle verb in that sentence is not "tongues;" it is "pray." If I *pray* in a tongue, my spirit *prays*. The fact that this is about prayer automatically makes it important–unless you are a person who thinks prayers are useless!

Tongues are a supernatural way for the deepest part of you, your spirit, to be fully released in prayer to God. In America, we assume that the brain is the most important part of a person. We put our little kids on the school bus at age five and send them off to program and train their brains. But no one ever talks about training the human spirit. What a shame!

God's Word says the deepest part of you is not your mind. The Greek word for "soul" is "psuche." Psychology says the center of you is your psyche, or your soul. Medical science as a whole treats mankind as two-dimensional: body and soul. But, the Bible says you are body, soul and spirit and that the deepest part of you is your spirit.

When you pray with your mind, the deepest part of your center is not praying! Paul said, in essence, "As I pray with the spirit, the deepest part of me prays, but my mind cannot understand." By praying in the spirit, or in other tongues, you can always go a step deeper than your intellect or your emotions will allow.

When someone does evil against you, you don't just get hurt in your soul. You often are injured in your spirit. It is deeper than your mind, deeper than your brain, even deeper than your emotions. People get wounded in their spirits. Jesus said, *"He has sent Me to heal the broken hearted...To set at liberty those who are oppressed"* (Luke 4:18). He was talking about people's spirits, which affect the mind and emotions.

"Now may the God of peace Himself sanctify you completely; and may your whole spirit, soul and body be preserved blameless at the coming of our Lord Jesus Christ" (I Thessalonians 5:23).

Notice the order here. It says, "<u>whole</u> spirit, soul and body." Wholeness begins at the spirit. And, tongues allows the deepest part of you to pray. This is where inner healing begins.

2. A supernatural way to sing a new song to our Lord Jesus

"What is the conclusion then? I will pray with the spirit, and I will also pray with the understanding. <u>I will sing</u> with the spirit, and I will also sing with the understanding" (I Corinthians 14:15).

Paul was saying here, "I refuse to be limited! I will sing with my spirit and I will also sing with my mind. I will express myself to God through both outlets." Singing in tongues is a powerful way to worship the Lord. With just these two methods of supernatural communication–singing and praying in the Spirit–how could anyone say that tongues is the least of the gifts?

3. The unique gift identified with the New Testament Church

"And these signs will follow those who believe: In My name they will cast out demons; they will speak with new tongues; they will take up serpents; and if they drink anything deadly, it will by no means hurt them; they will lay hands on the sick, and they will recover" (Mark 16:17-18).

Of all the gifts of the Holy Spirit, only the gift of tongues and the interpretation of tongues are unique to the New Testament. Examples of all of the other gifts can be found in the Old Testament. The only two gifts that are not present in the Old Testament are speaking in tongues and the interpretation of a tongue. In some ways, we could say that if you don't believe in tongues and their interpretation, as far as supernatural things of the Spirit go, you are still an Old Testament Christian.

Now, there are obviously many other things different about the New Covenant. The Messiah has now come. He has died and risen on the third day. We have a better mediator in Jesus; we have a better covenant based on better promises (Hebrews 8:6). But in the realm of the grace gifts, only tongues and the interpretation of tongues are unique to the New Testament era following the New Birth as an experience.

4. A supernatural way to bless others in the Spirit

"Otherwise, if you bless with the spirit, how will he who occupies the place of the uninformed say

'Amen' at your giving of thanks, since he does not understand what you say?" (I Corinthians 14:16).

The phrase, "occupies the place of the uninformed," in the Greek language flows from the word "idiotus," from which we get the word "idiot" today. The literal translation would be: "occupy the place (or room) of the idiots." "Idiots" could be translated also as "illiterate," "uneducated," "ignoramus," "morons," and so on. The point Paul is making is that these people just do not understand—yet!

I personally occupied that room as a Baptist pastor for ten long years. I was ignorant when it came to the gifts. I was saved. I was sincere. I was a good "brother in the Lord" too. All of those things were true in my life. But when it came to the gifts of God, and the Baptism in the Holy Spirit, I didn't know very much. I occupied the room of the unlearned.

There are wonderful Christians who are in that room now. We don't have to be mean about it, but it is still a fact. The truth is, we've all spent some time in that room.

5. A supernatural way to release thankfulness

"For you indeed give thanks well, but the other is not edified" (I Corinthians 14:17).

Paul says speaking in tongues is a way not only to bless but to give thanks. You can lay your hands on someone, pray over them in tongues and bless them! You can bless people! You can bless your children before they go to school. You can bless people without even laying hands on them! It is the way to give thanks well. Speak to God in tongues and give Him thanks.

6. A supernatural way to enhance your private devotions

"I thank my God I speak with tongues more than you all; yet in the church I would rather speak five words with my understanding, that I may teach others

also, than ten thousand words in a tongue"
(I Corinthians 14:18-19).

Paul says that tongues are primarily for use as a private devotion gift and prayer tool. In a church or in any public forum I would much rather speak in a known language. But when I am alone in my prayer closet and I need answers, I will pray with my spirit and my understanding.

7. A supernatural sign to those who do not believe in the Baptism in the Holy Spirit

> *"Therefore <u>tongues are for a sign</u>, not to those who believe but to unbelievers; but prophesying is not for unbelievers but for those who believe"* (I Corinthians 14:22).

I'm going to put a spin on this that you may not agree with. If you don't, that is perfectly okay with me. Just consider this thought for a moment: I don't necessarily think Paul is talking about believing for salvation here. I think he's talking about believing in the Baptism. Because that is the context of the passage. The whole context is about the Baptism in the Holy Spirit and speaking in tongues. Paul is saying, "tongues is a sign, not to those who already believe in the Baptism, but to those who <u>don't</u> believe. Prophesying is not for unbelievers in the Baptism, but for those who already believe in the Baptism."

That has come to be my understanding of that verse. And although other people might see it differently, I think it deserves consideration... the clue to the meaning is always in the context.

8. Praying in tongues, a supernatural means of resisting the devil

> *"But if there is no interpreter, let him keep silent in church and <u>let him speak to himself and to God</u>"* (I Corinthians 14:28).

You can blot out everything around you and just have a direct relationship with the Lord by praying silently in the Spirit–momentarily blind to your surroundings. No one even knows that you are speaking. While you're at work, you're not going to speak out for interpretation; it is just between you and God. Just turn it on and live free of all the garbage surrounding you.

Let me give you an illustration. John Osteen was a great Baptist minister in Texas. He was standing in line to pay his gas bill while another fellow in front of him was expressing his anger toward the gas company. He began to scream, and yell and cuss with "four-letter" words. Brother Osteen said the whole room turned blue with this guy's anger and overtly obscene language. John clicked on the tongues silently and then out loud he suddenly said, "Hold it, wait a minute. Praise God, hallelujah, glory to Jesus. Bless Your Holy Name."

Everyone in the place turned and looked at John like he was nuts and Brother Osteen simply said, "I just wanted God to get some equal time!"

There was filth and strife all around him and still he tuned in to God. He just gave the interpretation which was worship and praise. We need for God to have equal time in a lot of our work situations today. We must resist the devil to win life's battles and I know of five particularly effective ways to do this:

1. Ignoring the devil;
2. Rebuking the devil;
3. Speaking in tongues;
4. Rebelling against the devil, doing exactly the opposite of his temptation; and
5. Quoting scripture.

Most Christians think that the only way to resist the devil is by rebuking him: "I rebuke you, Satan." Jesus did that when He confronted Peter about His going to Calvary. In the wilderness Jesus quoted scripture, but there are at least five ways to resist the devil. Meditate on them and think about it.

I love to rebel against the devil. I challenge you to do exactly the opposite of whatever the devil is pressuring you to do. Everyone innately likes to rebel, and this flavor of rebellion is not against God, but the devil. You want to punch somebody out? Bake them a cake instead. And make sure it is a good cake! Watch Satan cringe!

9. A supernatural way to speak mysteries to God that the devil can not understand

> "For he who speaks in a tongue does not speak to men but to God, for no one understands him; however, in the spirit he speaks mysteries" (I Corinthians 14:2).

God said to me one day, "The only way the devil could possibly know what you were saying is if I gave him the gift of interpretation; and that is not going to happen!"

10. A supernatural way to build up your inner man

> "He who speaks in a tongue edifies himself, but he who prophesies edifies the church" (I Corinthians 14:4).

We need to build ourselves up in order to effectively build others up. We need to be so full of God that we overflow— like a gushing waterfall of joy, wisdom and encouragement. A lot of our understood prayers are selfish and very limited. When we pray in tongues our batteries are recharged so that we can be a blessing to those around us.

11. A supernatural way to give a prophetic message that will edify the whole church

> "I wish you all spoke with tongues, but even more that you prophesies; for he who prophesies is greater than he who speaks with tongues, unless indeed he

interprets, that the church may receive edification"
(I Corinthians 14:5).

A tongue and an interpretation together are like the two nickels that equal a dime. Prophecy is like a dime standing alone. A tongue with an interpretation ends up being equal in value to prophecy. And when someone speaks out in tongues, it brings the prophetic aspect of ministry alive in a powerful way.

12. Tongues brings the "rest" and "refreshing" of the Lord

"In the law it is written: 'With men of other tongues and other lips I will speak to this people; And yet, for all that, they will not hear Me,' says the Lord"
(I Corinthians 14:21).

This New Testament scripture comes from Isaiah 28:11:

"For with stammering lips and another tongue He will speak to this people, To whom He said, 'This is the rest with which You may cause the weary to rest,' And, 'This is the refreshing;' Yet they would not hear."

Many folks today are weary, and the prayer language is a way for them to tap into God's rest.

Have you ever awakened from a fitful night's rest? It is so refreshing to wake up fully energized and refreshed for the coming day. Tongues is a heavenly "refreshing" that allows the Holy Spirit's life to flow into you.

The best way to refresh yourself is to enter into that spiritual level of refreshing by praying in the Spirit. And as you pray in the Spirit, your emotions, mind and body will be refreshed. This is because you tap into the energy of God down at the spirit level. God Himself said it, *"This is the rest with which You may cause the weary to rest."*

It is a Holy Ghost coffee break!

It will do more for you than any nap ever could. A "power" nap may refresh your body, but when you pray in the Spirit you refresh your entire being. What a tremendous tool!

In I and II Timothy we read, *"Do not neglect the gift that is in you,..."* (I Timothy 4:14); and *"...stir up the gift of God which is in you..."* (II Timothy 1:6). As with every Gift of God, we need to stir up the gift of tongues within us. I write this to release you in God. Understanding this concept of spiritual refreshment will help you move forward more powerfully in God.

13. A way of preaching the wonderful works of God in a language you never learned

Most everyone is familiar with the events surrounding the Day of Pentecost. If you read the story in Acts 2:1-47, in the King James, we read, the Holy Spirit fell on them all and they all began speaking in tongues and "it was noised abroad." You see after they were baptized in the Holy Spirit it was not till several hours later that they spoke the Gospel in other unknown languages. The initial outpouring so shocked everybody that they spread all over Jerusalem getting the crowds together. When all were gathered together there was only Peter speaking, but 14 different language were heard!

You may ask, "Why doesn't that happen today?" Well, it does!

At the Evangelistic Center in Kansas City, Missouri, one day a man stood up and gave a mighty message in tongues. But it wasn't interpreted, so it was assumed that somebody was completely out of order.

However, it turned out that there was a Jewish Rabbi in the service. He said to the pastor, "I want you to tell me about this man. Has he ever had training in Hebrew?"

The pastor said, "No, he hasn't even been to college. He's just basically your average Joe Christian. Why do you ask?"

The Rabbi answered, "He was speaking in perfect Hebrew, saying that Jesus Christ, the Messiah, is coming back soon." This is evidence that people today <u>do</u> give messages that are in known languages that they themselves do not understand.

14. A supernatural way to magnify God

Acts 10:46 says, "...*they heard them speak with tongues and <u>magnify God</u>.*" So, tongues are a supernatural way of worship and praise, and a unique way to exalt and glorify the Lord.

15. A supernatural way to intercede when you do not know how to pray

"Likewise the Spirit also helps in our weaknesses. For we do not know what we should pray for as we ought, but he Spirit Himself makes intercession for us with groanings which cannot be uttered. Now He who searches the hearts knows what the mind of the Spirit is, because He makes intercession for the saints according to the will of God" (Romans 8:26-27).

We had a woman in our church who was a registered nurse at a local hospital. Her name was Anna Flowers. One day, as she was doing her dishes and drying her hands on a towel, the Spirit fell on her and she began to speak in a harsh and guttural language—something totally different from her normal prayer language. It shocked her and even disturbed her a bit. She said, "God, what was that language?"

God simply replied, "Swahili." She called me and asked, "Where do people speak Swahili?"

I answered, "Well, Swahili is spoken in some parts of Africa."

To make a short story out of it, several months later we found out that at the precise moment of time when Anna had that season of spiritual intercession in tongues, they were loading an Assemblies of God missionary (her friend) with breast cancer onto an airplane that was to fly her back to the United States to die. <u>But</u>, the woman did NOT die! Instead she was healed at that instant. That was a totally amazing experience, demonstrating that God <u>does</u> use intercession in tongues to work miracles among us!

16. It brings visions and mental pictures while you intercede

In Ephesians we see that the purpose of the armor in spiritual warfare is prayer. You rarely hear anybody talking about,

> "...<u>praying always with all prayer and supplication in the Spirit</u>, being watchful to this end with all perseverance and supplication for all the saints..." (Ephesians 6:18).

Yet all of the armor is to be taken up as a prelude to its intended purpose of "praying always" in the Spirit.

It is good to have the shield of faith. It is good to have your loins girded with truth. It is wonderful having your feet shod with the Gospel of peace. However, an army stands or falls with its lines of communication. When a squadron gets cut off and out of communication with its command structure, people always die and missions are unsuccessful. Without communication you can't direct the artillery. Air support can't be called in. And <u>today</u> we <u>need</u> air support.

The same is true in the Spirit. Nothing is more important to spiritual warfare than intercession. Here Paul says to us, *"praying always with all prayer and supplication in the Spirit being watchful."* Today that would read, "See to it that you <u>always</u> do this above anything else."

If you have a teenager in trouble, pray in tongues and into your mind will come mental pictures of God's analysis of the situation. It could be your pastor or someone in your church who is struggling. God not only has a better plan, but a <u>victory</u>

plan! It could be a relative. It could be somebody at work. God wants to show you what is going on and work with you to bring victory to others.

A friend of mine once owned a pool hall. At their grand opening he was showing some expensive cues to a number of people, but lost track of which cue was with which customer. Suddenly he realized that one of the more expensive cues, worth about $300, was missing. Fearing the wrath of his partner, and having no idea where the cue was, my friend began speaking in tongues and "saw" the cue in the closed trunk of a certain car. My friend then went and spoke to the man who owned the car. The man denied any knowledge of the whereabouts of the cue, but a few minutes later came under conviction and brought the cue back to one of my friend's employees. It made an impression that my friend has never forgotten!

17. A supernatural way to build and increase your faith

How many folks do you think would like to have more faith or confidence in God? There are at least two ways to increase your faith. The one we hear about most often is, *"So then faith comes by hearing, and hearing by the word of God"* (Romans 10:17). We've all seen how reading the Bible can bring about a sudden surge of faith in God.

But Jude 20 says, *"But you, beloved, building yourselves up on your most holy faith, praying in the Holy Spirit."*

We don't hear about this aspect of building and releasing faith so often and it's too bad. When you pray in the Spirit, you are on the Spirit level where faith begins to flow into you. That is why it is always good to pray in tongues as you pray for someone's healing. Pray in the Spirit a while and let faith and revelation start to flow.

18. A supernatural way to keep yourself in the love of God

Jude 20-21 go on to say, *"...praying in the Holy Spirit, keep yourselves in the love of God."* Praying in tongues will both fill you with faith and keep you in love. Have you ever felt anger come up your esophagus? You can just feel it rising up. Can you identify with that? The Lord once told me to do three things in response to this sensation: "Shut up, pray in tongues, and don't say anything until I do!"

Now, that is how to control your temper! Bite your lip, pray in tongues silently – so folks don't know what you're doing – and don't say a word until you get a word of wisdom. I have found it to work every time. God always knows exactly what to say and do in every situation.

19. A supernatural way of staying full of the Holy Spirit

Jesus once said to me, "When people say that tongues are the evidence of the Baptism in the Holy Spirit, they are understating the issue. When you teach that, people will pray in tongues that one day and never use them again." Jesus said, "Tongues is FAR MORE than mere evidence of being baptized in the Holy Spirit. It is the supernatural means of staying full of the Holy Spirit."

My wife and I were praying for a lady once who was having all kinds of problems. My wife asked, "Do you have the Baptism of the Holy Spirit?"

She said, "Yes I do."

"Do you pray in tongues regularly?"

The lady said, "I prayed in tongues when I got the Baptism 18 years ago." We were shocked! This is akin to being a military officer with an automatic sidearm that has been fired but once. Can you imagine a fighter pilot who never flies again, once he gets his "wings?" It just doesn't happen! A military man who never uses his weapons will lead his men into captivity or death! It looks kind of like the church of today, doesn't it? Many have been taught this fallacy that "tongues are a trophy" in our Christian walk.

This lady had been taught that tongues was only evidence and that once you had the evidence, you lay it on a shelf like a trophy.

Tongues is so much more! You need to use that gift every day on the way to work, when you get up in the morning and whenever a problem comes. The gift of tongues is the supernatural means of staying full of the Holy Spirit!

Now, tongues is an evidence of the Baptism, but not just an evidence. It is the prayer part of the Baptism in the Holy Spirit.

20. The gift of tongues, a gateway to operating in all the other gifts of the Holy Spirit

"As it is written, eye hath not seen nor ear heard nor hath entered into the heart of man the things which God has prepared for those who love Him" (I Corinthians 2:9).

We often hear this Scripture misquoted and applied at funerals but it has absolutely nothing to do with funerals.

"But God has revealed them to us through His Spirit. For the Spirit searches all things, yes, the deep things of God. For what man knows the things of a man except the spirit of the man which is in him?" (I Corinthians 2:10-11).

The Spirit searches all the deep things of God. That includes gifts (power) and fruit (character).

What is your spirit like? What is my spirit like? If you do not know my spirit, you cannot know me. This says it is the same with God.

"Even so no one knows the things of God except the Spirit of God. Now we have received, not the spirit

of the world, but the Spirit who is from God, that we might know the things that have been freely given to us by God" (I Corinthians 2:11-12).

This verse says that the Spirit of God is the revealer of all things. The best way to tap into a revelation from God is to get in the Spirit. And the best way to do this is to pray in the Spirit. Suddenly the hidden things are revealed!

21. The supernatural way of taming the tongue

I think that just about every Christian has read James 3:8, where it says, *"But no man can tame the tongue."* Your tongue has been used to gossip, slander, complain, whine and even pronounce curses.

Isn't it ironic that when we get the Baptism in the Holy Spirit, the one part of us that can be made perfect in this life is our tongue. It <u>can</u> be "tamed" and we can pray a <u>perfect</u> prayer, releasing <u>perfect</u> worship.

Wouldn't you be disappointed if after you were filled with the Holy Spirit, God said He was just going to leave your tongue as it was before? God has not done that. He says, "I will reverse what happened at the tower of Babel. I will tame your tongue," which James said is *"full of deadly poison"* (James 3:8).

Tongues are that one unique spiritual gift identified with the New Testament Church. Tongues are the unique fulfilling event of Jesus' own prophecy about His Church, given with the great commission. With the exception of tongues and the interpretation of tongues, all of the gifts of the Holy Spirit, including miracles of healing, occurred first in the Old Testament. But these two gifts – tongues and interpretation of tongues – were given specifically to the Church, to the Body of Jesus Christ!!!

They are our birthright as New Testament believers in His matchless grace.

CHAPTER 6

THE TWENTY-FIVE GIFTS OF THE HOLY SPIRIT

"Now concerning spiritual gifts, brethren, I do not want you to be ignorant... no one speaking by the Spirit of God calls Jesus accursed, and no one can say that Jesus is Lord except by the Holy Spirit. There are diversities of gifts, but the same Spirit. There are diversities of ministries, but the same Lord. And there are diversities of activities, but it is the same God who works all in all. But the manifestation of the Spirit is given to each one for the profit of all: for to one is given the* [*literally: 'a'] word of wisdom through the Spirit, to another the* [*literally: 'a'] word of knowledge through the same Spirit, to another faith by the same Spirit. To another gifts of healings by the same Spirit, to another the working of miracles, to another prophecy, to another discerning of spirits, to another different kinds of tongues, to another the interpretation of tongues. But one and the same Spirit works all these things, distributing to each one individually as He wills" (I Corinthians 12:1, 3-11).

You may have been taught at one time or another about the "nine gifts" of the Holy Spirit, but when we look through the actual Greek for every usage of the Greek word "charisma," which is most often translated "gift," we will discover that there are actually 25 "charisma," or gifts of the Holy Spirit. So, we are going to take a long, hard look at each of these 25 gifts of the Holy Spirit!

It is important to realize that the normal Greek word used in the Bible for "gifts" is "doron," not "charis." The word "charisma" is a special word used only to define the gifts of grace that can only come from God.

The Greek word "charis," means "grace." You can take the same word and add an ending of "ma," and it means "gift of grace."

In English, we have added a "-tic" ending to charisma which forms the oft-used word, "Charismatic," applied most often to those people who believe that the "grace gifts" are available and operational today.

As we begin looking at these different gifts, notice first of all that the verb in verse eleven of I Corinthians 12 is "distributes," not "gives." When you receive the Baptism in the Holy Spirit, all of the gifts are potentially in you. God then sovereignly decides how to distribute these gifts in each situation or church service. For example, when a person speaks out in tongues for interpretation, the person who receives the interpretation may be a different person from Sunday to Sunday. The distribution of gifts on each occasion, as they are manifested, is completely dependent on the sovereignty and discretion of Almighty God.

1. ETERNAL LIFE

"For the wages of sin is death, but the gift of God is eternal life in Christ Jesus our Lord" (Romans 6:23).

In this very familiar passage the Greek word used for "gift" is "charisma." This means that anyone who is saved is actually a charismatic, because the "charisma" of God is eternal life! Like it or not, if you are saved, technically, you too are a charismatic.

The word "charismatic" has developed a somewhat negative image. This is due in part to the many extremes and excesses practiced by groups and individuals operating under a very broad and indistinct definition of the word, "charismatic." As is always the case, religious labels are often more harmful than helpful; the same word can have an entirely different meaning to each and every person. How does it feel to know that in the final analysis and <u>scripturally</u> speaking, <u>every</u> believer is a Charismatic?

2. JUSTIFICATION

"But the free gift is not like the offense. For if by the one man's offense many died, much more the grace of God and the gift by the grace of the one Man, Jesus Christ, abounded to many" (Romans 5:15).

Again, the Greek word, "charisma" is translated by the word "gift," in the phrase, *"the gift (charis) by the grace."* Also interesting is that this verse uses the Greek word "doron," initially: *"But the free gift (doron)..."* The first word, "gift," then is a "doron," whereas the second word for "gift" in this verse is "charisma." Justification is a <u>charisma</u> gift. In God, justification makes you just as if you have never sinned. That is what "justified" means. Can you see that if it were not for the "charisma" of God, we would be neither "saved" nor "justified?" We should all stop and thank the Lord daily for His <u>grace</u> gifts! Whenever someone is healed, that too is a manifestation of God's grace. When someone is delivered from demonic influences, that is grace. When someone gets a prophecy, again, it comes by God's grace. But, because of its primary importance, justification is a primary "grace gift."

3. A WORD OF WISDOM

We see "word of wisdom" in our key passage on the "charisma" of God, I Corinthians 12:4-8. As you take a fresh look at this scripture, I want you to note that in the original Greek text there is no definite article before the phrase, "word of wisdom." An <u>indefinite</u> article is used instead. Scripture speaks of *a* word of wisdom and *a* word of knowledge – not "the" word.

There is good reason why God did not use a definite article here. If Paul had said, "<u>The</u> word of wisdom," it would have meant that God is giving us generally wisdom or generally knowledge. But here, God is not giving us wisdom or knowledge as a gift. He is giving us "A word of wisdom," or "A word of knowledge." This means it is a specific word of wisdom to be applied to a particular situation that you or I may be facing. It is not general, overall wisdom or knowledge, but rather a special, specific "word" or message from the Lord.

4. *A Word of Knowledge*

Now, you may be thinking that a word of wisdom and a word of knowledge sound very similar, and you would be right. But there are some distinctions that clarify one gift from the other. In medical terms, a word of knowledge would correspond to a correct diagnosis of an illness, whereas a word of wisdom would correspond to a correct plan or prescription for treating the illness. A word of knowledge is the correct analysis. A word of wisdom is the correct solution.

In terms of auto mechanics: a word of knowledge would say, "Your brakes are going out," whereas a word of wisdom would say, "Replace that brake cylinder and the car will stop on a dime."

Sometimes you may not need a word of knowledge, but rather a solution. This is because the symptom or problem is obvious, but the solution is not so obvious. At other times you may need a word of knowledge telling you what is going on and you don't need a word of wisdom because simply understanding the problem will, in itself, present an obvious solution.

Not long ago, I was laying hands on a woman and as I did so she fell down, supposedly under the power of God. God gave me a word of knowledge, so I asked her, "Do you need to forgive your husband?" She said, "Yes."

Her problem was rooted in an ongoing condition of unforgiveness that was destroying her life! That was a word of knowledge. Once the lady had this piece of information, the obvious solution was that she needed to go through the steps of forgiveness. I didn't need a word of <u>wisdom</u> in this case; i.e. <u>how</u> to forgive. Rather, scripture already prescribes the treatment for unforgiveness.

A word of knowledge can be especially useful in the financial realm and in relationships as well. I personally love these three gifts: a word of wisdom, a word of knowledge and discerning of spirits. These are the three primary gifts that God has graced me to operate in. Being without these gifts in a hostile world is somewhat akin to being blindfolded on a military obstacle course. No wonder God doesn't want us to be ignorant! It really is a wonderful thing to know what is going on supernaturally. These three gifts are revelation gifts; they reveal the mind of God.

5. THE GIFT OF FAITH

The gift of faith is different from saving faith or the faith you exercise while waiting for an answer to prayer. Mark 11:22 describes this faith where it says, *"Have the faith of God."* Although the King James version of the Bible says, *"Have faith in God,"* the original Greek says, *"Have the faith of God."*

This gift manifests when faith comes rushing in, seemingly "out of nowhere," and it drops into you supernaturally.

What a difference one preposition can make in our understanding! The "gift of faith" is creative, in no way originating from your own being.

I was praying for a lady once who was an attorney's wife. She said, "I've got three very scary-looking lumps on my back."

Out of my mouth I heard myself say, "God <u>will</u> heal that... <u>right now</u>."

How did I know that she would be healed? Suddenly <u>faith</u> was given to me. It was a supernatural impartation of faith for her particular situation. She went home and asked her husband to give her a back rub. He was astonished to see that the growths were gone! He said, "How did these growths disappear?" Then she gave him her testimony.

The gift of faith is in action when you suddenly just "know" in your "knower" that something will happen. Ask for the faith "of" God. He has it to give and He isn't stingy about giving it out either. Jesus commanded, *"Have the faith of God,"* because there are times when we need a supernatural impartation of faith—faith that is beyond our own.

6. GIFTS OF HEALINGS

The original Greek literally says, *"energizes of healings."* Or *"the anointing and energy coming from God for various types of healings."* That is a powerful translation to consider.

My experience has brought me a glimpse into the diverse gifts of healings (note that both words – "gifts" and "healings" – are plural). No, that's not an error in grammar – gifts of healings is correct. We are going to spend some time, shortly, expanding our understanding of these particular classes of gifts, but, for a moment, I want to share with you the immediate relationship healing has with salvation.

You may not be aware that all of the Greek words for our eternal salvation also mean wholeness, health and healing. They are *sodzo, diasodzo, sotero, soterian* and the related compound words. In fact, there are several places in Scripture where these very same words are translated as "healing," "health," "wholeness" or "made whole" – when taken in their context. One such passage we have talked about briefly is in Ephesians 2:9,

> *"For by grace* (charisma) *are ye saved* (sodzo) *through faith, and that not of yourselves, it is a gift* (charisma) *of God, not of works lest any man should boast."*

If you believe in "salvation," you also believe in "healing" as well, for in Christ they are but one and the same – both are gifts (charisma) of God.

There are so many different people with different "gifts" in the realm of healing. Some have more success in one area of disease than others, e.g. emotional healing, cancer healing, heart disease healing, even financial healing. What I want you to realize is that "healing" is for us today, and is a gift (charisma) of God – not earned by works, but given by God's grace through simple faith.

In James 5:16 there is a very interesting connection between prayer and healing that is revealed to us:

> *"Confess your trespasses to one another, and pray for one another, that you may be healed. The effective fervent* (energeo) *prayer of a righteous man avails* (ischero) *much."*

James connected healing to prayer. And that (energeo) energy is effective.

It comes as no surprise that in I Corinthians 12 we see that the gift of miracles is actually called the "working" or "energeo" of miracles as well. It is the same Greek root word. Healing and miracles both flow from this "energeo" force of God which incidentally is the same root word translated as "working" and "worked" in Ephesians 1:19-20,

> *"...and what is the exceeding greatness of His power toward us who believe, according to the working* (energeo) *of His mighty power which He worked (energeo) in Christ when He raised Him from the dead and seated Him at His right hand in the heavenly places."*

Healing, miracles, resurrection all have an intimate relationship to this, the "energeo" (energy) of God at work.

7. THE WORKING OF MIRACLES

As we have just seen, the Greek word used here actually means the, *"Energizing of Miracles."* And the word, "miracles," is the Greek word, "dunamis," which I am sure you are probably already familiar with. It means superlative, dynamite or dynamic power; or, simply, <u>miraculous</u>!

This is one of the power gifts and includes all the various miracles that are not primarily healing. This would include Jesus' feeding the five thousand, turning water into wine, walking on the water and raising Lazarus from the dead! These kinds of miracles have always occurred in both the Old- and the New-Testament ages. But these "dunamis" miracles are part and parcel of the "charisma" of God–gifts <u>by</u> and <u>of</u> the Holy Spirit, given for our profit.

8. THE GIFT OF PROPHECY

In a particular church service I was receiving words from God. So I prayed, "Do You really want me to speak this out?"

God replied, "Prophesy according to your measure of faith, son!"

Prophecy takes faith! Whenever you are given a prophecy, for the Body, you must share it with the rest of the Body. It is given for their benefit.

You don't have to use King James language. In fact, it is much better if you just speak in your normal manner. Just say, "God is speaking this to me, and this is what He said." Then just share it.

I have found that if you begin, "Yea saith God," it seems to go right over the heads of those you are sharing with. They've heard that "yea and therefore ye must" stuff before.

I find it appalling that in many churches preachers will say, "Well, the gift of prophecy is really a gift of <u>preaching</u>."

If I ever pick up a translation of the Bible that translates I Corinthians 12:10 as the "working of preaching," it is a obvious tipoff that the translator is coloring the translation to favor his personal or denominational bias.

"Prophecy" in the Greek New Testament is the word "prophetao." Preaching is an entirely <u>different</u> Greek word, "kerugma," which has more to do with "heralding an announcement" than prophetic "forth telling." If somebody ever tells you that prophecy is just a manifestation of preaching, realize that they are either ignorant of the truth, have not searched the matter out, or they are willfully trying to deceive you. Preaching is used primarily in scripture to mean the proclamation of the Gospel. Prophecy relates most often to revealing what is hidden and calling forth the will of God to be done.

Prophecy can include telling folks about the "good news" and preaching can call on prophecy to reveal, expose and confront what is not always clearly seen. All of these gifts work together at times, blending with a simultaneous purpose of God. But they are not the "same" thing!

9. DISCERNING OF SPIRITS

This gift gives us the ability to know which spirit is operating in a particular situation. This gift is related to the "word of knowledge" or "word of wisdom." I have come to believe that every believer operates in this gift of discerning of spirits more than they realize. When this gift manifests itself, many of us think, "this is just my mind." But I would say that everyone has walked into an office, church or home where they have sensed, "Something is very wrong here!" You can sense a heavy spirit. On the positive side you can also sense when there is love and joy flowing.

A couple of years ago, I operated a courier business where I went from business to business making pickups and deliveries. It was interesting to note the spiritual climate of each different place I visited. Some places felt like hell was in their back room, all dark and gloomy inside. Others just seemed permeated with life and light. My sensing the spiritual climate of each place was an aspect of this spiritual gift operating in me!

We need to pray that God would reveal the spirits that are operating in the various areas and spheres influencing our lives. For instance, what spirits are operating in your child, spouse or parent?

When someone speaks out in a church service, one way to test the spirit is to ask under your breath, "You spirit speaking, do you confess that Jesus Christ came in the flesh?" You don't test the <u>person</u>. You test the <u>spirit</u>! Whenever you operate in the gift of discerning of spirits, you can compel the spirit that is speaking to answer this question: "Do you confess that Jesus Christ came in the flesh?"

On one occasion when I tested the spirits in this way, I heard them yell at me, "No I don't!" This was scary, but nevertheless vital for me to know at the time!

Derek Prince once said, "Discerning of spirits is the ability to hear and see in the spirit world." It can indeed be startling when you test the spirit, it shouts back at you and you hear it as loud as if it were audible.

Any spirit that does not confess that Christ has come in the flesh is Antichrist.

I met a fine young man once, I will call him "Bob," who got involved in a very strange cult group. And this cult group was really weird! Two of us who were pastors walked into the little church headquarters they had and it was filled with darkness and gloom. It was so eerie! As we looked around there was nobody there, or so it seemed at first. We started to flip out, because it turned out these people had a Bible school! And one of the courses was entitled "Caskets and Graves." I kid you not! They were really a cult that studied all about death and practised necromantic activity. Suddenly out of the gloom, there was standing behind us a little old lady all dressed up in a long flowing black gown.

She said in an ominous voice, "May I help you?" I mean, it was enough to curl your hair. This cult group would go around to all the widows and widowers in this small town and have the elderly people sign over their property to this "church." They owned over a dozen houses. They routinely took advantage of widows. So I asked this little old lady, "Where is Bob?"

"I don't know where Bob is. I have no idea, at all," she replied flatly.

We left to look elsewhere because we knew that this group also owned a restaurant in town. "Quite an enlightening little group, huh?" I mused with a smile. It was so weird. The waitresses at their restaurant all had this sort of distant, spaced-out look in their eyes. One of the waitresses said, "Well, Bob is doing some maintenance with a work crew at the local park."

So, we went to the park and there was Bob, along with two or three other men. These guys were pretty slick and tried to whisk him away. I said, "We just need to talk to Bob for five minutes." They granted me "just five" minutes.

I showed Bob this scripture,

"By this you know the Spirit of God: Every spirit that confesses that Jesus Christ has come in the flesh is of God, and every spirit that does not confess that Jesus Christ has come in the flesh is not of God. And this is the spirit of the Antichrist, which you have heard was coming, and is now already in the world" (I John 4:2-3).

I said to Bob, "I want you to pray right now and ask, 'You spirit speaking to me through Ernie Gruen, do you confess that Jesus Christ has come in the flesh?'"

And when he did that I asked him flat out, "What did you hear?"

He said, "I just heard a real soft 'Yes.'"

So, I continued, "Now, ask the spirit running this group of folks the same question. 'You spirit speaking through the such and such fellowship, do you confess Jesus Christ has come in the flesh?'"

Startled, he turned to me riveting his eyes on mine and reported, "I heard a voice shouting at me, 'NO, I DO NOT!'"

On that basis he decided, "I'm going with you, NOW, brother Ernie!"

But that wasn't the end of it. These other men actually said, "You can't take him!"

I said, "But, we ARE taking him!" and we drove back to the supposed "church" where he had been staying in a dorm upstairs. We told him, "You run in and grab your clothes; we're out of here!"

Well, he didn't come back out. When we went in after him, they announced, "Bob can't go."

I asserted, "He is going! I'll give you two minutes and we're calling the police, because we're not leaving here without him. And if you don't cooperate immediately, we're going to put the police on you! That's when he appeared with all of his possessions. We threw them in the trunk and sped off.

Now, what I want you to get is this: I John 4 <u>works</u>! That day I John 4 got a man – a very young, impressionable man – out of an extremely dangerous cult group.

Bob, became an evangelical missionary in Mexico! He made his whole decision to stay with Jesus on the basis that this scripture would work for his life. If he could do it in the face of a demonic cult system, <u>you</u> can actually examine the spirit underneath a simple prophecy or any other life situation or group.

10. KINDS OF TONGUES

The Greek word for "different kinds" here is "genos" which means "nation" or "race;" while the word for "tongues" is "glosa" or, in other scripture, "glosalalia." People who want to sound intellectual will call tongues "glosalalia." That just means "speaking in tongues."

We have already discussed the different uses of speaking in tongues for various purposes. Tongues used in prayer energizes and directs intercession.

11. INTERPRETATION OF TONGUES

Tongues with interpretation in a church service is the same as prophecy. Tongues are the "prayer language of the Spirit" and with the gift of interpretation are a source of great blessing.

Interpretation of tongues however is not translation. It is interpretation. I don't know if you've ever worked with translators, but the first thing you will notice is that they each will translate your words differently. One translator can take two paragraphs to interpret what another can interpret in two sentences. An interpretation basically gives the essence – the overall thought – or impression of what God's Spirit has spoken. Whether I say, "Water is a liquid" or I say, "Water is wet," the essence of my words remains the same. An interpretation is more like the Living Bible than a literal word-for-word translation of the New Testament.

(12.-16.—THE FIVE-FOLD MINISTRY GIFTS)

"And His gifts were [varied; He Himself appointed and gave men to us,] *some to be apostles* (special messengers), *some prophets* (inspired preachers and expounders), *some evangelists* (preachers of the Gospel, traveling missionaries), *some pastors* (shepherds of His flock) *and teachers"* (Ephesians 4:11, The Amplified Bible).

We are going to look at these special gifts in more detail in the next chapter, but we must at least touch on these briefly now. There are five of these gifts. All are both gifts to men and of men, for the Body of Christ. Jesus was the pinnacle of all five of these gifts, rolled into one person: Apostle, Prophet, Pastor, Evangelist and Teacher!

We can see in this passage that Jesus personally gives these individuals <u>to</u> us as His special gifts and He gives these men <u>by</u> calling them to a specific office or function of His choosing. You and I cannot "call" ourselves to these positions, although I have seen many folks who have tried to do just that.

12. APOSTLE

An apostle is one sent on a mission with a Divine Commission bearing authority from God. Their mission can be changed, amplified, or redirected at the will of God.

Jesus accomplished a lot in his ministry! But whatever He did, He first <u>saw</u> through the eyes of His Father's will. Apostle means "sent one" and Jesus was sent to do a lot. Jesus was "Apostled by God" as our high priest after facing Calvary's cross. We can learn much from studying His work, but as it relates to the ministry gift of "Apostle" we know at least this:

- Apostles do what they first see as being the Father's demonstrated will.
- The apostle's commission carries with it both the vision and the authority to get the job done!
- There is an application of the cross that precedes the call to this ministry in its fullness.

The Apostle Paul cried out triumphantly: *"I have been crucified with Christ; it is no longer I who live, but Christ, lives in me;..."* (Galatians 2:20). Paul was rejoicing in the fact that he clearly saw Christ's will flowing through his own life – accomplishing God's desire. Paul's goal was to attain to the resurrection of the dead. The life of Christ, flowing within, was to him a joy unspeakable and full of glory.

13. PROPHET

Now, prophets are a little different. They see the will of God, as well as hidden obstacles to progress; and with their vision, an indicated pathway to victory. But prophets don't just see the hidden path to God's victory for the Church; for lots of people see things. The very word, "prophet," means to tell forth. They have the ability to "say it right," with maximum impact. A prophetic word, spoken forth by a true prophet will absolutely come to pass. It will impact its intended purpose with certitude.

Prophets bring forth action, releasing faith in a group of believers, turning the believers toward God and miraculous levels of obedience. The prophet and his unique "gifts" speak to us, bringing growth, victory, and progress along God's ordained pathway. Always listen for the "I will..., if you will..." in the prophet's message. Some things God promises unconditionally; at other times, He adds a condition, which the prophet is sure to include in God's offer to us: *"Whosoever will may come,"* but *"whosoever will not,"* will never be forced!

This gift historically carries an awesome price tag, just like the apostolic gift. Jesus asked the leadership of Israel the rhetorical question: *"Which one of the prophets didn't you kill?"* (See Luke 13:34 and Matthew 23:31, 37). Prophets often give their lives to make sure that God's will is known to each generation. What the prophet has to say to God's people may be so critical to victory, that it costs the prophet his life.

14. PASTOR

The epitome of pastoral ministry was prophesied regarding Christ in the 23rd Psalm by David, who was also by trade a shepherd. In this Psalm we see Jesus as the Great Shepherd leading the flock of God. Pastors who are called and gifted by God should naturally exhibit these aspects of the life of Christ in their ministry to the sheep.

Can there be any doubt that we need more of these precious gifts to lead and protect the Body of Christ today? True pastors are not hirelings (mere employees) who flee when they first hear the "wolf" coming. Instead, they defend and provide for their flock. They truly care for the sheep personally, and will lay down their lives to protect them. *"I am the good shepherd. The good shepherd giveth His life for the sheep"* (John 10:11).

Pastors are, in a word, "shepherds," called to feed and lead God's precious sheep. Each of the other five ministry gifts has a pastoring component to go along with each gift. And pastors at times are called to do the functions of the other ministry gift as well. Timothy was a <u>pastor</u>, who the Apostle Paul instructed to "do the work of an <u>evangelist</u>."

Pastoral giftings enable the pastor to supernaturally find the various feeding grounds for meeting the sheep's needs – spiritually, mentally and even physically. In the Old Testament, as we shall see in the next chapter, pastors were chastised for not healing the injured and ill sheep. A true pastor is always looking for food and provision for the sheep entrusted to his care. Pastor's also have zero fear of "wolves" and possess the anointing to drive away dangers to the flock.

15. EVANGELIST

In their many different manifestations, all the gifts of the Holy Spirit carry at least one primary message: "The Good News!" In fact, "Evangel" means "good news." <u>So</u> good is that news that the prophet, Isaiah, said, *"How beautiful upon the mountains Are the feet of him who brings good news"* (Isaiah 52:7). Supernatural signs often follow their good-news message of hope. God confirms His Word with signs following.

In some measure, all saints are called to share the "good news." It is not surprising to me that "evangelism" seems to be the "port of entry" for many who are eventually called to other of the five-fold ministry gifts. Neither is it a surprise that God holds us all accountable for being His instrument of "evangelism" to others at one time or another. Aren't you glad somebody told <u>you</u>?

But all of these ministries aren't like separate and distinct "corporate job descriptions;" in ministry there is a flowing together of the stream of God's gifts and anointings.

Prophets make supernatural utterances that witness to God, Christ and the power of His resurrection. Sometimes evangelists prophesy in that manner. Stephen was just such a man. He both taught and prophesied in the day of his "testimony!" Scripture reports Stephen's wisdom and teaching were supernaturally "irresistible."

Stephen was a deacon, the first martyr recorded in Scripture. He did the work of an evangelist that day, but what really triggered his murder were his pointed prophetic utterances to the leadership in Jerusalem. He boldly spoke about what he saw and knew to be God's truth: *"I see the heavens open and the Son of Man standing at the right hand of God"* (Acts 8:56). Moments later we see Stephen falling to his knees, and falling asleep in Jesus' arms. There is a grace given by God to ministers that enables them to pay the price for their work and testimony – but it comes with a price tag. Never underestimate the power of a life sacrificed for service at the Master's behest!

The power of Stephen's testimony was the seed that God used to bring the Apostle Paul to his knees by faith in that very same living Christ! Paul heard Stephen say, *"Look! I see the heavens opened and the Son of Man standing at the right hand of God,"* for the rest of his days.

16. Teachers

Teachers in the "ministry-gift" sense are not necessarily of the Sunday-school or elementary-school variety, although those might be the avenues where one realizes, "I seem to have a 'special gift' for communicating truth to others."

Teachers in the Body of Christ: (1) know God's Word, (2) have an unction to teach with divine authority, (3) exhibit revelatory understanding of biblical truth and make it applicable in daily life, and (4) live what they teach.

They also often manifest the supernatural gifts of the word of knowledge and the word of wisdom. A skilled teacher can walk into a setting and quickly discern what is needed, what is missing and plot a course to meet the situation head on, making the maximum beneficial impact for the Body of Christ.

Teachers have the gift of impartation. They don't just teach others to memorize verses and curriculum.

A BASIC FIVE-FOLD MINISTRY SUMMARY

Five-fold ministry positions are not earned and the brief treatment we have given them here are not to be taken as "job descriptions." Instead, these are simply brief introductory discussions of the office functions that each ministry position has a tendency to fulfill! The truth is, none of these function in a vacuum as will be seen in the following chapter quite clearly. Neither are these ministry gifts "competitive" in nature, as can be seen in Acts chapter 13, at the calling and ordination of Paul and Barnabus as Apostles to Europe.

In this passage we can see that certain ministry groups flow, feed and play off of one another as vital ministries within the context of the Body of Christ. It is interesting to note that this group, meeting in prayer and fasting, were primarily, if not exclusively, "prophets and teachers." These are two groups that often interact in ministry to produce new direction. Prophets reveal obstacles, needs and divine direction; whereas teachers, recognizing needs, go about plotting the God-ordained and scriptural method for "getting there" by faith.

Prophets gain understanding of the way of God from teachers, and teachers grasp confirmation for the will of God revealed. The result in this case: the birthing of a new and vigorous apostolic ministry that rocked the foundations of western civilization!

I am not giving you a guaranteed formula, but in this passage: Prophets + Teachers + waiting on God = the Apostles, Barnabus and Paul! What is guaranteed is that ministry gifts flowing together will birth new and powerful ministry! But, they must function – together – with God's direction.

Prophets and teachers together in Acts 13 provided the "pastoral" gift of guidance to confirm what Paul and Barnabus already knew. Paul and Barnabus were willing to wait for that confirmation. Patience was a key element in the life and ministry of apostles in general and of Jesus in particular.

Remember, there is safety in numbers when it comes to walking in the ministry gifts. God gave five ministry gifts and He gives no gift in vain! Are you receiving the benefits of each?

In the Body of Christ we need these gifts today more than ever before in history. *"Many are called..."* but few are willing to pay the price of commitment necessary to also be "chosen" (Revelation 17:14, Matthew 20:16).

Are you willing to offer yourself as a living sacrifice to Jesus in one of these callings – as a gift of God, to his people??? Now is the time that multitudes of God's people need to begin counting the cost! A lost and dying world awaits our decision.

17. GIFT OF SERVING (DEACONS)

"Having then gifts differing according to the grace that is given to us, let us use them: if prophecy, let us prophesy in proportion to our faith; or ministry, let us use it in our ministering; he who teaches, in teaching..." (Romans 12:6-7).

The Greek word used here for ministry is actually "diakonia" or deacon. Deacons could be either feminine or masculine. I believe you should pray for this gifting. I believe every pastor should pray to be a servant. Every man or woman who holds any office in the church should strive to partake of this primary natural characteristic of Christ – that of being a servant. He came not to be ministered to, but to minister. The heart of those in leadership should be one of service.

18. GIFT OF ENCOURAGEMENT

"He who exhorts, in exhortation; he who gives, with liberality; he who leads, with diligence; he who shows mercy, with cheerfulness" (Romans 12:8).

The Greek word here for "exhort" is "paraclete" or comforter. It doesn't mean rebuke! It means to encourage, comfort, cheer or aid. Jesus never said, "I'm going back to heaven, and I will send you another rebuker?" This passage uses the same Greek word that Jesus used when He said, "I will send you another comforter."

One day God said to me, "People do not receive encouragement in the world, in high school, or on their job. If they come to church happy and leave sad, you have failed My people." He said, "I want you to be an encourager!"

Literally thousands of times I have prayed this, "Lord give me the gift of encouragement. I want to build people up." As I've looked around at the elderly people in nursing homes, they need so much encouragement. As I look at husbands, across the board, most of them really need encouragement. Most wives need encouragement as well. As I look at children, they are so often discouraged. The most favored gift for me to pray for would be, "Please Lord, help me to be an encourager."

I want to be that way. I want to be anointed to comfort people, to bring them good cheer. I want to have them go home full of joy. I like to laugh. I like to joke around. I like to have fun all week long. I hate being an up-tight "stick in the mud." I want to be encouraged. The Bible says that we will reap what we sow. I choose to sow encouragement. How about you?

Isn't that a gift you want to pray for? Everyone in your family and in your workplace, with maybe a few exceptions, are like dry sponges, waiting for someone to fill them up with joy or a positive word. We need to be encouragers, building people up. It is perhaps one of the most needed gifts in our world today.

19. GIFT OF GIVING

"...he who exhorts, in exhortation; <u>he who gives,</u> <u>with liberality</u>; he who leads, with diligence; he who shows mercy, with cheerfulness" (Romans 12:8).

This is the gift of giving with generosity. The New King James says, "liberality." This is a different thing than simply tithing.

You SHOULD enjoy giving presents. I love to give. I'm not necessarily even talking about church either. You can fill in the blanks on your own. Just being a giver is a wonderful blessing. If you're ever going to be like God, you will have to become a giver. Giving is a manifestation of His primary nature, *"...God so loved the world that He **gave** His only begotten Son,..."* (John 3:16). In plain English, love <u>gives</u>.

My daughter called one day, asking where most people go to have the turn signal bulbs in their cars replaced. I said, "Well, the place they do that is in your dad's garage."

I could feel her smile spreading across her face.

So, she came over, I took her old burned up light bulb out, bought a new bulb, installed it and put the whole light assembly back in place. There were about five other small things wrong with her car that I noticed at the same time. So, I fixed those things and, just for good measure, I vacuumed her car interior from top to bottom. Now, that vacuuming part took a good deal of Fatherly grace!

You know, they say, "Men are the 'messy ones.'" But I have news for you: that is just a cliché. Don't you believe it! Let's just say this car desperately needed vacuuming. There were actually things "growing" in there! Now, it was a great joy for me to serve my daughter like that. We must look for opportunities to do something for others. That's what life is all about – being a giver and an encourager!

20. GIFT OF LEADERSHIP

"...he who leads, with diligence; he who shows mercy, with cheerfulness" (Romans 12:8).

Again, looking at Romans 12:8, we find the Greek word for "lead" is "proistami." It is translated many times as "ruler" in the Bible, but the Greek word actually means "to stand in front of." This is sort of like the husband in a family. He is neither the ruler nor the dictator over his house, but he does get out in front to protect and deflect.

Everything hits him first. He is physically and spiritually a barrier of protection. He decides what stops at him and what goes through him to impact his wife and children.

Leadership in this context is the idea of a barrier of protection, not domination. This is how leadership is to be seen by all who hold the office of pastor or walk in <u>any</u> of the ministry gifts, for that matter. Pastors in particular should never dominate or control others. A pastor's responsibility is to get out in front and take the abuse, keeping it off God's family in the local church as much as possible.

Those called to "leadership" will follow his lead and take their place alongside the pastor to protect that Body - the family of God.

21. GIFT OF SHOWING MERCY

There are folks who actually love making hospital calls. They cannot wait to send flowers and cards. These people love showing mercy. Do you know someone who is a "card" person? There is a lady in our church who would always send two or three cards and a present as well. These people who are "card-sending-people" have the gift of mercy. God prefers mercy to judgment.

22. GIFT OF HELPS

This is a gift that manifests itself in people who love to clean the church and do things like that for others. I remember a wonderful Christian lady in a Baptist church where I pastored in Milton, Kansas. Her name was Grace.

We had a 3 ½-year-old, a 2-year-old and newborn twins – that was four children under the age of four and three still in diapers. Grace sat with my wife every day in church, helping with the twins. She was an "uncomplicated" person, and never asked for any of this world's acclaim. But, she was a woman of God.

In heaven, Grace will be sitting in the front row while the rest of us will be a couple miles back, if we even get that close. She was a true servant of God.

23. GIFT OF STEERING

"And God has appointed these in the church: first apostles, second prophets, third teachers, after that miracles, then gifts of healings, helps, administrations, varieties of tongues" (I Corinthians 12:28).

Most translations interpret the word "administrations," here in the New King James version as "government." However, the Greek word is actually a navy term meaning "to steer" or "to pilot" a boat. It carries with it the idea of having your hand on the rudder. As soon as I found out what that word, "steering," really meant, I asked that God manifest that gift in me immediately.

As you probably know, anybody who pastors desperately needs to have the gift of steering. Somebody has to make decisions and take responsibility while being willing to stand in judgment before God regarding those decisions. This steering gift is absolutely essential in leading a church or ministry service.

The Holy Spirit moves like a river, with many turns. If we are not sensitive to the flow, we will end up crashing on a sand bar. Someone has to make the decision as to how long to worship, who is to speak, and then be willing to stand and be accountable to God for those decisions.

This gift can also be applied beneficially in secular business affairs as well. If you carry any responsibility for a group of people, you can pray, "God, please give me the gift of steering." If you are under someone else's responsibility, you should pray that for them as well. You should make this request for your pastor because – gift or not – their hands <u>are</u> already on the rudder!

The church MUST be steered in the right direction on EVERY decision.

24. GIFT OF INTERCESSORY PRAYER

"Blessed be the God and Father of our Lord Jesus Christ, the Father of mercies and God of all comfort, who comforts us in all our tribulation, that we may be able to comfort those who are in any trouble, with the comfort with which we ourselves are comforted by God. For as the sufferings of Christ abound in us, so our consolation also abounds through Christ. Now if we are afflicted, it is for your consolation and salvation, which is effective for enduring the same sufferings which we also suffer. Or if we are comforted, it is for your consolation and salvation. And our hope for you is steadfast, because we know that as you are partakers of the sufferings, so also you will partake of the consolation. For we do not want you to be ignorant, brethren, of our trouble which came to us in Asia: that we were burdened beyond measure, above strength, so that we despaired even of life. Yes, we had the sentence of death in ourselves, that we should not trust in ourselves but in God who raises the dead, who delivered us from so great a death, and does deliver us; in whom we trust that He will still deliver us, you also helping together in prayer for us, that thanks may be given by

many persons on our behalf for the gift granted to us through many" (II Corinthians 1:3-11).

As you read this passage, notice that it is placed in the context of ministering out of one's own pain and suffering. As you yourself are comforted, you are able to comfort others and intercede for them.

25. GIFT OF CELIBACY

"But I say this as a concession, not as a commandment. For I wish that all men were even as I myself. But each one has his own gift from God, one in this manner and another in that. But I say to the unmarried and to the widows: It is good for them if they remain even as I am; but if they cannot exercise self-control, let them marry. For it is better to marry than to burn with passion" (I Corinthians 7:6-9).

Celibacy here is a grace (or charis) gift. We shouldn't joke about it because it takes much more grace to remain celibate and pure than it does to be married and pure. The body does make those demands! But there is a grace gift of God that is available to every single man or woman in the Body of Christ when it is needed or appropriate.

I know people who actually have this gift! Then there are people who receive this gift after they have lost their husband or wife. It requires a special anointing of the grace of God to be celibate.

These are the 25 gifts of the Holy Spirit and they are all given for our profit. You may not be a leader, but every man and woman, for example will need the gift of "steering" on one occasion or another. All of these gifts are for every believer, as the Holy Spirit distributes them according to His sovereign will and our human necessity.

Jesus said, *"For everyone who asks receives, and he who seeks finds, and to him who knocks it will be opened"* (Matthew 7:8).

We need to do just that in regard to God's gifts for us and others. Ask. Seek. And Knock! God wants to open the doors for us!

CHAPTER 7

THE FIVE MINISTRY GIFTS

To this point so far we have looked mostly at individual tools or abilities that God by His Spirit has made available to His children. We are awed by how much God has committed into our hands by His grace. But there is more – much, much more – because God, by His Spirit, not only gives supernatural gifts, He also gives out ministry giftings, or callings; each include unique aspects all its own.

Have you ever been to a Christmas celebration where one or more people were left out and did not receive a personal gift from anyone? Has that ever happened to you?

No person has been left out of receiving some combination of the gifts of the Spirit. God, it seems, is unwilling that anybody should be left out of having a unique calling, custom designed for each individual's abilities, cultural context and level of obedience. No one is left out, and every gifting, calling, or supernatural gift has been crafted by God in a uniquely designed package for each person. And unlike Christmas Holidays or Birthdays, God's giving never stops!

Oh, what a supreme joy it is to begin discovering *"the unsearchable riches of Christ!"* (Ephesians 3:8).

As with all gifts from His hand, grace and humility are the keys to understanding and receiving God's best. We have learned through experience:

"But he gives more grace. Therefore he says: God resists the proud, But gives grace to the humble" (James 4:6).

This concept of humility is vital in receiving all of God's gifts for you.

Pride has a way of shutting down all that God wants to do for us, in us and through us. Nowhere is this more important than in the understanding of the five ministry gifts.

The gifts of the Spirit that we have looked at so far are individual enablings or supernatural abilities, but the ministry giftings and callings not only carry special enablings, they each carry a unique commission.

In a ministry gifting, you not only receive supernatural gifts and abilities, you actually become the gift of God to others. The commission you receive from God, is one of those "words" from God that has the unique authority, or *exousia* to bring itself to pass. You become the calling – the calling that God has for you – to bless others.

Such a calling can be "heady" stuff for immature believers. This kind of power and authority in the hands of a novice can be destructive beyond words. History has been littered with God-ordained movements that strayed from His will through prideful sin. So, in consideration of the Holy Spirit's five ministry gifts, we must always focus on the humility of Christ.

Jesus is the Pattern

"Therefore, holy brethren, partakers of the heavenly calling, consider the Apostle and High Priest of our confession, Christ Jesus" (Hebrews 3:1).

When Jesus ascended, He divide out callings, ministry gifts and assignments to men. We see Him work through those men in the Church of the New Testament. Each person called of God into these positions drew his primary motivation from the life of our Lord Jesus Christ. As we look at them, we see Jesus at work. Jesus in His earthly ministry didn't come out and divide Himself into five parts. We have only one Jesus! Ministry must function together.

As we look at the gifts as He distributed them to men, we can see Jesus, the Apostle, being sent; Jesus, the Prophet, turning over the money changers' table in the temple and declaring what was about to happen. We can see Jesus the Evangelist proclaiming the "glad tidings" that "the Kingdom of God is in your very midst." We see Jesus, the Pastor, feeding His flock on the hills of Israel, defending them from the wolves. He declares, "I am the door of the sheep." We see Jesus, the Teacher, instructing "The Teacher" of Israel – Nicodemus – by night: "Ye must be born again."

No man but Jesus ever had all the gifts, all the time, functioning in perfect harmony. But in Him we see that unique pattern that binds them all together: a life of servanthood and humility. By God's grace, His Body, the Church, is on its way to reaching that level of maturity in ministry. The day is fast approaching when we will reach the God-ordained measure of the stature of His fullness. As we look at the five-fold ministry gifts, we need to try and see Jesus as He walked through all five of them. It is in following Him that we find our own place of calling and gifting.

THERE ARE FIVE GIFTS

*"But to each one of us grace was given according to the measure of Christ's gift. Therefore He says: 'When He ascended on high, He led captivity captive, And gave gifts to men'.... And He Himself gave some to be **apostles**, some **prophets**, some **evangelists**, and some **pastors** and **teachers**, for the equipping of the saints for the work of ministry, for the edifying of the body of Christ"* (Ephesians 4:7-8 & 11-12).

To appreciate and understand the five ministry "grace gifts," we first need to understand why they have been given. These gifts were given by Jesus for the primary purpose of equipping saints to do ministry, which builds up, fortifies and strengthens the Body of Christ. God wants every child of His to move into some aspect of ministry. These five ministries provide the resources to get them moving <u>now</u>.

Think about it: God wants you to minister to others for Him, here in the earth!

Now, these ministry gifts were ordained and set into motion when Jesus ascended on high, after His complete and total victory over death, hell, sin and the grave. These ministries are critically tied to manifesting the victory of Christ in the earth. They are part of God's plan for making the kingdoms of this world the Kingdom of our God and of His Christ, and for our reigning with Him for all eternity.

Furthermore, these gifts were given for specific purposes... *for the edifying of the body of Christ... till we come in the unity of the faith... to become a mature man... to reach the measure of the stature of the fullness of Christ... that we may grow up into Him in all things, who is the Head,* (my own condensed transliteration).

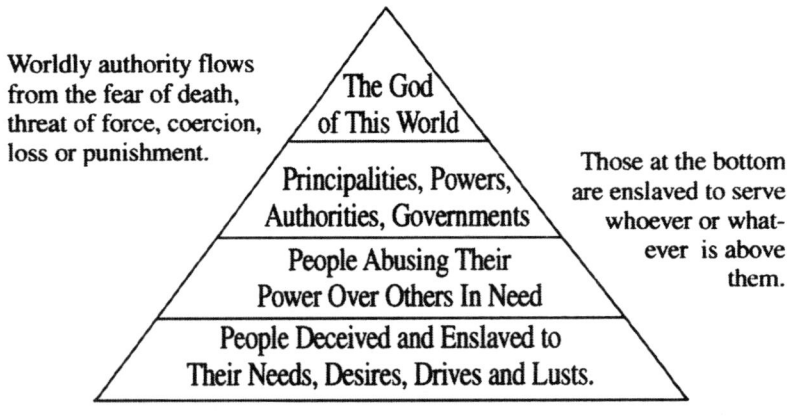

Worldly authority flows from the fear of death, threat of force, coercion, loss or punishment.

The God of This World

Principalities, Powers, Authorities, Governments

People Abusing Their Power Over Others In Need

People Deceived and Enslaved to Their Needs, Desires, Drives and Lusts.

Those at the bottom are enslaved to serve whoever or whatever is above them.

This World's General Paradigm of Power, Authority and Leadership.

Put simply, God gives these people as gifts, to us, so that we may grow up and be all He wants us to be.

Whenever a person is called to become one of these ministry gifts, serving the Body of Christ, he or she must always remember that the individual is not stepping up to some great and "high" position of supremacy. Always remember that there really is only one Head on this body – Christ.

Instead, the individual must realize that he or she is stooping down to a place of servitude in order to carry out a mandate from God for the benefit and deliverance of others.

It is immoral to take a ministry position for the sake of social prominence or financial gain. Ministry is intended to be a living demonstration of this scripture:

> *"Let nothing be done through selfish ambition or conceit, but in lowliness of mind let each esteem others better than himself"* (Philippians 2:3).

God's Economy for All Ministry Authority

We must also:

"Let this mind be in you which was also in Christ Jesus, who... made Himself of no reputation, taking the form of a bondservant... He humbled Himself and became obedient..." (Philippians 2:5-8, selected portions).

THEY HAVE A GOD-ORDAINED ORDER

"And God has appointed these in the church, first apostles, second prophets, third teachers, after that miracles, then gifts of healings, helps, administrations, varieties of tongues" (I Corinthians 12:28).

Just because the ministry gifts are to be accepted with all humility and a sense of esteeming others does not mean that there is no primacy in ministry gifts. Each has its place and its priority in God's economy. God has set these gifts in a very specific order according to His wisdom.

In this passage, the words for first, second and third, are ordinals – not just counting numerals like "one, two and three."

Each number here has a specific meaning. For example, the original Greek word for "first" here is the word, "proton" and you can probably guess what it means by how it sounds. It means primary, the first, one of a kind, the beginning of a set, and the most important. Nuclear scientists named the subatomic particles at the center of each atom "protons," to convey the primacy of the particles. Without protons, matter as we know it could not exist.

Jesus is the primary "Apostle and High Priest of our confession." He gave the ministry gift of apostles to us because they are primary; they follow the exact pattern His life laid down for us, and are foundational to all other ministries.

The Greek word for "second" is the word "deuteros" which means: second, and also, and afterwards. Prophetic ministry follows the Apostolic in priority, but it is interesting to note that many times we see in the Bible that apostles move in the prophet's calling and prophets are "sent" or "apostled" on a mission. In fact, they are almost inseparable and God usually blends people called into these two areas of ministry seamlessly, so as to make them one solid element of His grace.

The Greek word for "thirdly" is the word "tritos" and it means: "a third part of," like in the fraction one-third, except it is actually the third part. These three ministries, according to this scripture, make it possible for all the others flow thereafter – and for good reason. There are aspects of all three that put them in an order – a necessary order based on the work they all do together.

TWO OF THE FIVE ARE FOUNDATIONAL

*"...having been built on **the foundation of the apostles** and **prophets**, Jesus Christ Himself being the chief cornerstone"* (Ephesians 2:20).

Here is a key to understanding: God gave the five ministry gifts to build something very important to Him – His Body, the Body of Christ. The understanding of all five flows from the paradigm of God *constructing* something.

We are the building of God, His handiwork in the earth. But all construction requires first a foundation. Foundations require sitework, demolition and earth moving. Foundations require firm materials designed to support the weight of the structure they will undergird. And foundations have to be laid out according to a plan if a building is to meet the specifications of the architect's plans. They must stand the test of time, despite wind, rain, flood, earthquakes, hurricanes and tornadoes.

When this passage of scripture was written, the first foundation stone laid (Christ) had to be perfectly square and level with the site in order to form the building. Jesus was the perfected epitome of all of God's ministry gifts, – Apostle, Prophet, Evangelist, Pastor (shepherd) and Teacher. In Him, the pattern for every aspect of God's building was present in His perfect life, ministry, temptation, victory over sin, sacrificial death, victorious resurrection and His giving us each and every one of the gifts of His Holy Spirit.

THE APOSTLE

άποσγαλους, pronounced: "ap-os'-tol-os;" is transliterated, *apostolos*, as a noun and in its related verb forms. It actually means: an official delegate carrying authority; specifically an ambassador of the Gospel; officially a commissioner of Christ. It is translated as an *"apostle," or "messenger," or "sent"* (also having miraculous powers). Related Greek words are *apostole, apostello and apostellos*. The word(s) refer to the "one that is sent" and often the actual act of sending one with a specific commission or accompanied by given orders of a higher authority.

There are a lot of people today talking about the "Apostolic" ministry. I have heard, "So and so is our Apostle; he is so wonderful," or "Our church is under Apostle Smith or Jones." All of this is said in tones that go quite beyond basic respect, mutual submission and humility – approaching a level of worship. But the title is nothing to be worshipped. The truth is simply that the word "apostle" means "sent one" simple and plain. In basic terms, if I were to assign my daughter the task of going out every day to pick up the mail for me, I would be "apostoling" her with a commission. Now, "apostoling" is not really a word in our English language, but in the original language of the New Testament it would be transliterated very much like that, indeed!

In fact, in many of the times that the word "sent" appears in the New Testament, it has been translated from the verb for "apostle." The other word translated "sent" is *pempo*. It means to be sent on an errand. The difference is that being "apostled" carries with it the idea of a <u>permanent</u>, <u>long-term</u> assignment with accompanying orders and the necessary authority to carry out that assignment. In every case when Jesus said things like, "the Father has *sent* me, so *send* I you," He used the verb form for "apostle." In the other cases where someone is being *sent* to pick something up or deliver something, it is the word *pempo.*

When God calls and assigns an Apostle, there is a commission given to that person to undertake that assignment. That commission carries God's own authority and permission, enabling the necessary supernatural gifts and always laying a foundation for building the Body of Christ.

Because of the importance of each assignment that God makes, people are drawn at times to "try and be" an apostle. People can desire the prestige of an assignment "directly from God," just from watching apostolic ministry in action. People like Simon the Sorcerer in Acts 8:18 come to mind:

"And when Simon saw that through the laying on of the apostles' hands the Holy Spirit was given, he offered them money."

Now, here was a guy who was asking for trouble and who got exactly what he was asking for. Peter the Apostle told him what to do with his money:

"You have neither part nor portion in this matter, for your heart is not right in the sight of God. Repent therefore of this your wickedness, and pray God if perhaps the thought of your heart may be forgiven you. For I see that you are poisoned by bitterness and bound by iniquity" (Acts 8:21-23).

Simon, you see, was covetous of Apostolic power and prestige. With all the people today running around calling other people "Apostle," we need to keep in mind that laying claim on an office that one is not called to is dangerous business.

The Church of the end times will be held particularly responsible for testing those who claim to be Apostles of the Lamb. We see this in the book of Revelation:

"I know your works, your labor, your patience, and that you cannot bear those who are evil. And you have tested those who say they are apostles and are not, and have found them liars" (Revelation 2:2).

If this scripture means anything, it is saying that there must be a test for false apostles. Otherwise God wouldn't commend and reward this particular Church for doing just that.

The Apostle Paul referred to the necessity for testing those who claim such an office for themselves when he said:

"For such are false apostles, deceitful workers, transforming themselves into apostles of Christ. And no wonder! For Satan himself transforms himself into an angel of light. Therefore it is no great thing if his ministers also transform themselves into ministers of righteousness, whose end will be according to their works" (II Corinthians 11:13-15).

But where is the test mentioned in Revelation 2:2?

We see false apostles disguise themselves as apostles of Christ through deceitful works. They look real, so Paul laid down in Scripture the standard for discerning false apostles and he did it in the way he lived his own life as a pattern of apostolic ministry. It is no coincidence that the issue of testing to determine what is true once again revolves around the issues of ungodly gain, manipulation or misuse of others:

"Did I commit sin in humbling myself that you might be exalted, because I preached the gospel of God to you free of charge? I robbed other churches, taking wages from them to minister to you. And when I was present with you, and in need, I was a burden to no one, for what I lacked the brethren who came from Macedonia supplied. And in everything I kept myself from being burdensome to you, and so I will keep myself" (II Corinthians 11:7-9)

It was in the context of this real-life, sacrificial testimony of a man who went to jail (and death) for his Apostolic calling that he said, in essence, "Folks who say that they are apostles and yet fail to measure up to the standard God has laid out for you to see in my life, regardless of their deceitful works or miracles, are false apostles."

Paul's personal standard, summarized briefly in this scripture passage, would constitute a fair test – not only for apostles, but for all of those who have been called of God to be His gifts to the Body of Christ.

BASICS OF THE TEST:

a. Paul preached the Gospel and taught the Word at NO charge to those he served, taking no gain personally.
b. Paul's expenses were not extracted by edict from the place where he served. Other churches and ministry partners believed in and adequately supported his work.
c. Paul endured his lack without complaining about his mission in life to other people. He didn't beg for money and he placed no obligation on those who were under his charge.

"The laborer is worthy of his wages" (Luke 10:7) and God meets His servant's needs abundantly. Paul even said so at times, but the key was in Paul's attitude and Jesus' as well. Paul never saw the people of God like a flock of sheep to be shorn of their wool, or eaten in a time of need. He saw them as people in need of guidance and protection. From that "servant" attitude flows the divine authority of God.

Apostles have tremendous authority, directly given to them by God. God gives them insights that are simply not available to just anyone (see Ephesians 3:5). Apostles are rock-solid in character, being morally strong and worthy foundation material. They particularly are given special giftings, unique to their calling, whether it be the working of miracles or raising the dead. Their assignments can be to specific regions, or ethnic groups, or fields of endeavor. There are many, many apostles.

Titus was specifically "apostled" or "sent with a mandate" to handle financial matters related to the Church as a whole: collecting for, and distributing funds to, the saints at Jerusalem, according to Paul. His assignment for that season of time laid a firm foundation for the Church regarding financial support of others who experience need and abundance in the Body of Christ. It is the same pattern that serves us today, as we, too, seek to serve God from a pure heart by our giving.

I cannot find anywhere in scripture that Titus or Paul ever asked for or kept a specific percentage of the funds they collected for themselves. Titus obviously followed Paul's apostolic pattern of financial operation and integrity. His example was laid down by his mentor Paul, and recorded in scripture for us today. Paul later said of Titus:

"Did I take advantage of you by any of those whom I sent to you? I urged Titus, and sent our brother with him. Did Titus take advantage of you? Did we not walk in the same spirit? Did we not walk in the same steps?" (II Corinthians 12:17).

Apostles are "sent ones" directly commissioned of God to build various aspects of the Body of Christ and we are in sore need of these precious gifts today. I have met some apostles who don't carry their title around on their license plate or wear it on their sleeves. They don't spend time manipulating people, nor are they constantly trying to "get" money from them. They don't claim a right to a "percentage" of the offering, or property of those they serve. The primary calling cards of their calling seem to be patience, or perseverance, and personal sacrifice (see II Corinthians 12:12).

The Apostolic commission given by God is vital to us today and more important to our success than most Christians today realize. These humble servants need our support to get their job done, but by nature their calling precludes the manipulative nature of "fund raising."

The apostles I know are completely satisfied to fulfill the function of their office without having the title. That's why you can find them in many different walks of life. Because of the CEO mentality in the United States, local churches and non-profits, the five-fold ministries are all often referred to as Pastors.

But titles given by men can never overshadow the immense value these people are to the Body of Christ. We need to see them where they are, honor their God-given vision and support their work – whether they are called "pastor," or work at a local library.

In the appendix section of this book is a listing of scriptures regarding the ministry gift of the apostle, which includes references to the work of the other five-fold ministry gifts as well. By looking at these passages in God's Word you can begin to recognize these precious five-fold gifts in operation all around you. God calls these "people" to be His gifts as He wills.

THE PROPHET

προφήτης, pronounced: prof-ay'-tace; means a foreteller; or one who "tells forth," by analogy at times an inspired speaker; by extension:—prophet.

Whereas an apostle is sent with a commission or a divinely empowered assignment, a prophet is one who speaks forth a divine message that contains supernatural power. One interesting place the "foundational" aspect of a prophet's ministry can be found is in the commissioning of Jeremiah by God, in the Old Testament:

> *"Then the LORD put forth His hand and touched my mouth, and the LORD said unto me: Behold, I have put My words in your mouth. See, I have this day set you over the nations and over the kingdoms, to <u>root out</u>, and <u>to pull down</u>, <u>to destroy</u>, and <u>to throw down</u>, <u>to build</u>, and <u>to plant</u>"* (Jeremiah 1:9-10).

A prophet's assigned authority may extend to a nation, a kingdom, a local government or community, or, as described elsewhere in scripture, to specific authority over individuals. Nathan was a prophet who God sent to confront David about his murderous affair with Bathsheba, saying: "Thou art the man!"

Prophetic authority is a foundational activity in the Body of Christ.

RAISING FOLLOWS RAZING!

What do I mean? Well, rooting out, pulling down, destroying and throwing down, are followed by building and planting. That's four parts demolition (in construction terms) and two parts construction, a ratio of two to one. Prophets prepare the ground for foundational activities by rooting out, pulling down, destroying and throwing down obstructions to progress in God's building process. Only after the ground is made level and obstructions are removed can building and planting take place. Hence, prophetic ministries can at times be perceived as harsh – even confrontational. But, it is all constructive in its purpose. Prophets make building and planting possible by removing what offends and obstructs. No wonder this ministry is so critical and precious to God: No stone can be laid until the prophets have done their part.

In the New Testament, we see that apostles can at times be used in a prophetic role. In Acts 13:8-12, Paul confronted a sorcerer, Elymas, who was subverting a local government official (the equivalent of a mayor), through deceit and mischief. It was a hindrance to God's plans for the region. Paul "destroyed" and "threw down" the sorcerer's power publicly, in much the same way as Jesus did in the temple when he overthrew the changer's tables.

The sorcerer was using subtlety to oppose righteousness, and the changers were stealing a "percentage" from God's people. Prophets don't let that kind of stuff stand in God's

way. Once the obstacle is "destroyed," or "cast down," God's
construction process can go on unhindered.
There is much overlap in the ministry gifts. For example,
a prophet can be apostled, and an apostle can be called on to
do a prophet's work as well. Both are particularly foundational
in their work.

THE EVANGELIST

εὐαγγελιστής, pronounced "yoo-ang-ghel-is-tace;" a
preacher of the gospel; evangelist. The first part of the word,
"eu," means good. The second part, "angelistes," means
message. We get our word, "angels," from the same root, which
simply means messenger. An evangelist brings good news!
There is an Old Testament Scripture we often hear regarding
this particularly welcome ministry today:

*"How beautiful upon the mountains are the feet
of him that bringeth good tidings, that publisheth
peace; that bringeth good tidings of good, that
publisheth salvation; that saith unto Zion, Thy God
reigneth! Thy watchmen shall lift up the voice; with
the voice together shall they sing: for they shall see
eye to eye, when the LORD shall bring again Zion.
Break forth into joy, sing together, ye waste places of
Jerusalem: for the LORD hath comforted his people,
he hath redeemed Jerusalem. The LORD hath made
bare his holy arm in the eyes of all the nations; and
all the ends of the earth shall see the salvation of our
God"* (Isaiah 52:7-10, KJV).

We see a reference to this "good news" or "glad tidings,"
in the New Testament as well:

*"And we declare unto you glad tidings, how that
the promise which was made unto the fathers, God
hath fulfilled the same unto us their children, in that
he hath raised up Jesus again;..."* (Acts 13:32-33,
KJV).

The Greek construction here for "glad tidings" is the double use of the word for "good news," or *euaggelizo, euaggelizo,* which really means really, really; good, good; news. This double usage of the word actually <u>multiplies</u> the meaning; it does not simply <u>double</u> it!

There is plenty of reason to call this ministry one of good news. The message brings salvation, healing, seeing eye to eye with God, and not just for one small group of people but for "all the nations" and "all the ends of the earth!" This was the ministry of Jesus carried out in the lives of people all around Him in healing, salvation and deliverance. And, if I may say so, it is probably one of the ministries in greatest need of restoration today: soul-winning, healing-manifesting, demonic-deliverance-bringing, preaching of the really good news of salvation and deliverance for "all the nations" of the earth. It is a ministry that is designed by God to flow with deliverance and manifestations of God's healing graces.

Jesus was an evangelist, He demonstrated the work of an evangelist and He commanded His disciples to do the same. *"As the Father has sent Me, I also send you"* (John 20:21).

The ministry of the evangelist in the book of Acts is illustrated particularly in the life of Philip:

> *"Then Philip went down to the city of Samaria and preached Christ to them. And the multitudes with one accord heeded the things spoken by Philip, hearing and seeing the miracles which he did. For unclean spirits, crying with a loud voice, came out of many who were possessed; and many who were paralyzed and lame were healed. And there was great joy in that city...Now when the apostles who were at Jerusalem heard that Samaria had received the word of God, they sent Peter and John to them, who, when they had come down, prayed for them that they might receive the Holy Spirit. For as yet He had fallen upon*

none of them. They had only been baptized in the name of the Lord Jesus. Then they laid hands on them, and they received the Holy Spirit" (Acts 8:5-8 &14-17).

Philip, the evangelist, had taken the gospel to Samaria in a powerful way, but he needed help to lay the foundation of the Baptism in the Holy Spirit. God had ordained that there was further foundational work to be done in Samaria: demonic influence had been removed, healing had come forth in abundance, people had been saved and baptized in water, but the Holy Ghost had not yet been received.

That foundational work was carried out through the ministry of the two apostles from the "home" church in Jerusalem. And here we see the emerging concept of five-fold "team" ministry, where the several ministries work together to build what God desires. One plants, one waters, but God gives the increase; and He alone receives all the praise and the glory!

The key was that they all worked together toward God's goal, without any competition or pride. Evangelists don't just blow into town, get people saved, healed and delivered, and then leave them to fend on their own. Instead, they take part in the team-ministry concept of laying a foundation and planting the work of God in a community; they call for help to get the job done!

Even pastors must play an ongoing part in fulfilling the role of an evangelist. Paul charged Timothy to do the work of an evangelist while he was pastoring at Ephesus to prove his ministry:

"But you be watchful in all things, endure afflictions, do the work of an evangelist, fulfill your ministry" (II Timothy 4:5).

Part of the proof of a pastoral ministry is the manifestation of evangelistic ministry and winning the lost for Christ. By this we can see that the evangelist is part of local ministry along with the apostle, the prophet, and the pastor. All have areas where they overlap and depend on one another to complete God's plans in any given region. Foundations not only must be laid, but people must be shaped, corrected and directed in ways that will bring them to maturity and usefulness in the Body of Christ. This then leads us to the ministry of the Pastor.

THE PASTOR

ποιμήν, pronounced: poy-mane; means a shepherd, either literally or figuratively. It also means, "to guide." The word, "pastor," is derived in our language from the same word we use for "pasture" where sheep or cattle are fed, watered and nurtured for growth. The pastor leads the sheep to safe pasture. And doing so is his primary function. A good place to start looking at the ministry of Pastor is the 23rd Psalm, where the happy condition of the man in His care is recorded for us:

"The LORD is my shepherd; I shall not want. He maketh me to lie down in green pastures: he leadeth me beside the still waters. He restoreth my soul: he leadeth me in the paths of righteousness for his name's sake. Yea, though I walk through the valley of the shadow of death, I will fear no evil: for thou art with me; thy rod and thy staff they comfort me. Thou preparest a table before me in the presence of mine enemies: thou anointest my head with oil; my cup runneth over. Surely goodness and mercy shall follow me all the days of my life: and I will dwell in the house of the LORD for ever" (Psalm 23:1-6, KJV).

Much has been taught over the years about the ministry of Pastor, but no one lived the Pastoral ministry better than our "Chief Shepherd," the Lord Jesus Christ. David was speaking of Jesus when he wrote the 23rd Psalm. All that we know about the ministry of Pastor is wrapped up in Jesus, and regarding that shepherd ministry He said:

> *"I am the door. If anyone enters by Me, he will be saved, and will go in and out and find pasture. The thief does not come except to steal, and to kill, and to destroy. I have come that they may have life, and that they may have* it *more abundantly. I am the good shepherd. The good shepherd gives His life for the sheep. But a hireling,* he who is *not the shepherd, one who does not own the sheep, sees the wolf coming and leaves the sheep and flees; and the wolf catches the sheep and scatters them. The hireling flees because he is a hireling and does not care about the sheep. I am the good shepherd; and I know My* sheep, *and am known by My own. As the Father knows Me, even so I know the Father; and I lay down My life for the sheep. And other sheep I have which are not of this fold; them also I must bring, and they will hear My voice; and there will be one flock* and *one shepherd"* (John 10:9-16).

There are many aspects of the office of Pastor that Jesus drew attention to here, and that apply to us today. One of the first items is the relationship of the shepherd to the sheep. The shepherd takes responsibility for the care and well-being of the sheep. Many who are called "Pastor" today are not concerned much about the needs of the sheep, and are not genuinely called to the ministry title they carry. Do they care for the sheep, or are they just collecting the wool?

The good shepherd brings freedom to come and go, and to find good pasture. He prevents theft, killing and destruction in the lives of those committed to his care. He is unafraid of the wolf (figuratively), and gladly lays down his own life for the sheep.

God had a lot to say to about pastors who weren't doing right by Him or the sheep. The ministry of a shepherd is not new to the people of God. God has always held His pastoral leaders to a high standard. God had stern warnings for negligent and self-serving shepherds.

"Woe to the shepherds of Israel who feed themselves! Should not the shepherds feed the flocks? You eat the fat and clothe yourselves with the wool; you slaughter the fatlings, but you do not feed the flock. The weak you have not strengthened, nor have you healed those who were sick, nor bound up the broken, nor brought back what was driven away, nor sought what was lost; but with force and cruelty you have ruled them. So they were scattered because there was *no shepherd; and they became food for all the beasts of the field when they were scattered. My sheep wandered through all the mountains, and on every high hill; yes, My flock was scattered over the whole face of the earth, and no one was seeking or searching for them"* (Ezekiel 34:2-6).

Whatever may be said about the gift of Pastor, what should be apparent is this:

- The pastor/shepherd truly cares about the life and safety of the sheep, not issues of control and dominance.
- The shepherd cares more for the sheep than he does for himself, willingly laying down his life for them.
- His care goes beyond religious-sounding platitudes and spiritual-sounding clichés; it is physical, as well as spiritual. He seeks abundance for his <u>sheep</u>, not for <u>himself</u>.
- He protects the sheep from whatever would destroy or scatter them.
- He looks to bring rest, restoration, peace, provision, anointing, and righteous living to the sheep.
- A true shepherd, called of God, seeks to find the lost sheep and refuses to rule them with force or cruelty.

A pastor leads by example and is not called to rule by edict. The pastor's heart cannot be purchased, or learned, or earned; is given by God to those for whom it is prepared. These gentle souls must be honored – not scorned for their willingness to sacrifice for others. They have an anointing that enables them to find the lost sheep and to heal the broken and injured. They can face down the wolf without fear or timidity because it is Christ in them who fights for the sheep. He WILL lead his flock like a shepherd and carry them in His bosom; thus says the Lord regarding His chosen Shepherd.

Jesus had some things to say, just prior to His ascension that bear on this unique ministry in the life of His primary apostle, Peter. What Jesus said to Peter speaks volumes to us about the priorities of all five ministry gifts and particularly the links between the functions of apostles and pastors.

JESUS' SUMMARY TO PASTORS AND APOSTLES

*"So when they had dined, Jesus saith to Simon Peter, Simon, son of Jonas, lovest thou me more than these? He saith unto him, Yea, Lord; thou knowest that I love thee. He saith unto him, **Feed** (bosko, feed) my lambs. He saith to him again the second time, Simon, son of Jonas, lovest thou me? He saith unto him, Yea, Lord; thou knowest that I love thee. He saith unto him, **Feed** (poimaino, rule or direct so as to feed) my sheep. He saith unto him the third time, Simon, son of Jonas, lovest thou me? Peter was grieved because he said unto him the third time, Lovest thou me? And he said unto him, Lord, thou knowest all things; thou knowest that I love thee. Jesus saith unto him, **Feed** (bosko, feed) my sheep,"* (John 21:15-17, KJV).

Jesus, when confronting Peter after his betrayal, and after the resurrection, said to him twice (once at the beginning and again at the end) to *"bosko,* or feed my sheep (or lambs)" while reminding him to *"poimen,* or guide and direct them" only once. Two to one is the ratio of provision to direction, and such should be in the heart of any pastor.

Here, Jesus told Peter that the first and the final responsibility is the "feeding," the sustaining role of the ministry overall. Feeding and provision is a pastoral role, and ruling is a lesser part of that role, though it is one of the primary roles of apostles as well.

Such "ruling" or directing of the sheep is motivated towards the end of "feeding" the sheep what they need: encouraging them to graze and water in the areas where they (not the shepherd) have the most need.

Pastoral ministry conceivably would be part of helping someone find a better job, a godly mate or housing; not just spiritual provision is in view when God uses the title "pastor." Shepherds must find provision for their flocks and for their individual sheep.

God thinks the sheep are so important that He gave these specific pastoral gifts to serve their needs. He did not create sheep so that shepherds could have someone to govern or exploit.

The shepherd LEADS the sheep. Jesus put "doing" ahead of "teaching," as the primary ingredient of teaching a lesson (see Matthew 5:19). Just as Jesus had much to say to Peter about the ministry gifts and their focus, He had much to say regarding the other ministry gifts as well. His focus was on the function of the gifts, instead of their "positions" or "titles."

It is interesting that in Jesus' final personal appearances to His disciples in the first five books of the New Testament, important aspects of all five of the ministry gifts were touched upon.

This is because Jesus was preparing to distribute the fullness of HIS ministry among many different men who would need to follow in the same heart-attitude as Jesus.

JESUS' SUMMARY TO PROPHETS

"But you shall receive power when the Holy Spirit has come upon you; and you shall be witnesses to Me in Jerusalem, and in all Judea and Samaria, and to the end of the earth" (Acts 1:8).

"And I will give power to my two witnesses, and they will prophesy one thousand two hundred and sixty days, clothed in sackcloth" (Revelation 11:3).

See also Revelation 11:10: *"these two prophets."*

*"And you are witnesses of these things. Behold, I send the Promise of My Father upon you; but **tarry in the city of Jerusalem until you are endued with power from on high"*** (Luke 24:48-49).

In Acts 2:8, Jesus focused on the supernatural "martus" or "witnessing" His followers were to perform. We see from further usage of the same Greek word "martus" in Revelation 11, that such ministry is related to prophecy and prophets (we get our word, "martyr," from "martus"). We realize, upon reflection, that these men in Acts 2 were actually called to "prophesy" in Christ's behalf as "witnesses." And they were required to do so in such a way that it required special empowerment from above.

Jesus told them to wait for that power before they even thought about trying to do their job. It is very important for prophetic ministry not to get "ahead" of the Lord. Jesus talked to the Apostle Peter about the <u>pastoral</u> function of his calling. He talked about the prophetic witness that would be necessary for these "last days" we live in. In fact, Jesus had something to say in His final appearances about the function of apostolic, pastoral, and prophetic ministries, but He did not stop there. With Jesus, everybody gets a turn!

JESUS' SUMMARY TO EVANGELISTS

*"Go into all the world and preach the **gospel*** (euaggelion) *to every creature. He who believes and*

*is baptized will be saved; but he who does not believe
will be condemned. And these signs will follow those
who believe: In My name they will cast out demons;
they will speak with new tongues; they will take up
serpents; and if they drink anything deadly, it will by
no means hurt them; they will lay hands on the sick,
and they will recover"* (Mark 16:15-18).

The calling cards for evangelism or the preaching of the
"good news" are that people believe and are baptized. Signs
follow them who believe the message: miracles of deliverance,
healing and divine protection from intended harm.
Furthermore, the function of preaching the "good news" is
one that belongs to all believers. In one way or another, most,
if not every one of us, are called to be this ministry "gift" to
someone else. Those signs should be following us ALL. And
this passage has a sister passage in the first Gospel that we
hear all the time, usually quoted by evangelists, but that is
different in its nature and emphasis. In it, Jesus connects the
teaching ministry with the work of evangelism:

*"And Jesus came and spoke to them, saying, 'All
authority has been given to Me in heaven and on earth.
Go therefore and make disciples of all the nations,
baptizing them in the name of the Father and of the
Son and of the Holy Spirit, teaching them to observe
all things that I have commanded you; and lo, I am
with you always, even to the end of the age.' Amen"*
(Matthew 28:18-20).

This scripture is so similar, but says so very much more
about the remaining gift of ministry: the gift of the Teacher.
Although baptism is mentioned, just like the "good news"
commission, here we see another focus. The focus is discipling
and teaching the nations how to "practice" or observe every
thing Jesus taught His disciples to do. Here is the principle of
supernatural duplication in action. Jesus had said earlier: *"As
the Father has sent me, I also send you."*

Jesus was reminding the disciples of this command once again, emphasizing that the primary method for transferring HIS ministry gifts to others was to be that of teaching, and through the God-ordained office of the "teacher."

Jesus had twice as much to say about "teaching" at His ascension than He did regarding the other four gifts and for good reason. Virtually every time you see "master" or "teacher " in the New Testament, particularly referring to Christ, it is the word for teacher, *didaskalos*, or a derivative.

THE TEACHER

διδάσκαλος, pronounced did-as'-kal-os; is an instructor, a teacher, one who imparts, instills or explains something.

This Greek word appears in many scriptures, but in one of the most important ones it wasn't even translated that way in King James. It has a broad application to all of leadership in the local church and the other four ministry gifts as well.

"My brethren, let not many of you become teachers (didaskalos), *knowing that we* (teachers) *shall receive a stricter judgment. For we* (teachers) *all stumble in many things. If anyone does not stumble in word, he is a perfect man, able also to bridle the whole body. Indeed, we put bits in horses' mouths that they may obey us, and we turn their whole body. Look also at ships: although they are so large and are driven by fierce winds, they are turned by a very small rudder wherever the pilot desires. Even so the tongue is a little member and boasts great things. See how great a forest a little fire kindles!...Who is wise and understanding among you? Let him show by good conduct that his works are done in the meekness of wisdom"* (James 3:1-5, 13).

In context, with the proper word "teacher" used, it sheds great light upon the powerful methodology God has invested in the office of Teacher. James said that whenever God wants

His Body to change direction He uses the mouth of His Body, who are, in context – you guessed it – Teachers.

Years ago, God raised up a teacher who taught: "the just shall live by his faith." And that justification by God Almighty was by "faith alone." His name was Martin Luther. Others have been raised up to correct the church's misdirections over the years as well, and have brought repentance (changes) to the Body of Christ that God desired. In fact, Church history is filled with the efforts of God-given teachers who were called, placed, and anointed for the purpose of bringing about a specific change in direction that God desired.

These are important "Gifts of the Spirit" and fruit of the Spirit that need to be present for teaching ministry to occur. James 3:17 draws particular attention to: wisdom, knowledge, an upright lifestyle and purity of communication, meekness and, once again, wisdom. The word of wisdom and word of knowledge are absolutely critical in a teaching ministry.

But gifts alone "do not a teacher make," for the demeanor and personality characteristics of the teacher are equally important. A teacher must realize the tremendous power committed to his trust and hold it in meekness ("meekness" means gentle and humble). A teacher must also live a lifestyle that is befitting of the office to which he is called.

A bad teacher can wreck a local body of believers or destroy a new Christian. False teaching leads people astray from the plan and purpose of God for their lives; it also puts them directly in harm's way.

Even accurate teaching, when mishandled, can damage God's precious sheep. Too much light, given at the wrong season, can blind those it was intended to help. No wonder we need the Word of Wisdom in teaching ministry.

Jesus once said to his disciples, *"I have yet many things to say unto you, but ye cannot bear them now,"* knowing none of us can handle all of God's truth at once. We need the gentle and meek teacher to spoon-feed us until we gain maturity.

"For though by this time you ought to be teachers, you need someone *to teach you again the first principles of the oracles of God; and you have come to need milk and not solid food"* (Hebrews 5:12).

There comes a time when we must all begin to grow up. God has a call on each life for a specific task or collection of assignments to be done – and done well. With the passing of time, people should grow up under good teaching. They should grow to the point where they, too, can hear the call of God to serve others, and teach effectively what they have learned. All Spirit-led teaching will begin with the first principles and oracles (prophecies and scriptural doctrines) of God, and lead on to the "meatier" matters of God's eternal plan for mankind and release of supernatural power.

We must all grow beyond the stage of being milk-drinkers to becoming meat-eaters. Such is God's plan for each and every one of us! We get there through exposure to all five of the ministry gifts. A major component of each of the five is teaching.

No matter how "high" one's perceived call in life is, we are all called to teach others what we KNOW, making them stronger at our own expense. Each of the five-fold ministry assignments from God includes teaching in some measure. Each contains the components of speaking forth (a prophet's chief duty) or following a specific commission using divine authority (apostolic assignments), or leading others to Christ and healing their sicknesses (in body or soul), as in evangelism.

Whatever may be gathered about the details of any particular calling from Scripture, the overarching truth to be incorporated is found in scriptures like Philippians 2:3-8:

"Let nothing be done *through selfish ambition or conceit, but in lowliness of mind let each esteem others better than himself. Let each of you look out not only*

*for his own interests, but also for the interests of others.
Let this mind be in you which was also in Christ Jesus,
who, being in the form of God, did not consider it
robbery to be equal with God, but made Himself of no
reputation, taking the form of a bondservant,* and
*coming in the likeness of men. And being found in
appearance as a man, He humbled Himself and
became obedient to* the point of *death, even the death
of the cross."*

The key trust of this passage is that the five-fold ministries
are not being called up to rule over others. We, instead, are
called down to a place of servitude and submission to the
needs and hopes of others less mature or qualified than
ourselves. We must not let anything be done through selfish
ambition, but rather seek the opportunity to bring God's very
best into the lives of others.

We are, after all, only God's gifts to the Body of Christ,
given by His Spirit, to bless all we come in contact with, and
to be instruments of His marvelous grace.

CHAPTER 8

THE GIFT OF PROPHECY

"Now concerning spiritual gifts, *brethren, I do not want you to be ignorant: You know that you were Gentiles, carried away to these dumb idols, however you were led. Therefore I make known to you that no one speaking by the Spirit of God calls Jesus accursed, and no one can say that Jesus is Lord except by the Holy Spirit. There are diversities of gifts, but the same Spirit. There are differences of ministries, but the same Lord. And there are diversities of activities, but it is the same God who works all in all. But the manifestation of the Spirit is given to each one for the profit* of all: *for to one is given the word of wisdom through the Spirit, to another the word of knowledge through the same Spirit, to another faith by the same Spirit, to another gifts of healings by the same Spirit, to another the working of miracles, to another prophecy, to another discerning of spirits, to another* different *kinds of tongues, to another the interpretation of tongues. But one and the same Spirit works all these things, distributing to each one individually as He wills"* (I Corinthians 12:1-11).

Paul says, *"Pursue love, and desire spiritual gifts,..."* (I Corinthians 14:1).

Most people who refer to this next verse don't consider the context at all: *"God has not given us a spirit of fear, but of power and of love and of a sound mind"* (II Timothy 1:7). This verse ties in with the context of the verse just before it:

*"Therefore I remind you to stir up the gift of God
which is in you through the laying on of my hands.
For God has not given us a spirit of fear, but of power
and of love and of a sound mind"* (II Timothy 1:6-7).

Paul said, in essence, "You receive the gift through the
laying on of hands." Spiritual gifts often can be imparted by
the laying on of hands of those who are anointed. It is in that
context that we read, "God has not given us a spirit of fear,..."
God does not want us to be fearful of prophecy or speaking in
tongues. We should not fear moving in the gifts of healings.
Dealing with the gifts is a very interesting aspect of this
passage of scripture.

In I Corinthians 12:1, Paul said, *"Now concerning spiritual
gifts, brethren I do not want you to be ignorant:..."* As you
read the key scripture for this chapter, did you notice that the
Holy Spirit is mentioned nine times? Verse 11 concludes by
saying, *"But one and the same Spirit works all these things,
distributing each one individually as He wills."*

What point is God making here? He is saying that these
gifts are of the Holy Spirit and distributed by the Spirit. It is
redundant. Those people who fight the Baptism in the Holy
Spirit are dangerously close to blaspheming the Holy Spirit.
They can be guilty of attributing the things of God to the devil.

There are three "Vocal" gifts representing the mouth of God:
tongues, interpretation and prophecy. Then, there are three
"Power" gifts: healings, miracles and faith. These are the arm
of God extended. The third category comprises the "Revelation"
gifts. This category includes the word of wisdom, the word of
knowledge and the discerning of spirits. These gifts reveal the
mind of God. So, taken as a whole, we have the mind of God,
the mouth of God and the arm of God extended.

PROPHECY DEFINED

Prophet: As we mentioned earlier, a prophet is a person
who speaks for God – one who is divinely inspired to

communicate God's will to His people and to disclose the future to them. A prophet's words are not the production of his own spirit, but come from the <u>Holy</u> Spirit! God loves and respects prophets!

"He who receives a prophet in the name of a prophet shall receive a prophet's reward. He who receives a righteous man in the name of a righteous man shall receive a righteous man's reward. And whoever gives one of these little ones only a cup of cold water in the name of a disciple, assuredly, I say to you, he shall by no means lose his reward" (Matthew 10:41).

This scripture says that there is a special reward for prophets. If you receive a prophet, you will receive the reward of a prophet. We must be very careful to receive those whom God sends.

The Hebrew word for prophet (nabi') means to declare or announce. The word literally means, an "announcer" or a "declarer." Two other Hebrew words, "ro'eh" and "hozeh" are translated prophet. These words mean, "one who sees," and are sometimes rendered, "seer," by the translators.

THE SEER

Now, a seer is a person who sees or hears things that do not lie in the domain of natural sight and sound. Fifty percent of the time when the word "seer" was used in the Old Testament it was in reference to the prophet, Samuel. He was a "seer." We should pray for this gift: "Lord, I want to see. I want to be a see-er. I want to see and hear in the spirit realm." It is a tremendous advantage to know what God is doing.

PROPHECY

The gift of prophecy is used to speak forth supernaturally a message from God. A prophet does not prophesy out of his or her own heart, nor can prophecy originate in personal reflection and calculation. It is not to be the product of feelings, fears or hopes. In Jeremiah 23:16-18 we read,

"Thus says the LORD of hosts: 'Do not listen to the words of the prophets who prophesy to you. They make you worthless; They speak a vision of their own heart, Not from the mouth of the LORD. They continually say to those who despise Me,' The LORD has said, 'You shall have peace;' And to everyone who walks according to the dictates of his own heart, they say, 'No evil shall come upon you.' For who has stood in the counsel of the LORD, And has perceived and heard His word? Who has marked His word and heard it?"

GREEK WORD "PROPHETEUO"

This literally means to stand in front of another; or to be a spokesperson for another. It is to be God's mouthpiece.

The word "prophet" was actually just transliterated into English. It is not even a <u>translation</u>, per se; it's a <u>transliteration</u>. "Phemi" means to make known one's thoughts or to declare. Pro means before. To stand before God as His mouthpiece is very similar to the role of Aaron as he spoke for Moses. The responsibility of speaking for God is an awesome thing. Most of us would rather have God in front, with us hiding far in the corner.

Prophecy is primarily "forth-telling" rather than foretelling. A prophecy can deal with the past, present or future, but its primary role is to say things as they are. The office of a prophet <u>does</u> include prophesying future events, but there are many other purposes for prophecy.

Scripture also shows the principle of double fulfillment in the words of a prophet. An initial fulfillment in one historical incident does not rule out another application later in history. Take for instance the prophecy in Joel 2:30, *"And I will show wonders in the heavens and in the earth: Blood and fire and pillars of smoke.*" Peter applied this passage to the Day of Pentecost where Jesus applied this prophecy to His second coming.

A prophet is able to discern the signs of the times. Amos 3:7 says, *"Surely the Lord GOD does nothing, Unless He reveals His secret to His servants the prophets."* God will not do anything without His true prophets first seeing where He is going. Jesus rebuked the Scribes and Pharisees, saying, "*...You know how to discern the face of the sky, but you cannot discern the signs of the times*" (Matthew 16:3). They were completely clueless as to what God was doing.

According to I Corinthians 14:3, prophecy does three things: edifies, exhorts and comforts. The Greek word for comfort means a gentle cheering. What a delightful word.

WHAT THE GIFT OF PROPHECY IS NOT:

One necessary way to define the gift of prophecy is to point out what it is <u>not</u>. It is not fortune telling, ESP, clairvoyance, the "Psychic Network" on TV, mental telepathy, or parapsychology.

Horoscopes are not prophecy, either. I believe it is a <u>sin</u> to read the horoscope in the newspaper. When you do, you are asking a demon to prophesy to you. You are in fact opening yourself up to demon spirits. If you open the doors, demons will move in at your invitation.

Prophecy is not making decisions for other people; that is witchcraft. Any attempt to <u>control</u> another person or situation with any spirit other than the Holy Spirit is witchcraft. True personal prophecy will usually act as a <u>confirmation</u> to an individual, touching on things that the Holy Spirit is <u>already</u> dealing with them about.

"For as many as are led by the Spirit of God, these are the sons of God" (Romans 8:14). When you experience the new birth, you are given the Holy Spirit as an internal guidance

system. You should never let someone else make decisions or direct your life by personal prophecy. What is said should be a <u>confirmation</u> to you of what you have already sensed from God. If you fail to understand this principle, you can easily be manipulated and controlled by other people and even demonic spirits!

The <u>gift</u> of prophecy is not to be mistaken for the <u>office</u> of a prophet. I Corinthians 12:29 says, *"Are all prophets?"* A person can genuinely prophesy every Sunday without being gifted or called to the office of a prophet. In similar fashion, we all have a pastoral function – with our children, for instance. With kids, even if you do not hold the office of "pastor," you still fill a pastoral function. The office and the ability of each calling are two different things. This is a very important distinction.

Prophecy is not simply inspired preaching. There are two words in scripture that can be translated preach. The most common Greek verb for preaching is "euangelizo," meaning, "to proclaim glad tidings." The second Greek word for preaching is "kerusso." It literally means to preach. The word "prophetuo" definitely means, "to prophesy." Scripture is specific on this, especially in the original text. If anyone ever tells you that prophecy is merely inspired preaching, know that this person is twisting the scripture, either willfully or ignorantly.

Prophecy is not oratorical ability or human charisma. Prophecy is primarily <u>revelation</u>, not <u>preparation</u>. It is not something a person prepares ahead of time at home, and then delivers at a church service.

II Peter 1:21 reads, *"...for prophecy never came by the will of man, but holy men of God spoke as they were moved by the Holy Spirit."* Prophecy does not originate in the will of a person. It comes through moving in obedience to the Holy Spirit of God.

Prophecy is not quoting a book or system of theology. There was a young man at our church who came in one night as a visitor. He walked in and as the worship service came to a close, he began to prophecy, "Yea saith God, when Jesus was in the tomb, He was recreated. Yea, Jesus was born-again in the tomb." Everybody in the church knew that it was not really prophecy.

I corrected from the pulpit, "The Son could not have been recreated because He was never created in the first place. What you are saying denies the deity of Jesus. This prophecy doesn't agree with Scripture. We love you brother, and do not want to be cruel, but Jesus was never lost. He didn't have to be born-again. We cannot accept the prophecy. It does not agree with God's Word."

The next day, one of my staff came in and showed me a book by a well-known charismatic evangelist. What amazed me was that it was verbatim what had been prophesied. I sent this young man who prophesied a letter. I told him he was welcome to come to our church and that there were no hard feelings. We weren't angry with him. I did however, let him know from which book his prophecy originated. I Xeroxed off the pages (and sent them with the letter), which he had quoted as if it was revelation from God.

Prophecy is not an opportunity to take revenge and say publicly what you do not have the courage to say in private. The Bible says that if you have ought against your brother, to go to him privately. In the late sixties and early seventies, it was a cool thing for young men to have long hair. We had a wonderful lady in our church who could not stand long hair on men. Each Saturday night, at a prayer meeting, she got all worked up like a steam engine and began praying against long hair. Every week she got a little more pumped up, a little more excited. Finally, one Sunday morning came around and she prophesied, "Yea, saith the Lord God, I hate long hair on men!"

I wanted to laugh out loud. I could have prophesied that she would prophesy that! Anyway, she was out of order and at the time it was a bit upsetting. That prophecy was coming out of her human frustration, irritation and a judgmental attitude toward the dress and appearance of others. No matter how tempting it is to share your feelings as though they were God's, realize that no matter how strongly you feel, you are not God and your feelings are not prophecy!

I used to go over to special meetings in Kansas City on a particular weekday morning. There were always a lot of prophesies in those meetings. One morning there was a guy who prophesied a new wave of revival. On the following Sunday, one of the guys who attended that meeting and heard that prophecy came to my church and repeated the exact same prophecy. He even used the same examples in his prophecy!

In Jeremiah 23:30, we read, " '...I am against the prophets,' says the Lord, 'who steal My words every one from his neighbor.' " This fellow at my church stole those words and then prophesied them himself at the very next opportunity. That is not prophecy. I'm sure the original prophecy was true and its repetition probably didn't hurt anybody. But you cannot copy someone else and still call it prophecy.

Prophecy is not an opportunity to be seen or get attention—to stand in the spotlight. Some people with hurts and wounds have a great need to be accepted but self-glorification must be avoided like the plague.

There was a woman we knew quite well who came from a dysfunctional family. She had a good heart but was always over-burdened and carried a sense of rejection. She would prophesy and give testimonies that flowed out of her wounds. She was really hurting, so she gave phony or embellished prophecies to gain approval and acceptance.

Around Christmastime, the town where she had relocated had a singing Christmas tree—actually a choir arranged in a pyramid to look like a Christmas tree. It collapsed, injuring a lot of the people. When she came to visit our church, she stood up and shared how she had healed all the people who had been hurt on the singing Christmas tree. She really played her story up, too, saying, "Everyone I laid hands on was instantly healed! The paramedics were saying, 'Oh wow, awesome, cool!'" According to her story, she prayed for 10 or 15 people and they were all instantly healed.

As time went on, she continued embellishing her stories, which were obviously not true. You know, a real quarter has a certain ring to it when it hits the floor, and what this lady was throwing out definitely did not ring true. Consequently, some of our church staff did some investigation. I then confronted her. She said to me, "Brother Ernie, it wasn't true. I was lying." She had wanted only to be accepted.

We should never be mean-spirited when we correct things. We must always realize that there is probably something pushing people to fabricate prophecies, stories of healing and miracles. Remember, the church is a hospital for sinners. It was never meant to be a refuge for the saints. Whenever I correct a prophecy, I will attempt to be as loving as I can be. I always make sure the other person knows that I still love them before telling them they were out of order with their "prophecy."

WHAT THE GIFT OF PROPHECY IS

"'I am not able to bear all these people alone, because the burden is too heavy for me. If You treat me like this, please kill me here and now; if I have found favor in Your sight; and do not let me see my wretchedness!' So the LORD said to Moses: 'Gather to Me seventy men of the elders of Israel, whom you know to be the elders of the people and officers over them; bring them to the tabernacle of meeting, that they may stand there with you. Then I will come down

*and talk with you there. I will take of the Spirit that
is upon you and will put* the same *upon them; and
they shall bear the burden of the people with you,
that you may not bear* it *yourself alone'"* (Numbers
11:14).

God told Moses, "I want to take the same spirit that is on
you, and put it on 70 other men." Many people would answer,
"Please don't do it Lord. Don't give anybody the spirit I've
got."

That was a tremendous compliment to Moses!

His spirit was obviously the Holy Spirit. Later, in verse
25, we see God do the transplant procedure as it happens.

*"The Lord came down in the cloud, and spoke to
him and took of the Spirit that was upon him, and
placed the same upon the 70 elders; and it happened,
when the Spirit rested upon them, that they prophesied,
although they never did so again."*

The first evidence that the Spirit had fallen on these 70
leaders was that they began to prophesy. You could say that
the evidence of the Holy Spirit being in a man here was God
speaking through him. Continuing in verse 26 through verse
29,

*"But two men had remained in the camp: the name
of one* was *Eldad, and the name of the other Medad.
And the Spirit rested upon them. Now they* were *among
those listed, but who had not gone out to the
tabernacle; yet they prophesied in the camp. And a
young man ran and told Moses, and said, 'Eldad and
Medad are prophesying in the camp.' So Joshua the
son of Nun, Moses' assistant,* one *of his choice men,
answered and said, 'Moses my lord, forbid them!' Then
Moses said to him, 'Are you zealous for my sake? Oh,
that all the Lord's people were prophets* and *that the
LORD would put His Spirit upon them!'"*

Of course, Moses' prayer request here was answered on the Day of Pentecost. Moses revealed to us the attitude of God. God wants to share the Holy Spirit with us all. He doesn't just want the Holy Spirit to rest on a select few. He wants His Spirit resting on every man and woman that they might have a word from Him.

He likes you just as much as He does everybody else. You can have the gift too! Some nice day go park your car somewhere and get under a tree with a tablet. Write down about six or seven questions. Say, "God, I've got to have answers. I don't want to hear from my own mind or myself. I am asking You, in Jesus name, for the answers to these questions."

You may not get them all right then. A key to prayer is to ask God questions. Prayer is a dialog. Get in a position to listen for God's voice by asking. We all know what we think. We hear our own thoughts in our heads every waking moment. We need to hear from God!

Many times, as a person prophesies, they will get the first sentence of the first phrase or concept, and they begin to speak. They have no idea how the prophecy is going to continue or even when it will end because the Holy Spirit is speaking through them.

In prophecy, the words are coming out of your mouth as soon as they reach your spirit. You begin saying things that you would have never thought before.

Most of what we call prophecy today, is really a long word of knowledge or wisdom. You get a word and you speak it forth as if it were prophecy. Prophecy is the flow of the Holy Spirit. Whether it be a creek or a river, it all flows from the same source. Both will quench a man's deepest thirst. Both are channels of life and refreshment. The only difference is that one channel has a greater depth than the other. As we grow, God deepens us and our capacity to minister. If you have only a brief prophecy to speak, speak it. God will increase it.

COVET THIS GIFT

I Corinthians 14 tells us a lot about the gift of prophecy. Starting in verse 1 it says, *"Pursue love, and desire spiritual gifts, but especially that you may prophesy."*

If you want a spiritual gift, the one you should desire the most is prophecy. Now continuing in verse 2 it says,

> *For he who speaks in a tongue does not speak to men but to God, for no one understands* him; *however, in the spirit he speaks mysteries. But he who prophesies speaks edification and exhortation and comfort to men. He who speaks in a tongue edifies himself, but he who prophesies edifies the church. I wish you all spoke with tongues, but even more that you prophesied; for he who prophesies is greater than he who speaks with tongues, unless indeed he interprets, that the church may receive edification,* (I Corinthians 14:2-5).

These verses shout at you to seek prophecy. It is a greater gift than tongues. Paul desired that the whole church would prophesy. Verses 24-25 tell us,

> *But if all prophesy, and an unbeliever or an uninformed person comes in, he is convinced by all, he is convicted by all. And thus the secrets of his heart are revealed; and so, falling down on* his *face, he will worship God and report that God is truly among you."*

I have seen this very thing happen. There was a liberal seminary holding a series of symposiums nearby. One night they decided they would visit a large charismatic church of about 2000 members. They wanted to have something else to discuss. (The previous night they had visited a gay bar for their insights.) So they slipped in the back and the Spirit got on them. I prophesied, "You have come to spy out the land. Take a big bunch of grapes home with you!"

Remember the story in the Old Testament where they carried grapes back from spying out the promised land? I continued, "Gather as much fruit as you want to take back home with you, saith the Lord." Nobody knew that this group was even there.

The preachers from this other denomination later had to say, "Of a truth, God is in your midst." Their hearts were exposed!

That is exactly what the gift of prophecy does. It exposes what people try to hide from the Body of Christ and the Holy Spirit. We should pray for prophecy. We should earnestly covet it.

Prophecy is a powerful way to build up your brothers and sisters. If you've never moved in the gift of prophecy, ask God to anoint you. And, as you begin to operate in this gift, never allow anybody to tell you, "Well, don't go off the deep end!"

Remember, you must always go off the deep end. If you try diving into the shallow water you will break your neck. Plunge right in. If you make a mistake, God is gracious and we can all help one another. Besides, God knows how to swim!

One of my favorite passages is John 6:63, *"It is the Spirit who gives life; the flesh profits nothing. The words that I speak to you are spirit; and they are life."* The flesh and all its ability, profits nothing. When someone comes and asks you a question, they don't really want to know what you think. They need to hear a word from God that will bring them life. They need to hear Jesus talking through you.

If our words do not bring life to others, we need to learn to zip them up—until God gives us a word by the Holy Spirit.

HOW TO JUDGE/DISCERN PROPHECIES:

Scripture says, *"The testimony of Jesus is the spirit of prophecy"* (Revelation 19:10). That means Jesus is testifying whenever a person prophesies. Whenever you hear a prophecy, ask the simple question: "Did Jesus really say that?"

It is so simple to discern a prophecy. If somebody prophesies, ask yourself this question, "Would Jesus say that?" I've heard some prophesies and thought, "There is no way Jesus said that."

All true prophecy brings edification, encouragement and comfort. However, sometimes a negative word edifies. A battery, after all, has a negative pole and a positive pole. Sometimes the negative statement and rebuke can have a very positive effect. Prophets are also called: *"...to root out and to pull down, to destroy and to throw down, to build and to plant"* (Jeremiah 1:10), at times a little "Holy Spirit" demolition crew is required before construction can resume.

John the Baptist was just such a prophet. Jesus called him a forerunner. Yet John the Baptist had many negative things to say. He said that God was sweeping His threshing floor clean. He called the people to repent, which is the most positive thing a person can do. The greatest blessing that we have is the ability to repent of sin and get beyond it.

Negative demonic "prophecies" are about such things as predicting death, divorce and accidents. Prophecies about these flow from within the occult. You should run from that kind of negativism. Never accept it. It isn't Jesus.

Scripture specifically says, *"Do not despise prophecies"* (I Thessalonians 5:20). The Greek word for "despise" here means to make of no account, to despise utterly, to hold in contempt, or scorn.

Let the internal witness of your spirit be a primary test of prophecy.

I John 2:20 says, *"But you have an anointing from the Holy One, and you know all things."* Everyone should have what I call a "pending" file. It is a personal file for items "to be considered." Whenever you get a prophecy that just doesn't seem to sound right, don't despise it, instead write it out and place it in your "pending" file. As time passes, consider the word and evaluate the prophecy. Do not throw it away. You may find that though the prophecy was not for you, it was for someone else who needed it at the time.

Think of this process as a "Polaroid" picture. When you first look at prophecy, it looks fuzzy. Then after a while, as you are reading Scripture, you might realize, "That was God. It really was a word from the Lord, for me." At this point, take the prophecy out of your pending file and accept it.

This works because ultimately all prophecy must agree with Scripture. This should be obvious. In Isaiah 8:20 God tells us, *"If they do not speak according to this word, it is because there is no light in them."* That means if someone doesn't speak according to Scripture, there is no light in them.

As you discern prophecies, remember as well that religious spirits love legalism. (All demons are religious spirits!) There is a constant struggle in most of us between grace and works; faith and law; receiving and earning. This is a another valid way of testing any prophetic message. Many times a religious spirit will prophesy with compliments and praise followed by condemnation as it relates to our works. The prophesy always permeates the hearer with fear instead of faith. It focuses on you and your own efforts. This is very subtle and may require several years of listening before you learn to spot it. The clue to discerning here is to find the prophecy's focus. Do you end up focused on yourself and your deeds, or is your focus centered on your Lord and Savior and the "spirit of faith."

I hate the current, emphasis on works in the sense of religious legalism. There is a great difference between legalism and living holy, which includes works as a by product. Real holiness flows from the grace of our Lord Jesus, Who is living through us.

Holiness has little to do with promises and commitments we make. Jeremiah 23:33-36 says,

> *"So when these people or the prophet or the priest ask you, saying, 'What is the oracle of the LORD?' you shall then say to them, 'What oracle?' I will even forsake you," says the LORD. And as for the prophet and the priest and the people who say, 'The oracle of the LORD!' I will even punish that man and his house. Thus every one of you shall say to his neighbor, and every one to his brother, 'What has the LORD answered?' and, 'What has the LORD spoken?' And the oracle of the LORD you shall mention no more. For every man's word will be his oracle, for you have perverted the words of the living God, the LORD of hosts, our God."*

In Jeremiah's day, this burdening people with prophetic commands was common and God hated it. This Scripture says that if you go prophesying burdens onto people, you will be cut off from God. Legalism is a burden, as is humanistic religion. You need to watch out for "works and self-effort" in prophecy. When a prophecy is of God, instead of it being a burden, there is a spirit of faith, encouragement and direction. We can tell that God has been in our midst whenever that occurs.

I Corinthians 14:29 instructs us, *"Let two or three prophets speak, and let the others judge."*

Be careful when a person waits until no pastor or elder is around to give a prophecy. It is God's way to have someone listen and judge prophecy. If the individual is married, the spouse should be present in addition to the pastor or elder. A true prophecy does not have to be given in secret. Obviously there are private matters that require some discretion.

We used to have a person who would wait until the service was over and then go back and prophesy in the hallway or bathroom where they thought no one would be listening to them. Beware of bathroom prophesies, they may need to be flushed!

They wanted to avoid being "discerned" by others. If you've got a prophecy for somebody, it should be put out, right in the open where reasonable people can consider it. If you have a prophecy for somebody's spouse, their mate if possible, should be present!

I've heard some truly weird prophecies in my time. There was one guy who loved to jump and dance and hop and jump around. He actually prophesied one Sunday morning saying, "'Yea,' saith the Lord, 'I'm greater than Jane Fonda. Yea,' saith the Lord, 'I am greater than Richard Simmons. Come work out with Me!' saith the Lord."

The pastor said something like this, "Well, you know, we love brother so-and-so, and he is a new Christian, and he's just learning. We've got to give him some time to get hold of his faith and gain some understanding. We all know that wasn't the Lord."

You have to laugh at some of these types of things, but prophecy does need to be judged.

IN CONCLUSION

Would to God that all God's people prophesied!

God's desire is that we would participate in using the gifts that God has freely given them, especially prophecy.

Paul said, "I wish that you all spake in tongues, but much more, that you all prophesied." Since this is God's Word, you should be confident in praying to move in the gift of prophecy. Ask that God would give you a word of encouragement for your brothers and sisters – or even yourself.

As we ask believing, we will receive!

CHAPTER 9

PROPHETIC VISION

"Where there is no revelation, the people cast off restraint; but happy is he who keeps the law" (Proverbs 29:18).

This word for "vision" in the Hebrew language means prophecy. Vision is not simply the setting of goals. It is having a living word from the Lord. Without a word from the Lord people in fact do perish, by casting off restraint (direction) and losing their way.

Of course, I have also seen people perish with a vision. A vision out of their own ego! They form a vision out of their own grandiose opinions of themselves and what they imagine they could do. Before you start setting goals, you had better have a prophetic word from the Lord.

"Thus says the LORD of hosts: 'Do not listen to the words of the prophets who prophesy to you. They make you worthless; They speak a vision of their own heart. Not from the mouth of the LORD'" (Jeremiah 23:16).

Verse 18 that follows poses a series of questions, *"For who has stood in the counsel of the LORD, and has perceived and heard His word? Who has marked His word and heard it?"*

To these false prophets God says in effect: They haven't been alone with Me. They never heard a word of wisdom, word of knowledge or a prophecy. "Who has stood in the counsel of the Lord?" A good question to ask!

"'I have not sent these prophets yet they ran. I have not spoken to them, yet they prophesy. But if they

had stood in My counsel, and had caused My people to hear My words, then they would have turned them from evil of their doings!" (verse 21-22).

God says that when a prophecy is true, it will have the result of holiness. People will turn from sin and error.

"I have heard what the prophets have said who prophesy lies in My name, saying, 'I have dreamed, I have dreamed!' How long will this be in the heart of the prophets who prophesy lies? Indeed they are prophets of the deceit of their own heart, who try to make My people forget My name by their dreams which everyone tells his neighbor, as their fathers forgot My name for Baal. The prophet who has a dream, let him tell a dream; And he who has My word, let him speak My word faithfully. What is the chaff to the wheat? says the LORD. "Is not My word like a fire?" says the LORD, "And like a hammer that breaks the rock in pieces?"' (Jeremiah 23:25-29).

God is not saying that all dreams are wrong. The prophet Joel tells us that old men should dream dreams!

I had a dream not too long ago about a political leader. He was riding a black horse. The horse was bucking, but the leader would not fall off. Then the horse went into the water and tried to drown him but he stayed on the black horse. The horse came up on the land galloping and bucking but he still managed to stay on the black horse. The horse went down into the water a second time, and stayed under for a long time. You would have thought it had drowned, but it came up again galloping. Then I woke up.

If that is a prophecy, the black horse in revelation represents famine. This dream could mean that this particular leader is unable to get off the horse called famine. He will come to a place of financial, emotional, mental and physical famine. He won't be able to get off the horse. This could also refer to a famine of "character," a lack of healthy morality.

But notice, this dream is not scripture.

It could very well be nothing more than chaff. What is chaff in comparison to the wheat? It could have been a dream from the Lord or perhaps I had too many pickles before I went to bed. Dreams do not have the same authority as Scripture. The scripture is wheat, dreams may be chaff.

In Jeremiah 23 we see reference to occult prophets. They are of a whole different spirit. They are not praying. They are not standing in the counsel of the Lord. They are not marking His Word. They do not love the scripture. Jeremiah 23 is really a prophecy against false prophets who are trying to deceive the people of God with dreams of their own design. They are dreams to control and manipulate people. Today's false prophets are usually after two things—self-glorification and money, all attained by a controlling spirit of manipulation.

Dreams, even if they are of God, do not have the same authority as Scripture.

Always test dreams by asking three simple questions: Is this demonic? Is this fleshly? Is this of the Holy Spirit? Never throw out what is genuine just because there are counterfeits.

The essence of a prophetic ministry can be found in Jeremiah 15:16, *"Your words were found, and I ate them."* Jeremiah did not just read God's Word, he digested it. He ate it like food. *"And your word was to me the joy and rejoicing of my heart."*

This is how you become accurate in prophecy. Consuming the Word. Finding it and eating it. It becomes a joy and the delight of your heart.

Jeremiah continued, *"For I am called by Your name, O LORD God of hosts. I did not sit in the assembly of the mockers..."* (Jeremiah 15:16-17a).

While everybody else is laughing, telling jokes and carrying on, Jeremiah said, "I was like a duck out of water." He was on a different page than all of the other prophets, because he was seeking God and contemplating the Word.

People accused Jeremiah of being too sober minded. He replied,

"I did not sit in the assembly of the mockers. Nor did I rejoice; I sat alone because of Your hand, For You have filled me with indignation. Why is my pain perpetual and My wound incurable, which refuses to be healed?" (Jeremiah 15:17-18a).

That is how he came to be called the weeping prophet. God asked a question of him,

"Will You surely be to me like an unreliable stream, As *waters* that *fail? Therefore thus says the LORD: 'If you return, Then I will bring you back; You shall stand before Me; If you take out the precious from the vile, You shall be as My mouth. Let them return to you, But you must not return to them.'"* (Jeremiah 15:18-19).

God in effect said, "Jeremiah, you are hearing from Me. You are crying and everybody else is in the circle of merrymakers. As a prophet, your job is to separate the worthless from that which is truth."

Sometimes the work of a prophet is not appreciated. People would rather hear worthless jokes.

I have seen many dead and dry people come to life as a result of somebody laying hands on them and prophesying over them. A dead person <u>can</u> live again. Prophecy is creative. It brings life and resurrection, leading people back into fellowship with God – (See Ezekiel 37:1-14). Because we are grafted into the vine of Israel through Jesus, this Old Testament principle still applies to us as Christians.

It is no wonder Satan hates prophecy! God loves it! It creates life, spirit, breath and resurrection. What a joy to be able to give life and new spirit to somebody.

I would love to have seen Ezekiel's vision.

Can you image how noisy it was?

He saw an entire valley filled with bones. Then he started prophesying. Can't you almost hear the sound of those bones crashing against one another, each looking for its proper place? It says they stood up, an exceeding great army. I think this is the army of the Lord, perhaps the 144,000 evangelists mentioned in Revelation. They are not a military army conscripted by man, they are **THE** army of God. They are the sons of God... an army who will not compromise and will not be appeased. God needs such an army of the uncompromisingly righteous.

WARFARE AND PROPHECY

"This charge I commit to you, son Timothy, according to the prophecies previously made concerning you, that by them you may wage the good warfare" (I Timothy 1:18).

We should be striving to use prophecy to wage a good warfare according to this charge given by Paul to Timothy.

In January of 1997, I was attending a church where my mentor Bill Newby is the pastor. A prophet by the name of Gary Pack was sitting in the middle of the church. He didn't look like a preacher.

He took one look at me and said, "You, stand up. You thought God is through with you, 'but it has just begun,' saith the Lord. 'You will minister to young men, and you will not have to advertise. I will send young men into your life. You will not have to print out business cards. You will mentor them.'"

This prophecy continues to fulfill itself everyday. One guy lived in Manhattan, Kansas. He e-mails me several times a week asking for tapes. He's been saved for less than a year. He is so hungry for God. He wants to serve God full-time. He set up a web page with all my notes and it gets 200 hits a day, asking questions on his web site.

The prophecy went on, "You will move in healing and miracles like you've never moved before." Many that I have prayed for since then have been healed. Not instantly every time, but healing has come in many cases. Because of this prophecy I have more faith for healing than ever before.

Whenever you get a prophecy, get a tape of it, type it out and look at it. You will be able to do spiritual warfare once you've heard God's voice and seen where He is going. That prophecy will minister to you. You can look at it, whenever times of trouble come. And as Satan tries to steal your vision, you can look at God's Word for your life, and begin to act on it, bringing victory out of discouragement.

IMPARTATION

"Do not neglect the gift that is in you, which was given to you by prophesy with the laying on of the hands of the eldership" (I Timothy 4:14-15).

Elders can impart gifts simply by the laying on of hands. It is one thing to hear a sermon, it is another thing to have something imparted into you that becomes an actual part of your spirit. Impartation is better than knowledge! God is not impressed with what we know. So, don't neglect that gift you have received. Something was imparted to me when Gary Pack prophesied over me. Something is imparted as anyone prophesies, by the spirit, over another.

PROPHECY IN A PUBLIC MEETING

How is it then brethren? Whenever you come together, each of you has a psalm, has a teaching, has a tongue, has a revelation, has an interpretation, (I Corinthians 14:26a).

We see that everyone in Corinth had a psalm, a teaching, a tongue, a revelation, etc. This is not the New Testament model for a church service. Notice that the verse is describing how it is, not how it should be. Paul was rebuking them. Then he gave instructions!

"If anyone speaks in a tongue, let there be two or at the most three, each in turn, and let one interpret. But if there is no interpreter, let him keep silent in church, and let him speak to himself and to God. Let two or three prophets speak, and let the others judge. But if anything is revealed to another who sits by, let the first keep silent. For you can all prophesy one by one, that all may learn and all may be encouraged" (I Corinthians 14:27-31).

To this, there is always someone who will say, "Well, bless God, if God puts it on me, I'm going to speak it." To them, Paul would say, "The spirit of the prophets are subject to the prophets. Control yourself!" The enemy is always at work to promote confusion!

"For God is not the author of confusion but of peace, as in all the churches of the saints. Let your women keep silent in the churches, for they are not permitted to speak; but they are to be submissive, as the law also says. And if they want to learn something, let them ask their own husbands at home; for it is shameful for women to speak in church" (I Corinthians 14:33-35).

"Let a woman learn in silence with all submission. And I do not permit a woman to teach, or to have authority over a man, but to be in silence. For Adam was form first, then Eve" (I Timothy 2:11-13).

This verse further explains what is meant by order in the church. Here we see three things that women are not permitted to do:

- Teach adult men
- Usurp authority over men
- Interrupt public worship services

In stating these we must remember to esteem those Christian ministries who hold different views.

There are three basic views:

The first view states that the Holy Spirit is the same in a man or woman, therefore a woman is free to do anything in the church realm a man can. This view takes the position that the restrictions on women found in I Corinthians 14, and II Timothy 2 are underlined cultural, and thus do not apply to women today. In this view, the only verse that applies to us today is Galatians 3:28, *"There is neither Jew nor Greek, there is neither slave nor free, there is neither male nor female; for you are all one in Christ Jesus."* Many sincere, Godly ministries say that this is the correct interpretation. We should respect, esteem and honor them.

The second view takes the position that a woman can do anything in the church realm, unless it involves occupying a governmental position such as being an elder. She can be a prophet, teacher or an evangelist, as long as she is under a "covering." She operates freely under her husband or the elders of the church as her "covering." People who take this view often word it like this: "The issue is usurping authority, and as long as a woman is under the authority of her husband or an elder, she can do anything." Most people who take this view believe that women cannot be apostles or pastors because these callings lie within the governmental realm.

The third view says, "A woman can do anything in the church realm, except two basic things: teach men or usurp authority over men." Obviously, neither a man nor a woman should be disruptive or interruptive in a public meeting. People with this view would say you cannot simply dismiss Scripture by assigning it to the cultural context. They would also say

Galatians 3:28, *"There is neither male nor female, for we are all one in Christ Jesus,"* is in reference to a person's standing before God and value to God, but does not apply to person's function or office in the Body of Christ.

Nearly everyone holds one of these three views. We must respect and honor one another, especially those who sincerely hold to a different view. I have heard people make fun of and actually preach against those who have a different view as to the role of women in the church. It must also be stated emphatically that the above restrictions would apply only to the church and not to employment in the secular world. Obviously, women can excel as CEO's and leaders throughout the business world or in the arena of politics.

CHAPTER 10

A WORD OF KNOWLEDGE AND WISDOM

"The Word of knowledge" as we discussed earlier is the correct diagnosis or analysis of a given situation or person. The "word of wisdom" is the correct solution or prescription for that situation or person.

These are both revelation gifts of the Holy Spirit. They are gifts that come in the form of a word! God drops "a word" into the mind, that could never have been known through study or natural acquisition.

I was once counseling a lady in her late fifties. She complained, "I've been receiving psychological counseling for the last two years." Apparently, the counseling was doing little to help her.

So, I said, "Well, let's just pray about this." I prayed in tongues for a few moments and announced, "Well, the Lord says it's guilt."

She said, "That's what my psychiatrist said. But he couldn't figure out why I feel guilty."

I told her, "It happened when you were sixteen-years-old."

A "Niagara Falls" of scalding tears started running down both of her cheeks. She said, "I got pregnant before I was married back when I was 16 years old."

I asked her, "Well, have you ever confessed that as adultery?"

She said, "It was not adultery. I wasn't even married."

I said, "It's fornication... Have you ever confessed that and called it what God calls it?"

She said, "No, I never have."

I led her in a prayer saying, "Lord Jesus, I am guilty of fornication, of committing sexual intercourse before marriage. I call it what You call it. It was sin and I ask that Your blood cleanse me from it."

She was immediately set free! End of guilt.

See, as soon as we had the correct diagnosis, we didn't need a word of wisdom to arrive at an appropriate solution. We already knew to go to the cross. The correct diagnosis pointed to the solution which set her free.

While counseling another lady, I kept hearing the word "murder." I thought that it had to be something in my own mind. I kept praying in tongues while she sat across from me at my desk. I finally said, "Sister, I'm not accusing you of this, but for some reason, I am getting the word murder."

She began to wail in anguish, "I had an abortion!"

I said, "Well, have you ever confessed to God that you are guilty of committing murder?"

She said, "I prayed about it, but I have never called it murder."

"To be free, you need to call it what God calls it," I continued.

She bowed her head and prayed, "Lord Jesus, I am guilty of murder," and she too was instantly set free of her guilt and depression. It is essential that we never get into rationalization or self-justification. Call sin exactly what God calls it.

I was called to a home to visit a lady who was extremely depressed. She was drawing a Santa Claus. It was a most beautiful drawing. She had a lot of artistic talent.

I can't draw a good stick man! The only 'D' I ever got in school was in art, and I am still upset about it! I did my best, but my hands just won't draw.

Here was this beautiful Santa Claus picture, and when it was complete, she took her pen and started scratching it all out.

I thought, "Well, that is a parable. God does things in your life, and you just run yourself down, scratching it all out." Then I received a word of wisdom from the Holy Spirit, "'Come now, let us reason together,' saith the Lord, 'Though your sins be as scarlet, they shall be as white as snow.'"

The Lord told me, "I will give you eighteen things that I want you to number 1 through 9, but don't go past 9 because it will upset her."

I said to the woman, "Let's just list the things that you are depressed about." We got to nine things and then I counted 10 through 18. In all, she had come up with 18 things. The Holy Spirit said to me, "Thrust your pen through the paper because these 18 items are symptoms on the surface pointing to something that happened eight years ago." I stuck my pen through the paper and I told her what I heard.

She said, "Nothing happened 8 years ago."

I said, "Well, the Holy Spirit says something did happen 8 years ago."

Again she said nothing happened 8 years ago.

The third time I said, "The Holy Spirit is not a liar. Something happened 8 years ago!"

The woman began making loud and chilling yelling sounds. I nearly took off running. It turns out that the woman had committed adultery at that time. All of the surface stuff had been pointing to that event.

I said, "Do you want to be free of that?" I took her to scriptures on how to forgive, and I began to rebuke these spirits of unforgiveness. She began to gag and choke and cough. She went off to the kitchen and started to vomit in the kitchen sink. I was praying and the Lord said, "Open your eyes *NOW*."

She had grabbed a butcher's knife and just as she was getting ready to plunge it into me, I said, "In the Name of Jesus, drop that knife!"

Slowly her hand unfolded and the knife dropped to the floor.

This is why I quite often pray with my eyes open. I want to see what is going on.

That particular word of knowledge saved my life!

How it Comes

A word of knowledge or wisdom can be dropped into your mind, it can be a visualization, a perception, a mental picture, a dream, or a "rhema" from Scripture that suddenly comes alive to you. There may be other ways to receive a word, but these are the most common.

Most of us operate in the "word" gifts. We are just unaware of it. As things come to us, we often take credit. Women often say, "It's my woman's intuition," when in fact it is God, the Holy Ghost, tipping them off.

Sometimes people are called out in worship services through the use of "a word of knowledge or wisdom." This does not imply that these people are more spiritual, but more likely that they are more timid.

It is not necessarily a compliment to be called out. It might be that we are being hesitant or even disobedient. God so much desires to heal us and bless us. Satan, so much wants to block that.

Don't wait until someone calls you out! Come forward whenever you feel the need to.

What could be more important than knowing God's will? What has more importance than a supernatural diagnosis and prescription? These two revelation gifts are the key to effective counseling. They are also very practical in terms of personal relationships, maintaining unity, handling finances, receiving direction and in witnessing. They are the key to good parenting. Pray in tongues until you get a word for your daughter, or your son—or whoever has a special need.

WHAT THESE GIFTS ARE NOT

They are not gifts of wisdom, knowledge, or intellectualism. Many people have abundant God-given knowledge and wisdom, but do not move in these gifts. Supernatural revelation is the key to understanding the nature of these gifts.

These gifts are not mental telepathy, ESP, clairvoyance, divination, or fortune telling; which are satanic counterfeits. You can identify these individuals because they speak about destruction, death, caskets, divorce, fear and accidents, while pursuing self-exaltation.

There was a false prophet in the Kansas City area who prophesied over people, telling them they were either apostles, prophets, or something else great. These people became egotistically inflated about how important they were. He said, "The anointing is on my thumb, which means you are an apostle! Oh, I feel the anointing on my pointing finger, that means you are a prophet."

I listened to tape after tape and noticed the consistent pattern. It fed self-glorification and false ego and people just ate it up, flocking to his meetings.

The exact opposite of the egotistic extreme, is the undue emphasis of prophetic utterances regarding death and destruction.

While preaching in Iowa, I was teaching about the fact that if you've been to a fortune teller, you need deliverance. If you've ever submitted yourself to a spiritist, you need to confess it as sin and have it removed. One of the key ladies in the church said, "Well, I've been to a fortune teller, and I don't need deliverance." (She was really a neat person and a committed Christian.)

I said, "Oh yes you do." I didn't want to argue with her, so I let it lay.

Two days later, at a covered dish dinner, she ended up sitting across the table from me. I had been praying about this for two days, so I asked her, "Have you ever had a dream regarding someone in a casket?"

It was a supernatural word of knowledge!

She said, "That's funny. I had a neighbor, across the road who I did dream was in a casket. Three days later she died." She continued, "And you know, I had a dream that my brother had drowned and just a few months later, he drowned in front of my eyes. Coming home from the funeral, my husband said to me, 'Well, I wonder who will be next?' I heard it coming out of my mouth, 'You will. You will tip over the tractor and be killed.' Within a year he tipped the tractor and it killed him!"

I said, "That is that foul, filthy demon of divination. When do you want to get rid of it."

She gasped, "Right now!" She just hadn't realized it till that point.

We just left our covered dinner plates there and went to the sanctuary and cast the spirit out and it came out screaming! This Christian leader was saved and had the Baptism, but she had opened up an area in her life where she was exposed supernaturally to evil.

If you've messed with tarot cards, had your hand read, practiced fortune telling, read a horoscope or any of those kinds of things, you must pray specifically and confess each of those as sin. Tell God you were walking in the wrong kingdom, the satanic one, and ask specifically for the blood of Jesus to cleanse you.

You have five senses: sight, smell, taste, hearing and touch. Any communication between two people other than the five physical senses involves a spirit: either the Holy Spirit, a human spirit or an evil spirit. People with companion spirits function like magnets. They either attract or repel each other. There is a flow of communication between them. For example, two homosexuals or two lesbians instantly know each other. I've heard them testify that they can instantly spot someone else who is a sexual pervert. They have a companion spirit which provides them with instant recognition.

There is one very interesting verse which had puzzled me for years. It is Luke 7:35, *"But wisdom is justified by all her children."*

Jesus was saying, "Look at the results, <u>see what is conceived</u>, and then you will know what spirit is at the root of something. Ask yourself what is the child or fruit of this relationship?"

What is coming forth from your business? Wisdom is known by what it is producing. Is it love, joy and peace? Is it hate, anger and frustration?

These gifts are not just for those called to the ministry gifts. Everyone needs to move supernaturally in the word of knowledge and word of wisdom. We need them to make proper decisions. We need them to raise our children. We need them in business. We need them in relationships with people. If you can know what is going on in the spirit realm, you can stay on target.

HOW TO MOVE IN THESE TWO GIFTS

You must have a Spirit-filled walk of life, if you want to hear God talk. If you are not walking in the Spirit, you will always wonder who it is you are hearing from. We are talking about having a pure heart, absence of pride, anger, lust and wrong motives. We must fear the deadly sin of pride. It has the power to destroy all who embrace it.

To receive from God you must spend time in the prayer closet, in the presence of God, listening and talking to Him.

The false prophet in I Kings 22:24 arrogantly asked, *"Which way did the spirit from the LORD go from me to speak to you?"*

God's true prophet Micaiah replied, *"Indeed, you shall see on that day when you go into an inner chamber to hide!"* Micaiah knew that would never happen with those phonies!

Jesus instructed His disciples, "Go into the prayer closet and shut the door." He's not talking about a literal closet, He is talking about a place of prayer and quietness where you are shut in and alone with God. God wants to talk to you!

Have you realized yet that all the gifts of the Holy Spirit are potentially yours? It's true.

During the Pentecostal revivals years ago, people would pass out flyers saying, "I have seven gifts," or "I have five gifts," or "I'm a nine-gifted man."

These were all examples of self promotion. The gifts are not a product to be advertised like orange juice or soda. We have the Spirit of Jesus. Is He a product, commodity or a person?

Jesus didn't leave half of His gifts and fruit in heaven when He came into your life. Everything that God is, in terms of His gifts are already resident in Him, and in you. We actually just have one gift: Him!

In Him is the potential of releasing all 25 gifts of the Holy Spirit. We are completely full of the Holy Spirit in Christ. Each gift or fruit of the Spirit is actually just a matter of releasing what is already in us through Christ.

"Therefore let no one boast in men. For all things are yours: whether Paul or Apollos or Cephas, or the world or life or death, or things present or things to come; all are yours" (I Corinthians 3:21-22).

The forenamed were the three spiritual "heavyweights" of Paul's day. But Paul said, *"You are Christ's, and Christ is God's."*

I was reading this verse one day, when I first received the Baptism and I said, "that is true and I believe it." This Scripture says in effect, Don't look to men, or glory in men, and don't talk about this great evangelist, or this guy on TV or even your pastor. All things are yours in Christ. Talk about Christ!

GET YOUR TONGUE LANGUAGE GOING!

When you are trying to make a decision, working at your job, as you need a word, turn on your speaking in tongues just underneath your breath. The gift of tongues is the key to moving in all of the other gifts. It is Spirit-prayer and it gets you into the Spirit immediately. Be logical about this: If you want to be in the Spirit, why not pray in the spirit?

When you start moving in these gifts, make no declarations as if you were some great and mighty prophet.

Instead, ask people questions. For example: "Do you have a sinus headache?" If they say, "Well, yes I do," then you know that you heard from God.

When I first requested the word of wisdom and word of knowledge, I just started asking folks things – 100 times out of 100, the word God gave me was correct. I learned that this experience was not originating in my mind. It was the Holy Spirit.

Asking others is sweet and kind. It doesn't exalt you. At times, you will find that it was your mind instead of the Lord. If folks claim infallibility here, they are not being honest with you. To move in these gifts, you must give all the glory to God.

BOASTING IS FORBIDDEN

"It is doubtless not profitable for me to boast. I will come to visions and revelations of the Lord: I

know a man in Christ who fourteen years ago; whether
in the body I do not know, or whether out of the body
I do not know, God knows; such a one was caught up
to the third heaven. And I know such a man; whether
in the body or out of the body I do not know, God
knows; how he was caught up into Paradise and heard
inexpressible words, which it is not lawful for a man
to utter. Of such a one I will boast; yet of myself I will
not boast, except in my infirmities. For though I might
desire to boast, I will not be a fool; for I will speak the
truth. But I refrain, lest anyone should think of me
above what he sees me to be *or hears from me. And*
lest I should be exalted above measure by the
abundance of the revelations, a thorn in the flesh was
given to me, a messenger of Satan to buffet me, lest I
be exalted above measure. Concerning this thing I
pleaded with the Lord three times that it might depart
from me. And He said to me, 'My grace is sufficient
for you, for My strength is made perfect in weakness.'
Therefore most gladly I will rather boast in my
infirmities, that the power of Christ may rest upon
me" (II Corinthians 12:1-9).

The point of this passage is that revelation gifts tend to puff us up, and get us off track.

Paul said, "because of the abundance of revelations, I was given a thorn in the flesh." The point of the passage is not to argue over what the thorn in the flesh is, but that God was trying to keep Paul from falling into ruin. Apparently it worked!

I was preaching up in Canada once, and was moving in the gifts of the word of wisdom and word of knowledge. An elderly minister of God told me, "I have never seen anyone move in these gifts who didn't eventually fall away."

To stay safe, we must give 100% of the glory to Jesus, and walk in all humility.

BIBLICAL ILLUSTRATIONS IN THE OLD TESTAMENT

One of my favorite passages is found in I Samuel. Samuel was just a boy, but he kept hearing the voice of the Lord one night. Whenever God spoke, he thought that it was Eli calling instead. Finally, Eli who knew better said, "Go lay back down. It is the Lord."

Look at I Samuel 3:7, *"(Now Samuel did not yet know the LORD, nor was the word of the LORD yet revealed to him.)"*

Is that a key passage or what?

It says Samuel didn't yet know the Lord and the Word of the Lord was not revealed to him. Yet, if a special little boy could hear the Word of the Lord in the Old Testament times, shouldn't you desire for God to reveal His will to you today? I want the Word of the Lord!

Later the Bible says, *"So Samuel grew, and the LORD was with him and let none of his words fall to the ground."* This is a tremendous statement, to us by God... about a mere man. Every word he spoke; happened!

Two harlots brought a baby to Solomon's court. Both had a child and one rolled over hers in the middle of the night, suffocating the child. They both came to Solomon, both saying, "This is my baby."

He said, "Give me a sword and we'll cut the child in two and give each exactly half."

The woman who was the mother of course said, "No, give it to the other woman." So, Solomon received a word of wisdom. A supernatural solution was given to Solomon right on the spot. It was not the intellectual genius within him. It is now a famous word of wisdom.

In the Bible, you can read, *"Your ears shall hear a word behind you saying, 'This is the way, walk ye in it'"* (Isaiah 30:21). This speaks of a supernatural knowing. God leads us saying, "Cut that off. Stop that, start this!"

You can hear a word from the Lord!

These things happened selectively in the Old Testament but we are under a better covenant. We can all hear the "still small voice." When you hear the Word of the Lord, it won't be through your two ears. It will be louder than audible hearing but on the inside of you. It is peaceful and silent. It is a "knowing." It is found in the presence of God.

BIBLICAL ILLUSTRATIONS IN THE NEW TESTAMENT

In the Gospels there is an account where Jesus explains the issue of taxes and their application to His followers (see Matthew 17:25, 22:17, Mark 12:14, Luke 20:22, 23:2). The disciples had come to Jesus and asked, "Do we have to pay taxes to the Romans?"

Jesus immediately had a word of wisdom. He said, "Give me a coin... Whose image is on the coin?"

They answered, "Caesar's."

He said, "Render unto Caesar the things that be Caesar's and render unto God the things that be God's."

Now, that was a word of wisdom in answer to that situation. He spoke by the Spirit. He did not use some strange supernatural powers that are unavailable to us today. He overcame and lived His life as a human being full of the Holy Spirit. God gave Him that "word of wisdom."

We have a wonderful Jewish friend named Art Katz. Before he was saved, he was on a ship traversing the Mediterranean sea. He decided he would read the New Testament. He read Matthew, Mark and Luke and on into the Gospel of John. By this time, he was on Jesus' side, but had not yet accepted Jesus. As he saw the controversies between the Scribes and Pharisees against Jesus, he said, "I was on His side. I was actually wanting Jesus to win."

Then Art came to John 8, dealing with the woman caught in adultery. The Pharisees had caught her in the very act of adultery. They said to Jesus, "The law says stone her, what do you say?"

My friend closed the New Testament at that point and said to himself, "Jesus is trapped. They've got Him. There is no way He can get out of this." Art sat for about two hours on the deck of that ship with his great philosophical and genius mind. Art can out reason anyone I've ever known. He concluded, "There is no answer for Jesus this time. They've got Him." He started weeping because He thought Jesus had been trapped. Then he opened John 8 again and read Jesus' words in verse 7, *"He who is without sin among you, let him throw a stone at her first"* Art was shocked and he said, "This is the Messiah."

Art told us, "I didn't accept Him right then, but I knew that Jesus was the Messiah." Over the next six months he struggled with the fact that it was going to cost him his family – to be disowned if he accepted Jesus as his Messiah.

It is always astonishing to me what scripture God uses to get someone saved or filled with the Spirit. Here is Art Katz reading the most evangelistically "unlikely" verse in the Bible, and yet that turned his light bulb on. It was the word of wisdom from Jesus!

SAMUEL AND SAUL

Let's look at some very specific words of knowledge. These are found in I Samuel 10:1-7. In context Saul has lost his father's herd, and as he went to search for it, he came to Samuel. Here are the step by step directions that Samuel shared with Saul:

When you have departed from me today, you will find two men

by Rachel's tomb in the territory of Benjamin at Zelzah;

and they will say to you, 'The donkeys which you went

to look for have been found.

And now your father has ceased caring about the donkeys and is worrying about you, saying, "What shall I do about my son?"'

Then you shall go on forward from there and come to the terebinth tree of Tabor.

There three men going up to God

at Bethel will meet you,

one carrying three young goats,

another carrying three loaves of bread,

and another carrying a skin of wine.

And they will greet you

and give you two loaves of bread, which you shall receive from their hands.

After that you shall come to the hill of God where the Philistine garrison is.

And it will happen, when you have come there to the city,

that you will meet a group of prophets

coming down from the high place

with a stringed instrument,

a tambourine,

a flute,

and a harp before them;

and they will be prophesying.

Then the Spirit of the LORD will come upon you,

and you will prophesy with them

and be turned into another man. "And let it be, when these signs come to you, that you do as the occasion demands; for God is with you."

There are at least 25 different specific details given in the prophecy. I want you to realize from this that God knows <u>exactly</u> what is going on in your life. He alone knows what troubles you, what is really important and HOW to bring His best to pass in your life today.

He desires to tell you what you can do about your life, your situation and your problem. God wants to bless you with these two wonderful words today: The word of knowledge and the word of wisdom. You need but ask Him. Today, I challenge you to hear His voice and receive your deliverance.

"Therefore, as the Holy Spirit says: 'Today, if you will hear His voice, Do not harden your hearts as in the rebellion, In the day of trial in the wilderness'" (Hebrews 3:7-8).

Today is your day to hear from God!

CHAPTER 11

DISCERNING OF SPIRITS

"But the manifestation of the Spirit is given to each one for profit of all, for to one is given the word of wisdom through the Spirit, to another the word of knowledge through the same Spirit, to another faith by the same Spirit, to another gifts of healing by the same Spirit, to another the working of miracles, to another prophecy, to another discerning of spirits..." (I Corinthians 12:7-10).

Discerning of spirits is that gift which enables us to hear and see into the spirit world. Many times as I pray with someone, I will actually hear in the thought realm—the sarcastic tones of demonic "voices." It is not an audible voice, and it is not the normal thought processes.

You get the sense of them smarting off and making rude statements.

Kenneth Hagin was once praying when he suddenly saw these little green imps on one guy's head. He said, "You foul devils be gone in the name of Jesus." He saw them jump down on the floor, run down the aisle, out the back door and the door slammed behind them.

What was that?

He could see what no one else could. It was a supernatural ability to see and hear things in the spirit world.

THERE ARE COUNTERFEITS

There are people who see auras which is of the occult. You might hear them say something like, "Oh, I see a blue aura around you." Or, "I see a red aura." I get nervous quick when people talk like that to me. It is a counterfeit of the Holy Spirit's gift: the discerning of spirits.

Discernment of spirit is not the gift of "suspicion." People will often say things like, "I think they've got a demon." But, discerning of spirits is not the gift of suspicion, or accusation, or speculating about people.

We must be able to discern between human spirits, evil spirits, angelic spirits and the Holy Spirit. There are several passages of scripture that refer to angels as "spirits." Sometimes there is something angelic going on so you've really got a possibility of discernment in those four realms.

One day I was praying and God said, "If you know what the Holy Spirit is doing, you don't need to know what the demons are doing!" Discerning the "Holy Spirit" is the most important discernment.

That really refreshed my thinking! It was refreshing because I never thought of discerning of spirits as applying to the Holy Spirit. But the first thing we want to discern is what God is doing. When we truly know what God is doing, we need not worry much about "old Scratch."

The devil will often condemn you for getting "checks" in your spirit. A check is an alarm or sense that something is not exactly "right." Years ago, there was a couple who attended another church. A traveling speaker there was saying all the right things, but they were hearing bells go off in their spirits. They sensed that they were being warned that there was something seriously wrong with this guy. The devil tried to put them in condemnation saying, "Well, you are just judging unfairly. You are just condemning people you don't know."

It came out a couple weeks later, that this visiting evangelist was traveling with a woman who was not his wife. He was living in open adultery with her. It turned out that the

Holy Spirit "check" in their spirit was right. You can trust the Holy Spirit.

When "bells and whistles" are going off and something seems wrong, don't quickly throw that away. It is often the discernment of the Holy Spirit.

IT'S NOT LIKE HUNTING QUAIL

A couple years back, I went quail hunting on Thanksgiving Day. I'm not a very good hunter, but a guy loaned me a shotgun. We were off along a road hedge and ten or twelve quail jumped out together. I thought, well, if I fire towards the middle of a dozen or so quail, I'm bound to hit something. Of course, I missed every single bird.

This happened about five times and the other guys were getting a little upset. They jokingly said, "All the quails are on your side of the hedge because they know you can't hit them."

That is exactly how it is when you cast out demons. You can't just fire your pistol into the air to rebuke the devil. You need discernment to aim your weapons.

You must ask: What is the principality? What is the primary motivator controlling this person? Is a spirit of rejection operating? Is it a controlling, dominating spirit? Is this an occult spirit or an unclean spirit?

Don't just shoot into the flock of quail. Get lined up with your spiritual sites, by using spiritual discernment as to what the problem truly is.

This has happened to every Christian. You'll be praying for somebody and something drops into your mind suddenly. You pray about it, and then you know how to bring it up with the person. This is a word of knowledge, but it's also discernment.

The key to deliverance is to submit to and draw nigh to God.

"Therefore submit to God. Resist the devil and he will flee from you. Draw near to God and He will draw near to you" (James 4:7-8).

Before James ever mentioned casting out demons, he said, "submit to God." Then after he mentions resisting the devil, he says draw near to God.

Deliverance is absolutely worthless if somebody doesn't submit to God. Only when you submit to God are you in a position to resist the devil. Without submission, rebuking the devil is like sending him out a swinging bar room door. You can cast demons out but they come right back in. The key to maintaining deliverance is submitting to God. Being in close proximity to God makes you a very unattractive target for any demonic activity and it is a key to staying free.

As you wake up in the morning and get out of your bed, draw near to God and He will draw near to you. You can live in safety that way all day long. Deliverance will not work for someone who doesn't want to be near to God. When you are hugging God the demons will not dare to put their hands on you.

DECEIVING MANY

In Matthew 24, the word "many" occurs six times. Verse 5 says, *"For **many** will come in My name saying, 'I am the Christ' and will deceive **many**."* Jesus is saying there will be a large group of false teachers who are going to deceive large groups of people. There will be many false teachers and they will have great influence.

Verses 10-12 go on to say,

*"And then **many** will be offended [or stumble], will betray one another, and will hate one another. Then **many** false prophets will rise up and deceive **many**. And because lawlessness will abound, the love of **many** will grow cold. But he who endures to the end of things shall be saved"*

In light of this passage, the Church in these last days especially needs discernment. Without discernment, you will be deceived. Deceivers will come in Jesus' name and there will be a whole lot of them.

Not too long ago, there was a group in my community that did nothing but get together and dance before the Lord. One of the "spirit filled" dancers applied for a job but didn't show up for work. Then she made a frontal, verbal attack against the person who hired her. She called the Governor of the state to get that employer in trouble.

The person who hired her, being a Christian, went to the woman's home to try to reconcile, but instead got the door slammed in their face.

Here was somebody who is supposedly full of God, a great worshipper and supposedly in love with Jesus. She was living a life that did not demonstrate Jesus.

She may not have been representative of the group as a whole. But the point is, not everything that dances, preaches or quotes Scripture is of God. There is a lot of false stuff out there and it is only going to get further and further "off track." When Jesus spoke about the signs of the times here in Matthew 24, He emphasized false prophets more than anything else. And we cannot consider false prophets and deception without mentioning the demonic influence all around us today.

The Greek word for demon is "daimonion." The plural form of the word, demons, is "daimonia." These two words occur 65 times in the New Testament. They are translated in the King James 64 times as "devils," and one time as "gods."

The King James should have translated it consistently as "demons." Unfortunately, many translations fail to distinguish between the word Diabolos, which means the Devil, and the word for demon. For example, Mark 16:17b in the King James reads, *"In My name shall they cast out devils..."* But the Greek word is not "devils," but the Greek word for demons.

"In My name they will cast out demons!"

This is important because when you are casting out demons, you are not casting the Devil out. You are casting the demon out. There is only one Devil, and I doubt that he himself would inhabit anyone other than the Antichrist. Christians today are primarily working against demons.

Think about that word "diabolos." We get our English word "diabolical" from it. Dia means "through," bolos means "to throw." The word devil literally means "to throw through or to slander."

In I Timothy 3:11, it says, *"...the wives* (of deacons) *be grave, not* <u>*slanderers*</u>*..."* It could also be translated, *"the wives of deacons are not to be devils."*

Now, as a long-time pastor, I have to say that is really interesting!

When we slander someone, we demonstrate the very nature of Satan himself. The devil is the accuser of the brethren. The word "devil" means to "throw remarks through somebody." That is fairly graphic.

The Greek word for Satan is "satanas," meaning adversary. The Greek word for spirit is pneuma and can be used in an evil sense, especially when it is preceded by the adjectives "unclean" or "evil."

The actual phrase "demon possession" does not occur in the Greek New Testament. The Greek word "daimonizomai," simply means "demonized." The use of the word "possession" is unfortunate indeed! The very concept of "demon possession" is unscriptural. It denies personal accountability and responsibility for one's actions.

The verb "demonized" however, occurs through out the New Testament. One instance is the man who was "demonized" by thousands of demons and who was living in the tombs. When Jesus and His disciples landed ashore, this demonized man ran out of the graves and fell at the feet of Jesus.

The Bible says he worshipped Him. Those demons did not run the man to Jesus. The demonized man still had his free will. He still had the ability to go to Jesus and he was instantly and permanently set free.

The concept of "demon possession" implies that people are not accountable. There is no one so "demonized" that they are no longer responsible for their actions. Mankind will always be responsible. No one is so controlled by a demon that they cannot choose to be saved. Each and every man or woman can choose to repent, turn from sin to Christ.

CAN A CHRISTIAN HAVE A DEMON?

This is really an over simplified question that actually contains four sub-questions:

1. "Can a Christian have a demon in the sense of demon possession?" No, a Christian can't be demon possessed.
2. "Can a Christian have a demon in their spirit?" No.
3. "Can a Christian have a demon in the sense of a demon exercising some influence or control on their mind or emotions?" Yes.
4. "Can a Christian have a demon affecting them physically or in their body?" Yes.

The question "Can a Christian *have* a demon?" is so vague as to be dangerous to answer! When you ask that question, the answer is really no, no, yes, yes.

To answer it properly one must discover first what the asker means by the word "have."

The answer is relative to any one of the four sub-questions I just listed.

When the Holy Spirit comes into our human spirit, we are born of Spirit of God. A Christian cannot have a demon in their spirit. That is the Holy Spirit's territory. Can a Christian have a demon affect them in their soul, psyche, emotions or mind? We've all seen many Christians who were depressed, suffering from rejection and a terrible self-image. The truth is, demons influence Christians all the time.

Many times, people go without healing because no one can "heal a demon." Demons must be rebuked. Many times I have rebuked a demon just once, and the person was instantly healed. What the sick person needed was deliverance from a demon, not healing.

CAN A DEMON HAVE A CHRISTIAN

Now that is an interesting question, and it is the **real** question. The issue is not whether a Christian can have a demon, but whether a demon can have a Christian! Think of it by picturing someone who has a cloud all around them; a cloud of demonic oppression and vexation. They are under that cloud. In Mark 1:23, we read, *"Now there was a man in their synagogue with (literally "in") an unclean spirit. And he cried out..."* It doesn't say the spirit was in him, but this scripture says he was in that unclean spirit.

"But I fear, lest somehow, as the serpent deceived Eve by his craftiness, so your minds may be corrupted from the simplicity that is in Christ. For if he who comes preaches another Jesus whom we have not preached, or if you receive a different spirit which you have not received..." (II Corinthians 11:3-4).

If someone tells you, "Well, a Christian can't receive a different spirit," do not believe them. The Bible says they can! And it gives explicit warnings on how to keep it from ever happening to you.

Did you ever notice that false teaching is always complicated? Counterfeit teachers always claim to show us the *"deeper truths"* of God. In the "deeper truth" process I have seen Christians receive spirits of legalism, spirits of works and spirits of self-condemnation.

In Matthew 16:23 we see Jesus rebuke Peter, *"But He turned and said to Peter, 'Get behind Me, Satan.'"*

Jesus was not saying that Peter was Satan!

But, Peter was telling Jesus that He did not have to go to the cross. Those words were not in alignment with God's will. Jesus was explaining emphatically to Peter that he was speaking under the influence of Satan. In some sense, Peter's mind and emotions had gotten under the control of the devil. Peter didn't want to see Jesus die, or suffer, or go through pain. This was just moments after Peter had boldly stated, *"You are the Christ, the Son of the living God."* Isn't that an irony? Jesus had just finished acknowledging, *"...Flesh and blood has not revealed this to you, but My Father which is in heaven"* (Matthew 16:17).

Peter must have had his chest up so high at that moment of time. He was so happy! Then about ten minutes later, this "Satan speaking" passage shows up.

We are all subject to spiritual influences.

SATAN COMES IMMEDIATELY

Why is it so significant that Satan chose to show up in Peter's dialogue with Jesus regarding the rapidly approaching death of the cross?

We can see rather clearly that "pride" which goes before destruction could have been what opened the door for Satan's temptation. But why should Satan be so motivated to move in so immediately to add his "two cents" worth?

Obviously, Satan did not want Jesus to finish His mission. But what is not so apparent is the fact that when the gifts of the Spirit start to flow, Satan has to move in immediately for therein lies the route to his final defeat.

That is to say, when the word of knowledge, word of wisdom or discerning of spirits starts to flow freely, regarding the plan, purpose and the wisdom of God's plan... Satan's kingdom is immediately threatened. Such is always the case. That is why the plan of deliverance for mankind, wrought in the life, death, sin bearing and victorious resurrection of Jesus must be suppressed, attacked or distorted by Satan at any cost.

Satan must come immediately to "take away" the Word of God, before it has a chance to reveal the true meaning and effect of the Death of Christ. For in His death, we find life to provide us with victory. And so we need to look at the shed blood of Jesus Christ as it relates to our lives, our ministries and the impending victory of God's Kingdom in the earth.

CHAPTER 12

THE BLOOD OF JESUS

The shed blood of Jesus is the basis for our lives as Christians. With respect to that, it is interesting to study the last twenty-four hours of Jesus' life, where He shed His blood at three different locations. Each was in or around the city of Jerusalem. Each of their names starts with the letter 'G,' as they are listed in the Bible.

At Gethsemane; He shed His blood for our sorrows.

At Gabbatha; He shed His blood for our sicknesses.

At Golgotha; He shed His blood for our sins.

Each place where Jesus shed His blood was vicarious, which means "for us, as a substitute." In each of those places, Jesus substituted His blood for our own! Jesus endured all of that suffering on our behalf so that we could be set free from sorrow, sickness and sin.

GETHSEMANE

"Then they came to a place which was named Gethsemane; and He said to His disciples, 'Sit here while I pray.' And He took Peter, James and John with Him. And He began to be troubled and deeply distressed. Then He said to them, 'My soul is exceedingly sorrowful, even to death'" (Mark 14:32).

This passage describes the scene in the Garden of Gethsemane. Here Jesus acted as our sorrow bearer. He not only bore our sins at the cross. We have all experienced deep sorrows for a multitude of reasons. Sorrows may be caused by our own sins, stupidity, folly and foolishness, and also by the failures and hurts of others.

Jesus looked into the cup the night he offered his disciples communion. He realized that He was going to die. His time with them was nearly over. It filled His heart with sorrow.

The Bible goes on to tell us in Mark 14:35, *"He went a little farther..."* As a brother or sister in Christ, don't we all want to go a little farther, a little deeper into Jesus? Mark continues by saying, *"...and* (Jesus) *fell on the ground,..."* The other Gospels say Jesus, *"fell on His face"* in Gethsemane.

"And He said, 'Abba, Father, all things are *possible for You. Take this cup away from Me; nevertheless, not what I will, but what You* will'*"* (Mark 14:36).

Jesus was considering the price He was about to pay - the cup of His shed blood to be poured out in death. There was no other way for us to go to heaven. He knew He had to die. Had He not died, you and I would be irrevocably destined to hell. Jesus was on His face praying about this; He cried out, *"If it be possible let this pass."*

God the Father evidently said, "It isn't possible, son. Either You die or they die and go to hell."

Jesus was wrestling with His destiny as our Savior. He took a moment to check on His disciples.

"Then He came and found them sleeping, and said to Peter, 'Simon, are you sleeping? Could you not watch one hour? Watch and pray, lest you enter into temptation. The spirit indeed is *willing, but the flesh* is *weak'"* (Mark 14:37-38).

This is a good verse for all of us today. Because we may have a willing spirit, while our flesh is still weak. According to Jesus, we must all watch and pray because our flesh is so weak.

"Again He went away and prayed, and spoke the same words. And when He returned, He found them

asleep again, for their eyes were heavy;..." (Mark 14:39-40).

This is much like the church today. It seems to be sound asleep with heavy eyes.

The disciples, who were only half awake, did not know what to answer Him. I have been in that position myself, where I did not know what to say because I had failed. What a sad position to be in!

"Then He came the third time and said to them, 'Are you still sleeping and resting? It is enough! The hour has come; behold, the Son of Man is being betrayed into the hands of sinners. Rise, let us be going. See, My betrayer is at hand.' And immediately, while He was still speaking, Judas, one of the twelve, with a great multitude with swords and clubs, came from the chief priests and the scribes and the elders" (Mark 14:41-43).

Here came Judas, the whole Jewish Sanhedrin and the religious leaders. The legal representatives of the whole Nation of Israel were just getting ready to reject Jesus.

"Now His betrayer had given them a signal, saying, 'Whomever I kiss, He is the One; seize Him and lead Him away safely.' As soon as He had come, immediately he went up to Him and said to Him, 'Rabbi, Rabbi!' and kissed Him" (Mark 14:44-45).

In the Greek, the word "kiss" means, "kissed again and again with great affection." It was the Hebrew custom to kiss on each cheek, but Judas laid it on heavy. It was utter and total hypocrisy! The same word for "kiss" was used when the lady came to Jesus and washed His feet with her tears and her hair. *"And they laid their hands on Him..."* (Mark 14:46).

Can you lay hands on God, the Creator? He obviously permitted it. Any one of us would think, "Get your hands off of me," but Jesus was letting them crucify Him.

In Matthew we see more, *"But Jesus said to him* [Judas], *'Friend, why have you come?'"* (Matthew 26:50).

Jesus did not call Judas brother, but He was still trying to get Judas to repent! Ever faithful to the last and beyond.

In Luke 22:44, we read of Gethsemane, *"And being in agony, He prayed more earnestly. Then His sweat became like great drops of blood falling down to the ground."*

Here we find something that is very interesting indeed! We see no description at the crucifixion of the emotional pain Jesus endured. Scripture just reports He died. But here, in His emotional and mental agony, the scripture describes Jesus as sweating drops of blood.

The word Gethsemane actually means "olive press." An olive press, back then, was made up of two stones. They would put the olives in the center and would have a beast of burden hooked up to the top stone with a pole to go around and around. These stones would crush the olives and the oil would flow out of them into a trough. Jesus was crushed in the Garden of Gethsemane, so that the anointing oil of His Spirit would be poured out upon us.

This passage about Jesus in Gethsemane shows us that Jesus not only died for our sins, and our healing, but for our sorrows. The twin stones of grief and sorrow crushed His mighty heart and it showed on His bleeding body. In Luke 22:43, just before we read that Jesus sweat great drops of blood, it says that angels appeared to Him to strengthen Him. But, even with angelic strength, the blood poured out of His pores.

The Bible says, *"Therefore God, Your God, has anointed You With the oil of gladness more than Your companions,"* (Hebrews 1:9b). Jesus had more joy than anybody. Why? Because He did the will of God perfectly and consistently. How joyful are you when you are not living in sin? When sin is absent, you are not depressed or in a bad mood. Jesus was never out of the Spirit. He was one happy guy.

Why then does the Scripture call Him a "Man of Sorrows?" Isaiah 53:3-4 reads,

"He is despised and rejected by men, A Man of sorrows and acquainted with grief. And we hid, as it were, our faces from Him; He was despised, and we did not esteem Him. Surely He has borne our griefs And carried our sorrows..."

That blood spilled in Gethsemane was vicarious. Jesus not only died for our sins, but He died for our sorrows. He bore our sorrow. He surely has borne our griefs and carried our sorrows. Yet we esteem Him stricken, smitten by God and afflicted.

Now the word "sorrow" used in the Hebrew text of Isaiah 53, means: regret for past misconduct and disappointment over unfinished tasks.

Jesus had no regret for His own past conduct. There was no personal anguish. He wasn't marred. But vicariously, He bore our sorrows. He was sorrowed for our sins – in that instant of time He voluntarily associated Himself with the sorrow of all our failures whether by child abuse, verbal abuse, sexual abuse; or any other way we may have been marred. Marred simply means to be made sore. We still use the expression, "I am really sore about that." As Jesus began to sweat drops of blood, that blood flowed off His sinless body and was poured out on the earth. Right then and there, He became the Man of our sorrows and He began to die for our misconduct, our regrets and our unfinished tasks. In the garden Jesus experienced the sorrow of rejection.

Speaking of Judas' rejection, there is an Old Testament verse that says, *"...Who ate my bread, Has lifted up his heel against me"* (Psalm 41:9).

Some might say, "That is not true. Judas didn't lift up his heel against the Lord. He kissed Him."

Oh yes he did! Judas kicked Jesus right in the guts, right in the Spirit. It was in the inner man that Judas stomped on Jesus. Scripture is not talking here about a physical heel, but the emotions of rejection.

Have you ever been rejected? Have you ever been kicked in the spirit and wounded in your emotions? Jesus understands.

Jesus not only understands that, He died for it.

Peter failed Jesus too. His entire inner circle failed Him and Jesus died for that failure as well. Jesus said, "When I needed a friend, my elders were sleeping. They slept when I needed a prayer. I had to bear it all by Myself. My blood fell to the ground as I was crushed in the olive garden. I shed My blood so not only sins can be gone, but sorrows as well.

Jesus says to us today: "You can forgive! Ask that My blood wash your unforgiveness away."

He intimately understands rejection better than any of us ever will.

Nothing hurts worse than a divorce. Jesus understands covenant betrayal. A covenant was broken in the garden. When Judas kissed Him, it was more than rejection, it was covenant betrayal.

All of us, in some way, have felt utterly betrayed. Jesus says, "I have borne your griefs, and I have carried your sorrows. You must bear them no more. Carry them no longer!" Ask the precious blood of Jesus, shed in the garden, to wash that away.

Jesus journeyed the thorny road of sorrows to cleanse us of ours!

Following Christ invokes a principle that ensures us: every believer will go through Gethsemane. Most of us have already been there. Many have to go through it several times. Here, we too are crushed, so the anointing oil can flow out of us. That oil flows as we lay aside of our own lives and follow

Christ. As a result, we can be more gentle, less judgmental and less self-righteous. In the Garden, self-righteousness gets crushed. Even broken promises to God are crushed. In the garden we learn as we pray, "not our will, but Yours." It is God Who changes us, as we lose faith in ourselves.

I've heard people say, "Well, I can't be healed, I was marred beyond repair. I was forced to be a victim."

The blood can turn you from a victim to a victor because of its power to cleanse away all of your sorrow. The blood's power to cleanse from sorrow is the same as its power to cleanse sin. Jesus became the Son of Man, so we would become sons of God!

He took our sin so that we could have His righteousness. He took our sorrow, so we could have His joy. He took our sickness, so we could have His health. He took our nakedness so that we could be clothed with wholeness. He came to Earth, that we might go to Heaven.

> *"The Spirit of the LORD is upon Me, Because He has anointed Me To preach the gospel to the poor; He has sent Me to heal the brokenhearted, To proclaim liberty to the captives And recovery of sight to the blind, To set at liberty those who are oppressed"* (Luke 4:18).

Did He mean it? Isaiah 61 (which is where Jesus was quoting from) continues in verse 3 where Jesus left off,

> *"To console those who mourn in Zion, To give them beauty for ashes, The oil of joy for mourning, The garment of praise for the spirit of heaviness; That they may be called trees of righteousness, The planting of the LORD, that He may be glorified"* (Isaiah 61:3).

"To *give them beauty for ashes,"* means that Jesus will take your old ash heap and make you beautiful.

I have prayed for many people, having gone through rape, abortion, drug abuse and other terrible things. My prayer has been, "Jesus, do what I can't, heal this person's broken heart!"

Their sorrow leaves them instantly! Because Jesus shed His blood for all of our sorrows in Gethsemane. It is all Him. He shed His precious blood for our sorrow!

GABBATHA

"While he was sitting on the judgment seat, his wife sent to him, saying, 'Have nothing to do with that just Man, for I have suffered many things today in a dream because of Him'" (Matthew 27:19).

"From then on Pilate sought to release Him, but the Jews cried out, saying, 'If you let this Man go, you are not Caesar's friend. Whoever makes himself a king speaks against Caesar.' When Pilate therefore heard that saying, he brought Jesus out and sat down in the judgment seat in a place that is called The *Pavement, but in Hebrew, Gabbatha"* (John 19:12-13).

Here was another place where Jesus shed His blood... the judgement seat. Can you imagine sitting on a judgement seat to judge God? Looking at this in Scripture, you know Pilate was in big-time trouble right here as he sat down on that judgement seat. Anytime you sit in judgement, you are in trouble with God. He is the only Judge. I want to call your attention to three things: The judgement seat, the pavement (Gabbatha), and the whipping post.

The judgement seat was a raised platform with steps ascending to it. Pilate judging Christ would sit on this raised platform.

The pavement is the floor underneath the judgement seat which was a mosaic of small square blocks. And, the Hebrew word for that is Gabbatha or pavement.

"He was taken from prison and from judgment, And who will declare His generation? For He was cut

off from the land of the living; For the transgressions of My people He was stricken" (Isaiah 53:8).

Notice that Jesus was to be led from prison and judgement. In other words, Isaiah prophesied that at the place of crucifixion there would also be a prison.

In this judgment area, there was such a prison containing a whipping post. It was at Gabbatha that Jesus had his back ripped open by the scourge. He first shed blood at Gethsemane for our own sorrows. He shed blood a second time here at the tribunal, near Pilate's platform. This is the second place where Jesus shed His blood.

"Himself bore our sins in His own body on the tree, that we, having died to sins, might live for righteousness — by whose stripes you were healed" (I Peter 2:24).

The Bible says, *"by His stripes, we were healed."* Healing comes by the blood of Jesus. And it comes from the blood that flowed from His bleeding stripes and scourged flesh. The blood of Jesus and the Name of Jesus are the two things that will create faith in you!

SCOURGING

The horrible "flagellum" was a Roman implement of severe bodily damage. It consisted of a handle, to which several cords or leather thongs were affixed. These were weighted with jagged pieces of bone or metal, to make the blow more painful. It was designed to tear the flesh open, bringing a maximum amount of pain and damage.

The victim was tied to a post and the blows were applied to the back and loins. Depending on the cruelty of the executioner, scourging was also applied to the face and the bowels. So hideous was the punishment, that the victim often fainted and sometimes died. Because of this, it was illegal to apply the "flagellum" to any Roman citizen.

By this cruel weapon of punishment, secrets and confessions were extracted from a victim. This usually preceded capital punishment. We can conclude that Jesus received 39 lashes from the "flagellum." The Old Testament forbad more that 40 stripes—to be extra safe the Jews always stopped at 39.

"Forty blows he may give him and no more, lest he should exceed this and beat him with many blows above these, and your brother be humiliated in your sight" (Deuteronomy 25:3).

WHERE DOES OUR FAITH LIE?

The word "Atonement" is an <u>Old Testament word</u>. It means to "cover." The Day of Atonement was the day when sin was covered. That covered sin was waiting for the day when the Messiah was to come and cleanse it away. Sin was covered to avoid judgment, but still waiting to be cleansed. The word Atonement is not actually used in the New Testament at all (except a mistranslation in one verse). We should not use the term because it is no longer theologically applicable. Sin is no longer just covered; it is forever washed away!!

In the New Testament we focus on the shed blood of the Messiah, Jesus—the Lamb of God. There is power *in the blood of Jesus.* Our faith must be *in His blood.* Healing is received *by the blood of Jesus.* Nothing is received except by faith in the precious blood of Jesus!

We have seen that Jesus shed His blood at Gethsemane so that we could have our <u>sorrows</u> cleansed away.

He shed His blood at Gabbatha so that we could have our <u>sickness</u> cleansed away.

But finally, He shed His blood at Golgotha so that we could have our sins and guilt cleansed away. Because of His blood our sins are not just atoned for – they are no longer in existence.

Our faith must remain in the blood of Jesus! Our faith cannot rest in faith. I have no faith in faith. I do not have faith in myself. My faith rests in what Jesus accomplished when He shed His holy blood in the garden, on the whipping post and at Calvary. As we focus on His blood it will create faith in us!

Faith also comes from using the Name of Jesus as we pray. I have faith that when I attach the Name of "Jesus" to a prayer, something is going to happen because of Who He is. His Name and His blood have power. If you desire to move in the gifts, you must focus on His blood and His Name.

Now, let's take a quick look at Isaiah 53:1-12:

> *Who has believed our report? And to whom has the arm of the LORD been revealed? For He shall grow up before Him as a tender plant, And as a root out of dry ground. He has no form or comeliness; And when we see Him, There is no beauty that we should desire Him. He is despised and rejected by men, A Man of sorrows and acquainted with grief. And we hid, as it were, our faces from Him; He was despised, and we did not esteem Him. Surely He has borne our griefs And carried our sorrows; Yet we esteemed Him stricken, Smitten by God, and afflicted. But He was wounded for our transgressions, He was bruised for our iniquities; The chastisement for our peace was upon Him, And by His stripes we are healed. All we like sheep have gone astray; We have turned, every one, to his own way; And the LORD has laid on Him the iniquity of us all. He was oppressed and He was afflicted, Yet He opened not His mouth; He was led as a lamb to the slaughter, And as a sheep before its shearers is silent, So He opened not His mouth. He was taken from prison and from judgment, And who will declare His generation? For He was cut off from the land of the living; For the transgressions of My*

people He was stricken. And they made His grave with the wicked; But with the rich at His death, Because He had done no violence, Nor was any deceit in His mouth. Yet it pleased the LORD to bruise Him; He has put Him to grief. When You make His soul an offering for sin, He shall see His seed, He shall prolong His days, And the pleasure of the LORD shall prosper in His hand. He shall see the labor of His soul, and be satisfied. By His knowledge My righteous Servant shall justify many, For He shall bear their iniquities. Therefore I will divide Him a portion with the great, And He shall divide the spoil with the strong, Because He poured out His soul unto death, And He was numbered with the transgressors, And He bore the sin of many, And made intercession for the transgressors.

Notice the word iniquities in the fifth verse. The Hebrew word here is "Avon." He was wounded for our "Avon." This Hebrew word means, perversity, depravity, warped. The King James says he was "bruised" but the Hebrew word is much stronger. It means "crushed." He was crushed for our perversion and warped-ness. Jesus was totally smashed for our depravity and perversion. He was crushed in the Garden with such intensity that blood actually flowed from His sweat glands. He was tied to that whipping post and smitten again and again with blood spraying everywhere. The final crushing came on the cross—totally naked and humiliated in our place!

What a powerful Word from the Lord regarding our sorrows, healing and sin. He paid the full price. You and I do not have to be sorrowful. We can be sorrow free. He took our place.

He was crushed so that we could be healed in our bodies, in our emotions and in our spirits. He took care of sin, sickness and sorrow – the precious blood of Jesus.

Do you feel guilty for anything? Divorce, abortion, adultery, lying, hard feelings? Jesus was crushed for your healing. His soul was made an offering for your guilt. Have you ever grasped that truth, accepting it as your own?

You can pray, "Lord Jesus, with Your blood, cleanse away my guilt. I feel so bad about this." Take each guilty feeling before Him, and ask specifically that the blood of Jesus wash it away. Now pray and ask Him to heal you down where no man can see or understand. Ask Him to heal your broken heart, and to specifically wash away your sorrows by the blood of Jesus. Ask Jesus to cleanse away any physical sickness you are experiencing.

As you humbly pray through these three areas of your life: (do a thorough job, even if it takes several days). Freedom from sorrow and grief; freedom from sickness in your body; as well as freedom from guilt and sin!

CHAPTER 13

THE GIFT OF HEALINGS

As we saw in the previous chapter, healing is in the blood of Jesus. Isaiah 53:5 tells us,

> *"When evening had come, they brought to Him many who were demon-possessed. And He cast out the spirits with a word, and healed all who were sick, that it might be fulfilled which was spoken by Isaiah the prophet, saying: 'He Himself took our infirmities And bore* our *sicknesses'"* (Matthew 8:16-17).

Jesus had just put on a demonstration here. Demons departed and people were being healed instantly. The Bible declares that He healed <u>all</u> who were sick. He cast out the spirits with a word. <u>He did all of this that there might be a fulfillment of what Isaiah had prophesied.</u>

This has always been one of my favorite verses on healing. It has been made alive to me. I came to realize if Jesus bore it, I don't have to bear it. If He took it, I don't have to take it.

This attitude gets you in a fighting mode when it comes to healing. This is the Lord Jesus speaking, not just some "faith healer" preacher. We are talking about Jesus! And He was talking about us!

GOD'S WORD IS GOD'S WILL

> *"In this manner, therefore, pray: Our Father in heaven, Hallowed be Your name. Your kingdom come. Your will be done On earth as* it is *in heaven"* (Matthew 6:9-10).

Many people say, "I just want God's will to be done. Well pray the Lord's prayer." Did you know that no one is sick in heaven? Sickness is not God's will.

God is not schizophrenic!

He doesn't say one thing while actually wanting another!

If you really believe God wants you to have your sickness, then do not dare take any more medication. If it is God's will that you be sick, don't go to the doctor. That would be working against God! If it is God's will to be sick, stay away from the hospital. (Such thinking is ridiculous indeed!)

I have discovered that in relation to healing, God has a right hand and a left hand. His right hand is faith, healing and miracles. His left hand is medical science, doctors, medicine. God uses both hands to heal people. I never feel guilty about taking medicine. Likewise I never feel guilty for being healed in church.

I do not like legalism, rules and bondage. Scripture says, *"...and having done all, to stand"* (See Ephesians 6:13). Do everything you can nutritionally. Do everything you can spiritually. Do everything you can medically. One thing you should never do is accept sickness and quit fighting. Never become passive. Ministry in Jesus Name heals. Nutrition heals. Medicine heals. But Jesus heals today just as He always has, and He has the right to use any means that He decrees.

All throughout the ministry of Jesus, He was healing people. Now, if God the Father was making people sick, and God the Son was going around healing them, we would have a serious problem. The Trinity would be working against Itself!

That kind of thinking is ludicrous. God the Father and God the Son are one in purpose. God doesn't want you sick. Satan wants you sick. Sickness can come from many sources, demons, disobedience, sin and various other means. Never has it been God's perfect will for you to be sick. God the

Father's will was shown in God the Son's actions. Jesus said, "I and the Father... are one."

It is God's will to heal everyone, <u>unless and until God gives a revelation otherwise</u>, or it's time for the person to die. *"And as it is appointed for men to die once, but after this the judgment"* (Hebrews 9:27).

God's Word is God's will. It is God's Word that healing is for all mankind through the shed blood of Jesus.

IS SIN THE SOURCE OF SICKNESS?

ANSWER: YES AND NO!!!

"Now as Jesus passed by, He saw a man who was blind from birth. And His disciples asked Him, saying, 'Rabbi, who sinned, this man or his parents, that he was born blind?' Jesus answered, 'Neither this man nor his parents sinned, but that the works of God should be revealed in him'" (John 9:1-3).

A person's sickness is not necessarily a direct result of sin.

Because of this scripture, we cannot accuse a sick person, "You have sin or unbelief in your life. You left a window open for Satan to get you."

That is condemnation! This is judging! That is being an accuser of the brethren. *"There is therefore now no condemnation to those who are in Christ Jesus, who do not walk according to the flesh, but according to the Spirit"* (Romans 8:1).

If you have the flu, I'm not going to come visit saying, "You sinned, didn't you? You left the door to Satan open didn't you?"

Jesus says of this guy who was blind from birth, *"Neither this man nor his parents sinned."* That is what your Lord Jesus said. Now that makes sense because – how can you sin before you were born?

However, when you are walking in the Spirit, you feel good mentally, emotionally and physically. Obedience does bring divine health. Disobedience <u>can</u> bring sickness. Sickness in a person's spirit wraps around his entire personality. It affects them, warping them mentally, emotionally and physically.

I want to use HIV as an example. A practicing homosexual or drug user has a higher risk of contracting AIDS as a result of their alternate "death-style." They would acquire HIV as a direct result of living a perverted and sinful sexual life. However, right next to that person there may be a totally innocent person who got HIV through a blood transfusion. You can't honestly say everyone who has HIV has sinned. But you could say some people sinned and got HIV.

Sin can cause sickness. It depends entirely on the circumstances involved with each person. Never generalize in such cases. But, regardless of the cause, Jesus wants to heal.

"Now may the God of peace Himself sanctify you completely; and may your whole spirit, soul, and body be preserved blameless at the coming of our Lord Jesus Christ. He who calls you is faithful, who also will do it" (I Thessalonians 5:23-24).

God spoke something very precious to me years ago from this scripture. As you look at this verse, can you see that <u>if something is not peaceful</u>, then it is not from God? It is God that does the sanctifying, not our grunting. If you come to church and get beat up with legalism, ask yourself, "Where is the God of peace?" Make your life-decisions based accordingly. Maybe if the "God of peace" wasn't attending, you shouldn't either!

Notice how the above verse emphasizes spirit, soul and body. Never believe folks who deny that God is going to do something for your body!

From this verse, God spoke to me, "Man always starts with the body, and moves inward." If they can't get your body healed with medicine, the world concludes that you must need to see a psychiatrist. It must be a mental problem. Man starts with the body and then move to the mind, very rarely getting to the Spirit.

God said, "I am the Creator. I start with the spirit and work My way out!"

I am not putting down doctors and nurses. I am married to a nurse, my mother was a nurse, my daughter is a nurse practitioner!

However, the first thing God wants is for you to get right with Him. Be holy with no willful sin in your life. He wants you to be cleansed, having every evil washed away. When you are right with God, He will then go on to work on your mind, emotions and attitudes. This then will affect your body. God is really smart—first the spirit, then the soulish realm, and finally the physical.

DIVINE HEALTH

I have discovered that divine health is even better than healing! I am not kidding! I have listed twelve verses on divine health which show how obedience and health go hand in hand.

Exodus 15:22-27	Exodus 23:20-26	Deut. 7:11-15
Psalm 32:1-4	Psalm 41:1-4	Psalm 103:1-4
Psalm 107:17-20	Isaiah 33:24	Jer. 17:14
Mark 2:1-12	John 5:1-14, esp. 14	James 5:13-16

"...and said, 'If you diligently heed the voice of the LORD your God and do what is right in His sight, give ear to His commandments and keep all His statutes, I will put none of the diseases on you which I have brought on the Egyptians. For I am the LORD who heals you'" (Exodus 15:26).

It says here that obedience produces health. Exodus 23:20-26 is a very similar passage.

"Behold, I send an Angel before you to keep you in the way and to bring you into the place which I have prepared. Beware of Him and obey His voice; do not provoke Him, for He will not pardon your transgressions; for My name is in Him. But if you indeed obey His voice and do all that I speak, then I will be an enemy to your enemies and an adversary to your adversaries. For My Angel will go before you and bring you in to the Amorites and the Hittites and the Perizzites and the Canaanites and the Hivites and the Jebusites; and I will cut them off. You shall not bow down to their gods, nor serve them, nor do according to their works; but you shall utterly overthrow them and completely break down their sacred *pillars. So you shall serve the LORD your God, and He will bless your bread and your water. And I will take sickness away from the midst of you. No one shall suffer miscarriage or be barren in your land; I will fulfill the number of your days.*

However long you are supposed to live, you will get to live.

"I will bless your bread and your water;" is when <u>God</u> says grace over <u>your</u> meal.

"I will take sickness away," what a tremendous promise!

"Now a certain man was there who had an infirmity thirty-eight years. When Jesus saw him lying there, and knew that he already had been in that condition *a long time, He said to him, 'Do you want to be made well?' The sick man answered Him, 'Sir, I have no man to put me into the pool when the water is stirred up; but while I am coming, another steps down before me.' Jesus said to him, 'Rise, take up your bed and walk.' And immediately the man was made well, took up his bed, and walked. And that day was the*

Sabbath. The Jews therefore said to him who was cured, 'It is the Sabbath; it is not lawful for you to carry your bed.' He answered them, 'He who made me well said to me, 'Take up your bed and walk.' Then they asked him, 'Who is the Man who said to you, 'Take up your bed and walk'?' But the one who was healed did not know who it was, for Jesus had withdrawn, a multitude being in that *place. Afterward Jesus found him in the temple, and said to him, 'See, you have been made well. Sin no more, lest a worse thing come upon you'"* (John 5:5-14).

Here we recognize that sin can affect us physically. Here Jesus is telling a guy who could hardly move for 38 years, *"Sin no more lest a worse thing come upon you."*

Another New Testament scripture says,

"...not discerning the Lord's body. For this reason many are weak and sick among you, and many sleep" (I Corinthians 11:29-30).

Whenever we run down the other parts of the Body of Christ, whether it be other churches or people in a church, or when we get into gossip, and criticism, we will be made weak and sickly.

We must develop a healthy fear of both gossip and slander which are the primary indicators of not properly discerning the Body of Christ.

FAITH IN DISEASE

No matter their maturity or level of faith, a person who is suffering in their body, tends to believe their senses rather than Scripture.

I remember a meeting once where a woman was healed instantly. She had a bad back and so I asked her, "What is your need?"

She said, "I have this back pain."

I said, "Well, God is going to heal you."

I just knew it. I felt the "Spirit of faith" arise so I said, "God is going to heal you," again.

She said, "But I've had it for 18 years."

In other words, she was saying, "I've got to keep it. I've had it so long. It's part of me, I believe in it." I have discovered in life that you can't walk North and head South at the same time. You can't go two directions at once. As long as you are believing in your sickness, you will not be able to believe in Jesus for healing.

So, I led her in a prayer saying, "I confess to You Jesus, that I believe in my back trouble. This is negative faith, and it is sin. With Your blood, wash away this faith I have in my sickness."

Hundreds of people have been healed when they applied the blood to their negative faith!

The devil is jealous of your faith in Jesus Christ. He sees us trusting God and trusting Jesus. He wants the counterfeit of that for himself. He wants us to have our faith in him, in negativism, in sickness, and in fear. Negative faith is fear.

The reason the devil builds your faith in trouble, is to get your faith over into your sense realm. It is hard to receive healing when praying for yourself, because you can feel what is going on. Someone who doesn't feel what you do comes along and says, "Oh, that's nothing. Be gone in the name of Jesus." Oftentimes, illness leaves just like that because others don't have to overcome your faith in your senses. See what I mean?

Matthew 9:29 says, *"According to your faith let it be to you."* That scripture works in both kingdoms. If you say, "I am afraid I will get cancer," you are actually saying, "I believe that I will get cancer."

My dad died with a cerebral hemorrhage when he was 47. He collapsed in the bathroom hallway, and died a few hours later. For years the devil told me, "You won't live past 47." I am way past 47 now! I never believed that, but I had it thrown at me constantly.

This can happen in any realm. You could say, "Well, I've got red hair and my dad was always angry. Anger runs in our family." That is the faith that says, "I have to have a temper. My dad had it. It runs in the family. I believe in the family temper." That is a negative faith.

What do you do? You hit back by praying like this, "I confess to the Lord Jesus that I have been saying this, and this is faith in failure. Faith in sin. Faith in sickness. With Your blood, Jesus, wash that negative faith away."

It has to go. You cannot believe in your sickness and Jesus at the same time. They are opposites.

THE WORD "SYMPTOM" AND MOUTH CONFESSION

The word symptom does not occur one time in Scripture. Let's read Isaiah 33:24, *"And the inhabitant will not say, 'I am sick'; The people who dwell in it will be forgiven their iniquity."*

It is interesting that forgiveness and healing are both in this verse. Let's talk a little about mouth confession though. First of all, mouth confession must always be from Scripture. Don't go around saying, "I confess that that house is mine." Maybe God doesn't want you to have that particular house. You've got to get on a scriptural foundation.

"The inhabitant of Zion will not say I'm sick," is Scripture. You are not to say, "I'm sick." You should say, "I am trusting Jesus for my healing." The word symptom we hear today is an unfortunate word because it is unscriptural. Whenever we use unscriptural language, we will always end up with unscriptural concepts and unscriptural theology.

In the gospels there was a time when Jesus prayed for a blind man. The man replied, "I see men walking as trees!"

Jesus didn't respond, "That's just a symptom. Go your way. Confess that you are healed anyway." Jesus said in effect, "We are going to take another run at this."

Did any disciple ever say, "Well, you just have the symptoms of a disease?" No. That would be a denial of reality.

Christians don't deny reality. If you say, "I've got a symptom of cancer," and we take some cells of that "symptom," put them under a microscope, we will see your "symptom." It is not a symptom at all. It is an actual living cancer that can kill you dead. Don't play games like that. If it is cancer, say, "This is a cancer, I don't receive it. And I put the blood of Jesus against it." Diseases are a very real enemy. They are not symptoms.

For a long time, my wife was working at Bethany Hospital. One day, a Christian Scientologist came in. She had not had any bowel movement in a couple of weeks. She was totally impacted. Her intestines were like concrete. Her confession was, "This is not real. I am not impacted. This is not a problem." The doctor examined her, and they did all their tests, x-rays and sonograms. He said, "There is nothing we can do. She is too far gone. We can do nothing for her." In two or three days the woman died.

This confused my wife. She said, "Lord, if there was ever anyone that was stubborn in her faith, it was this woman. She went so far in faith and yet died. So God, while she was ironing one day, spoke to her saying, "healing is in the blood of Jesus."

It is more important what your faith is in, than how much faith you have. Jesus said, *"...if you have faith as a mustard seed,...* (Matthew 17:20). A mustard seed is the smallest little seed. It is not how big your faith is, it is what object your faith is resting on. This woman had faith, but not in the blood of Jesus. She died.

"Therefore, holy brethren, partakers of the heavenly calling, consider the Apostle and High Priest of our confession, Christ Jesus" (Hebrews 3:1).

Most people do not have a revelation of Jesus as their High Priest. They come to their pastor asking for prayer. What they are saying is, "Hail Pastor, full of grace, pray for me now in the hour of my need." This is the same error as Catholicism. We don't need to go to Mary, or to some pastor. We have immediate access straight to Jesus Himself. Many of us substitute a preacher and ask them for prayer. The thinking is, "My prayers aren't going to get off the ground. I have no intention on repenting. I have no intention of getting in God's presence. So here is my list. Maybe you are closer to God."

Why not go over man's head? Why not go to the headquarters? Why not go to the One seated at the right hand of God? Why not go to your best Friend? Why not go to the One Who gets every prayer answered? Why not say, "Jesus, High Priest, Savior of the world, pray for me now." He'll do it... just for you!

Notice in the above scripture how you can change what Jesus prays for you at the Father's right hand. He is the High Priest, not of His confession, but ours. You increase your confession, you increase His prayer.

When you get up every morning and say, "I am full of Joy." Jesus turns to the Father and says, "Ernie says he is full of Joy." He prays that for you. Then the Holy Spirit releases it. Joy is sent by God to boost you up.

When you get up in the morning and say, "I don't feel so good today. I'm just depressed," Jesus says, "Father, I would like to pray something, but I'm certainly not going to pray that." He is the High Priest of our confession.

What we say is extremely important. When you change what you speak, it changes what Jesus prays because He is the High Priest of what you speak. If you say, "I'm healed by the Blood of the Lamb," Jesus says, "that man believes he is healed by the blood of the lamb." Hebrews 3:1 is probably the best verse on "mouth confession" in the Bible. He is the High Priest of our confession.

Acts 10:38 is a great example of New Testament Healing,

"...how God anointed Jesus of Nazareth with the Holy Spirit and with power, who went about doing good and healing all who were oppressed by the devil, for God was with Him."

Peter was "preaching away" under the anointing. In the middle of his sermon, he said that God anointed Jesus of Nazareth with the Holy Spirit and power. He said Jesus went about doing good, and healing all who were oppressed by the devil because God was with Him.

This verse is a living prayer request. It is a <u>mouth confession</u>. It is a life verse. This is a verse to sink your teeth into.

God anointed Jesus!

We can do nothing without an anointing. But God anointed Jesus Christ of Nazareth with the Holy Ghost <u>and</u> power. We are anointed with power, too. And, Jesus went about doing good... let that be what we do with our lives. Let's go about doing good! Doing good, by healing all those oppressed by the devil.

In the Greek, the word oppressed means "mobbed under." It conveys the idea of having a mob of demons sitting on your head.

Jesus went about doing good, healing all those who were under a mob of oppression. He did this, *"For God was with him."*

Now here is something for us to confess and pray. "Lord, anoint me with the Holy Ghost and power. Help me do good for people and heal all those who are demonized."

God is with you. You can and should claim this verse!

Let every demon shudder when you walk in the room. Have them saying, "There is another one of those people Jesus anointed with the Holy Ghost and with His power. There is healing in their hands and their words. The Holy Ghost is on them."

FORGIVENESS: THE KEY TO HEALING

"Moreover if your brother sins against you, go and tell him his fault between you and him alone. If he hears you, you have gained your brother" (Matthew 18:15).

THE TEMPTATION IS ALWAYS, "TO LET THINGS SLIDE"

The basic key to healing is forgiveness. Matthew 18:15-35 is packed with meaning in relation to healing and forgiveness. As you read this passage in God's Word, you will find that there are seven major themes. I'm just going to hit them each real quick. The first major theme has to do with when we have had a falling out, what do we want to do? Let it slide.

But Jesus says, "No!"

"But if he will not hear, take with you one or two more, that 'by the mouth of two or three witnesses every word may be established'" (Matthew 18:16).

IF YOU DON'T CORRECT THEM, YOU WILL REJECT THEM!

If you can't get things settled, get two or three more to help you. If you still cannot get it settled, take it to the whole church. A relationship cannot survive resentment. It has to be dealt with. If you do not correct a situation, then you automatically reject. If you do not correct things in your marriage, you will reject your wife. If you fail to correct a child, you will end up rejecting that child. It is inevitable.

"And if he refuses to hear them, tell it to the church. But if he refuses even to hear the church, let him be to you like a heathen and a tax collector," (Matthew 18:17).

PENETRATING CLOSED CIRCLES

When someone sins, they draw a cloistered circle around them. They keep every Christian outside of it because they do not want to hear the Word. They become isolated to avoid the Word and correction.

I remember a woman in our church who got caught up in adultery. A couple of sisters went to work on her calling her all of the time. She eventually repented. She said, "I hated it every time you people called, but you kept after me and wouldn't leave me alone. You got inside my circle and God was able to deal with me. I repented."

"Assuredly, I say to you, whatever you bind on earth will be bound in heaven, and whatever you loose on earth will be loosed in heaven. Again I say to you that if two of you agree on earth concerning anything that they ask, it will be done for them by My Father in heaven" (Matthew 18:18-19).

SPIRITUAL WARFARE — SUCCESSFUL SPIRITUAL WARFARE REVOLVES AROUND RIGHT RELATIONSHIPS

The context is getting right with people. You can bind and loose until the cows come home, but <u>if you have hate and resentment towards people, you have already loosed some things that will never be bound</u>. Everyone likes to preach on spiritual warfare, but the number one step toward effective spiritual warfare is to get the hate, resentment and broken relationships healed and forgiven. This <u>is</u> spiritual warfare!

"For where two or three are gathered together in My name, I am there in the midst of them" (Matthew 18:20).

THE PRAYER OF AGREEMENT

Evangelists often come and talk about the power of agreement, but how can you agree when you've got people fighting? This is a magnificently complete passage of God's Word. The purpose of this whole passage is so that ministry can take place... so breakthroughs might occur for you or that something might happen to make you a different man or woman.

FORGIVENESS

Then Peter came to Him and said, "Lord, how often shall my brother sin against me, and I forgive him? Up to seven times? (Matthew 18:21).

Peter thought he was being really generous, magnanimous and full of mercy, "Hey, seven times is enough for any person," he probably thought, but not so.

"Jesus said to him, 'I do not say to you, up to seven times, but up to seventy times seven'" (Matthew 18:22). What a concept!!

Do you think Jesus meant to have us get a scroll and mark down your forgiveness tally? No. Jesus was saying "infinity," forever. It was a Jewish figurative expression. You can't keep a count of forgiveness. Jesus went on to tell a story in Matthew 18:23-24,

"Therefore the kingdom of heaven is like a certain king who wanted to settle accounts with his servants. And when he had begun to settle accounts, one was brought to him who owed him ten thousand talents."

The King is Jesus and a particular servant owes Him ten million dollars. Now, this guy had a debt he could not pay! The man in the parable represents all of us. We all have an incredible debt of sin. We are so far in debt there is no way we can ever pay it all.

"But as he was not able to pay, his master commanded that he be sold, with his wife and children

and all that he had, and that payment be made. The servant therefore fell down before him, saying, 'Master, have patience with me, and I will pay you all'" (Matthew 18:25-26).

The King said, "throw him in prison." The great prison is hell itself. The servant fell down and begged, "have mercy upon me."

Verse 27, *"Then the master of that servant was moved with compassion, released him, and forgave him the debt."*

Jesus hears us! He sent His grace our way!

God looks out and says, "I love you. I am moved with compassion for you. I release you. I forgive you." What joyous news. That is the Gospel. That is Calvary. That is the cross. When was Jesus moved with compassion? When He was hanging on the cross. All of our debt was put on Him. He was condemned for our sins. He suffered our hell and died as a substitute for us all. What a wonderful Savior!

But things turn dark in verse 28,

"But that servant went out and found one of his fellow servants who owed him a hundred denarii; and he laid hands on him and took him by the throat, saying, 'Pay me what you owe!'"

This particular guy went and found a neighbor who owed him the equivalent of about one hundred dollars. Basically it was a day's wages. He demanded, "Pay me what you owe me!" What would the ten million dollar debt man do?

"So his fellow servant fell down at his feet and begged him, saying, 'Have patience with me, & I will pay you all.' And he would not, but went and threw him into prison till he should pay the debt. So when his fellow servants saw what had been done, they were very grieved, and came and told their master all that had been done" (Matthew 18:29-31).

The fellow servants snitched on the unforgiving debtor. They said, "King, you know that guy you just canceled a ten million dollar debt for?"

"Yea."

"He went right out and had a guy who owed him a hundred dollars thrown in jail." The result:

"Then his master, after he had called him, said to him, 'You wicked servant! I forgave you all that debt because you begged me. Should you not also have had compassion on your fellow servant, just as I had pity on you?' And his master was angry, and delivered him to the torturers until he should pay all that was due to him. So My heavenly Father also will do to you if each of you, from his heart, does not forgive his brother his trespasses" (Matthew 18:32-35).

The King became really hot.

Jesus turned to Peter and to our astonishment says, "So likewise will my Heavenly Father do to you. You will be delivered to the tormenters if you do not forgive everyone from your heart."

The tormenters oftentimes turn out to be chest pains, stress, colitis, allergies, headaches, back problems, aches and pains, migraines, arthritis and blockages of healing, etc.

I was praying for a lady once and I started to rebuke her physical condition. The demon spoke out of her and said, "I don't have to let her go. She has hate in her heart." The devil has Matthew 18 memorized, folks.

The devil was saying, "<u>I have a scriptural and legal right to remain here</u> because the Word of God says that you will be delivered to me if you don't forgive." Many times, when a person goes through thorough forgiveness, they are healed instantly.

In Psalm 139:23-24 we can read: *"Search me, O God...And see if there is any wicked way in me."* Literally, in the Hebrew it says, *"If there be any way of pain in me."* If there is any way I have hurt someone or let them down. Oh Lord, I want to know.

The Holy Spirit has an awfully good memory! I've found that people who have not gone through forgiveness usually have a list of 40 to 400 names of people they need to forgive, revealed to them by the Holy Spirit. You must take the time to start with your childhood and work up to the present forgiving every single person, who has hurt you, let you down, rejected you, lied about you, stolen money from you, harassed you, or who did you dirty in any way. It will usually take several days or even weeks, but it is like being saved all over again.

ADMIT AND CONFESS

This is step one. If I ask you, "Do you hate anybody," you would answer, "I don't hate anybody." You would smile really big. But we are so very clever. We switch words to avoid conviction.

If I asked whether you have any hurts, your answer would probably be, "Hundreds of people have hurt me." So let's talk about hurts, wounds, resentments and anger. We are talking about forgiving everyone who has let you down, disappointed you or betrayed you; from your first conscious memory as a child to this very moment.

SPECIFIC PRAYER

A lady came to me for counseling once who was from Germany. She was going from one pastor or counselor to another, all the while suffering from severe depression.

She said on the phone, "God told me to have Ernie Gruen pray for me." I thought, "Well, what do I know?" She had been to four or five key pastors in the city. They were every bit as spiritual as I and I did not feel like I had anything special to offer her.

When she came into my office, I said, "Well, sister, I know one thing. I know what God has taught me about forgiveness. I will share with you what God has shared with me." I then went through Matthew 18 with her and told her the story of "the King," Jesus, who had forgiven this servant a ten million dollar debt. Then we looked at the wicked servant part. I asked her, "Do you have hatred towards any person."

She said in her broken English, "No, no, I do not have any hatred at all."

To tell you the truth, it almost made me mad. I thought to myself, "You are lying through your teeth." I said, "Would you be willing to pray and ask God by the Holy Spirit to reveal to you anyone that you need to forgive.

She said, "Yes, yes!"

So, I had her pray, "Father, by the Holy Spirit, drop into my mind the names or the faces of those who I need to forgive."

I waited a few moments and asked, "Did you get any names?"

She said, "No. I got faces." She continued, "Back in the village in Germany where I was raised, there was a marketplace and I saw every one I ever knew in that marketplace. I saw it, I saw it." She said, "And I hate every one of them!"

Sincerely, before she prayed, she said there was no one. After the prayer, she told me, "The vision from God, was a word of wisdom."

I said, "Well, let's name them." I took her names down one by one. It took us over 2 hours to go through her process of forgiveness. We did a thorough work. She began to forgive the people who had let her down and hurt her. She prayed and blessed each person.

When you do this, the first names you get will most likely be your parents. It doesn't mean you hate them. It means there has been a lot of friction, hurts and wounds. Next you will typically receive the name of your wife or your husband. You will get the names of your children. The first child you get will be the one who is most like you. You are irritated with them because they are just like you! You see your weaknesses and idiosyncrasies in that child. You will get their name. It doesn't mean you hate them. It does mean you have got some praying to do. (Can you tell, I may have done this a time or two, myself?).

I remember one girl I counseled received the face of a boy and said, "In second or third grade, he always pulled my hair. He sat behind me and pulled my hair. I really resented that kid." You may say, "Well, that's pretty insignificant, pastor Ernie."

Not to the Holy Ghost it isn't!

If you do not forgive every one from your heart, you will be delivered to the tormentors. This is real!

You will get the names of people who were "fast" on a date and horrified you. You will get the names of people who violated you. You will get names of people who have verbally abused you. You will get names of people who didn't love you. You will get the names of pastors and elders. You will even get the names of churches or denominations. You've got to clear all that rot out. You could also get the names of other organizations such as clubs, unions and political groups, etc., etc.

CHOOSE TO FORGIVE

I preached the funeral for a boy who was involved in a suicide pact with a girl. The boy shot the girl and then shot himself. I had to stand up and preach at that child's funeral.

What do you say?

Talk about hopelessness and darkness! There are situations where people, seemingly, just don't deserve to be forgiven.

You must choose to forgive them anyhow. Just do it! The scripture is clear, forgiveness is not optional. It is an imperative—an absolute must.

Pray aloud, "I choose to forgive them in the name of Jesus, and by Your blood Jesus, wash away this deep-seated rage, anger and resentment." I forgive them even if they do not deserve to be forgiven, just like you have forgiven me <u>when I did not deserve it</u>.

The blood of Jesus is powerful enough to cleanse us and release our anger to God. He can wash away all of your anger with His blood... so let Him do it.

You may think, "Well, they deserve judgment." Scripture says, "Vengeance is mine. I will repay, saith the Lord." You must learn to say, "Lord, this is your territory. I choose to forgive."

You don't forgive people because they deserve it. You forgive them because you were forgiven when you did not deserve it. And believe me, neither you or I deserved Jesus. You forgive them because the King of all creation canceled your ten million dollar debt.

You are forgiven. You have got to open up your personal jails and release those people who have hurt you in relationship or circumstance as well.

Somewhere in this process, you will find yourself praying and asking forgiveness, for your part in every situation—you must realize that you were not perfect either. You will pray, "Oh God forgive me for letting them down. Forgive me for hurting them." You will realize that no matter how big a jerk they were, you were also wrong and had a bad attitude. No matter how sincere we are, we are imperfect in word or deed.

PEACE, INSTANT HEALING, LIBERTY

I was in South Carolina, in February of 1997, and I preached on forgiveness. A lot of people were healed that day. I was at a conference since then and a choir director came up to me and said, "Do you remember that sermon you preached on forgiveness?"

I said, "Yes."

He said, "One of my choir members could hardly sing. She couldn't breathe. She had lung problems and while you were preaching, she began to forgive people and as she did, she felt that cloud simply pull off. She was instantly healed of her lung condition." Just by forgiving, without any ministry whatsoever from a human being, the tormenters had to leave.

The choir director continued, "My wife was in the meeting too. When we went to get married, the preacher had said something to me, because my wife was kind of a hippie. She had frazzled hair and big long dangly earrings. The preacher said of my fianceé, 'She's a floozy, and you could do a lot better than that!'"

Four or five years later, in a moment of anger, he had told his wife what the preacher had said. He realized, "I should never have done that."

His wife was sitting there during my sermon and the face of that preacher had popped into her mind. She said, "Jesus, I forgive him for calling me a floozy." She too, was instantly healed! All of her oppression lifted off of her. She went home free.

After going through the forgiveness process, I have had people say, "It felt like I got saved for the first time." I have had people say, "I never could pray in tongues until I did this." They were so full of resentment and anger that they couldn't get the baptism to flow in its fullness. When you clear your heart of all resentment, you will be flooded with peace!

My dad was a farmer. He sold his farm and bought an appliance store. Soon after that, my dad died of a cerebral hemorrhage. Two years later my mom sold the store and the guy who bought the place declared bankruptcy. From my perspective, he cheated my mother out of all my dad's life savings. While we couldn't prove it, we thought he had hidden the money. I was praying with someone and the Lord said to me, "You have never forgiven that man."

He may not have even done anything, but in my heart he had stolen my mother's well-being! Right then and there, as God revealed it to me, I forgave that man.

As you go through life, you are going to receive names. You will recall faces.

God desires that you forgive. If you want the best practical piece of advice I can give you, learn to forgive, and keep your heart clear of all hurts, wounds, and resentments.

CHAPTER 14

THE GIFT OF MIRACLES

"Ask, and it will be given to you; seek, and you will find; knock, and it will be opened to you. For everyone who asks receives, and he who seeks finds, and to him who knocks it will be opened" (Matthew 7:7-8).

In the original text, the verbs for ask, seek and knock are all present tense with continuous action. In a correctly translated amplified version this verse would read,

> *"Ask and keep on asking, and it will be given to you. Seek and keep on seeking and you will find. Knock and keep on knocking and it will be opened to you. For everyone who asks receives, and he who seeks finds, and to him who knocks, it will be opened."*

This is how the gift of miracles begins to operate. It operates in askers, seekers and knockers. All miracles start with an understanding of Matthew 7:7-8. When we get lazy, quit reading, quit praying, quit crying, quit praying in tongues, we begin to shut the door and close our hands so that we cannot receive. The door does not remain open when we do not continuously knock. We will not find when we do not seek.

Askers receive. Seekers discover and those who knock have things opened up for them. These are the three levels of receiving. They are the three levels of Christianity. You can backslide from being a seeker into just being an asker. You ask for your things when you are in trouble and receive some help. But, God desires us to do more than simply ask in times of trouble. He wants us to excel to seeking. It is His desire that we continuously discover and find. He wants us to pound on heaven's door with persistent insistence. That is God's will for us.

Think about the story of Jacob wrestling with the angel of the Lord. It is an incredible story found in Genesis, chapter 32. He persisted until he received his blessing. This is how the gifts originate and operate. This is how you move into the miracles of God.

All miracles have their start in prayer, persistence and some form of action. We have to ask. One way to ask is to turn on God's flow of tongues. We need to turn on the spigot. How can God flow through you when you have the faucet turned off?

THE GIFT OF MIRACLES DEFINED

Miracles are supernatural intervention by God. Any answer to prayer is miraculous. Never forget that! It is God showing up in your situation and doing something that you could not do. Since answered prayer is supernatural intervention, it is by nature miraculous. Things will be different from the way they would have been, every time you pray. I believe with all my heart that things change every time you pray. Prayer is an amazing changer of destinies!

The supernatural gift of miracles does not include "natural miracles" such as the birth of a child. I believe that every newborn baby is a miracle, but it is a natural miracle. If you do not believe me, just wait until you have a grandchild. It will give you a good "hallelujah fit." There is nothing like being a grandparent.

Supernatural miracle working power is available to every Christian. The proof is in John 14:12,

> *"Most assuredly, I say to you, he who believes in Me, the works that I do he will do also; and greater works than these he will do because I go to My Father."*

Jesus sent us the Holy Spirit. He ascended to heaven and put His Holy Spirit into the whole Church. Anyone can do the works that Jesus did. These include both the fruit of the Spirit and the gifts of the Spirit.

In Daniel 11:32 we read, *"...the people who know their God shall be strong, and carry out great exploits."* The condition once again is that we ask, seek and knock.

We should ask God the same question that Gideon did,

"...O my lord, if the LORD is with us, why then has all this happened to us? And where are all His miracles which our fathers told us about?" (Judges 6:13).

The Bible is a book of miracles. Our God is a God of miracles. Without miracles there is no Bible. Without miracles there is no God. There are well over 100 definite miracles of God recorded in the Bible. Of them, 88 are listed in Appendix II. The Bible holds miracles of deliverance, miracles of provision, miracles of judgment and miracles of healing.

The Red Sea being divided was a miracle of deliverance. From it we learn that God can make a way where there isn't any possible way. That happens all the time in prayer. I see it all the time!

What about miracles of provision? Some of the disciples had toiled all night fishing and caught nothing. They were professional fishermen from the sea of Galilee. Fishing was the number one occupation in the region. They knew how to manage their boats, nets and employ people. They were sharp men but they caught nothing. Jesus told them, "Go out in the deep, and throw your net over the other side." As far as we know, Jesus was raised in a carpenter's home, not a fisherman's.

They obediently said, "At Your word." As a result of their obedience, they could not even get all of the resulting fish on the boat! They had to call in other boats for help. Businessmen need to pray like this. Ask God where to cast your net. If you are working on the wrong side of the boat, you will work your fingers to the bone and accomplish nothing. If you get a Word from God, you will end up with such an abundance that you will need partners. You will have too much to handle on your own.

Then we also see miracles of judgment in scripture.

Annanias and Saphira were a prime example. They lied to the Holy Spirit. They wanted to be seen as "big money" givers. They wanted to impress people and look good.

Their sin was not in refusing to give all of their possessions. Their sin was that they lied about it. Annanias dropped dead and soon afterwards, his wife did too. That was a miracle! The message to be learned from their tragic story is this: no matter how embarrassing it is, or how bad you may look, just simply tell the truth.

How to Move in the Gift of Miracles

First of all, one must be saturated with the Word of God to move in the Gift of Miracles. Only a man of God who spends time in the Word becomes thoroughly equipped. That is a really awesome statement. You can be thoroughly equipped from what is in Scripture. We see this in II Timothy 3:17, *"...that the man of God may be complete, thoroughly equipped for every good work."*

Then one must also live in continuous consciousness of God's presence. Whether waking or sleeping, we must abide in Christ. *"If you abide in Me, and My words abide in you, you will ask what you desire, and it shall be done for you,"* (John 15:7). That is both an Old and New Covenant principle of God; *"For the eyes of the LORD run to and fro throughout the whole earth, to show himself strong in the behalf of those whose heart is loyal to Him,"* (II Chronicles 16:9).

This is a favorite verse of mine. We must be completely loyal to Jesus. God is looking for any sister or a brother whose heart is completely His. God desires to show Himself strong on this person's behalf.

I hope you are saying, "That's me Lord! My heart is perfect towards God!" If it isn't, make this your prayer now through the precious blood of Jesus.

THE IMPORTANCE OF A WORD

A Word of Wisdom or a Word of Knowledge is a major key to flowing in miracles.

Romans 10:17 says, *"So then faith comes by hearing, and hearing by the word* [rhema] *of God."*

Notice that the New Testament writer uses the word "rhema" here. This means a living word from God. This is a word that jumps right off the page and into you. This word has come alive. As you are reading a scripture, suddenly you realize, "That is awesome and it's for me!" That is "rhema." Faith comes by hearing, and hearing by a "quickened word" from God Almighty.

Now let's compare that with Galatians 3:5, *"Therefore He who supplies the Spirit to you and works miracles among you, does He do it by the works of the law, or by the hearing of faith?"* That question interests me, because the key to a miracle is not works. It flows from <u>hearing</u> a word of faith.

This is kind of like God managing the Holy Spirit Depot. He hands out Holy Ghost power. You ask God, "Well Father, how do I get a new supply of miracles?"

He answers, "It is not by the works of the law, but by the hearing of faith. Miracles are going to come when you hear something from Me!"

As you are praying, something may click inside your spirit and you will just know. God will drop a word of Scripture into you. As you are praying for a son, a daughter, a grandchild, your dad or whoever it is, there comes a hearing of the Word. You get the right mental picture. With this tool you can target your prayers. You are no longer firing arrows off blindly into the sky. You can better see your target. You know what forces are involved or what type of hurt is involved. This comes by the hearing of faith, that originates in a word from God.

"Then Jesus answered and said to them, "Most assuredly, I say to you, the Son can do nothing of Himself, but what He sees the Father do; for whatever He does, the Son also does in like manner" (John 5:19).

This is the conclusion of a story which started in John 5:1. A man had been lying crippled by a pool of water for 38 years waiting for the moving of the water. There was a tradition that whoever got in the water first, as the pool began to move, would be healed. Jesus sat down next to the crippled guy and they started talking. The crippled man said, "I do not have a man to put me in the water. For these last 38 years, someone else has always gotten into the water first!" Jesus ignored the past.

Jesus asked, "Do you want to be made well?"

The answer may be obvious, but not all people who are sick really want to be made well. They may and often do prefer to complain and receive sympathy.

The man said, "I've been lying here by this pool for nearly four decades." Notice that he didn't answer the question Jesus asked. He had been getting offerings and sympathy from people for his living. It had become his life.

Jesus commanded, "Take up your bed and walk," and being that it was the Sabbath the religious people all around Him got upset. They came to Jesus complaining, "Why did you heal this man on the Sabbath?"

Jesus answered them, "<u>I saw My Father do it and whatever I see My Father do, I do</u>." Out of that multitude of people waiting at that pool, Jesus healed one.

How did Jesus move in miracles? He did what He saw His Father doing.

Jesus did not do miracles on His own. The Son could do nothing of Himself. Now, if the Son can do nothing of Himself, where does that leave us? If Jesus did zero without God's revelation and anointing, what about us? Jesus lived with His ears and eyes turned towards heaven. He was always listening from His Father.

Whatever Jesus saw, He did. That is the pattern of the gift of miracles.

How can you and I move in miracles? Ask and keep on asking. Seek and keep on seeking. Knock and keep on knocking – until you receive a word from God. You will become His pipeline of blessing.

Luke 1:36-37 teaches us the same theme. An angel came to Mary in verse 36 saying,

"...Elizabeth your relative has also conceived a son in her old age; and this is now the sixth month for her who was called barren. For with God nothing will be impossible."

In the original Greek this last phrase actually reads, *"No rhema is void of power."* When you get a word from God, it is never lacking in power. Once you hear a word from God, anything can happen to bring it to pass.

Once again, the key to moving in God is to first hear His voice.

DIVINE-HUMAN COOPERATION

Earlier in this book we had an extensive discussion on divine-human cooperation. As it relates to the miraculous, this cooperation is absolutely essential. In order for you to release God's blessings in the lives of others, you must act as a vessel, a pipeline for God's power to flow through. This requires that you be in harmony with His will, and that you obey and act on God's Word.

The person who is receiving a miracle must also cooperate with God. One really good example of this principle was Naaman the leper. (See II Kings 5:1-19). He had a Jewish maiden serving him who told him to go see the prophet Elisha in order to get his healing. Naaman was not a Jew! He was not what we call a "believer," but he heeded the advice of this little Jewish girl and went to meet this prophet of God.

Naaman had great expectations. He thought that Elisha would come out, wave his hands in the air, begin to dance around and see the power of God fall on his leprosy from the sky. It turns out that when Naaman got to Elisha's house, Elisha didn't even come out to say hello.

He sent his servant instead saying, "Go take a bath in the Jordan river seven times and you will be healed." Well, Naaman got really upset. He didn't even get a personal audience with the great prophet. And Naaman was a major leader of his nation, Syria.

As you might imagine, Naaman was disappointed and headed home toward Syria with a bad case of "road rage." He was probably looking for somebody to run over on the way back to Syria in his chariot. The Jordan river is actually a very small body of water and it is very muddy. Let's just say you would not consider washing there if you wanted to feel "Zest-fully" clean! But, as Naaman was charging in his chariot home, his servant said in II Kings 5:13,

"My father, if the prophet had told you to do something great, would you not have done it? How much more then, when he says to you, 'Wash, and be clean?'"

It was a simple assignment – why not do it?

So Naaman went and dipped seven times in the river Jordan and when he came out of the water the seventh time, his flesh was restored to him as if it were that of a newborn child.

Here is a fully grown man dying of an incurable disease that eats your body parts off, being cured forever. Here is where we get to the waving and the shouting part of the miracle! Can you imagine his joy?

Here is the principle of divine-human cooperation in action. There was no healing in the Jordan. There was healing in acting in faith in obedience to God. Whenever someone is healed, I always say, "Run, or do something you couldn't do before. Stretch out your hand. Bend over and touch your toes." The power lies in God, but the obedience rests on us. Faith for miracles comes by hearing. Faith is released by action!

DON'T STOP NOW... PRESS ON!

In the appendices section of this book, is a large but not comprehensive list of the many different kinds of miracles in the Bible. Each one is a revelatory study in its own right. But each of the elements is there in each miracle, in one way or another.

There is always an asking, seeking or knocking soul. There is always a living word or "rhema," or a vision of God's promise – a demonstration to the seeker of His divine desire to bring deliverance, help or victory. And there is always someone who believes. And there is action that completes that divine flow. And the result is the Divine miracle done by the hand of the Living God our Lord and Savior, Jesus Christ.

As you examine the miracles, I want you to ask, seek and knock – for your own life and surrounding circumstances.

God has a word for you – Today!

Faith comes by hearing that rhema God has for you!

CHAPTER 15

THE GIFT OF FAITH

"But without faith it is impossible to please Him, for he who comes to God must believe that He is, and that He is a rewarder of those who diligently seek Him" (Hebrews 11:6).

If you are a believer you will love faith. And, however much faith you have, you will always want more. That is because faith pleases God and we all want to please God. One thing that truly makes God's heart jump for joy is when we trust Him, "I believe in You, Father."

With faith, you see, <u>it is possible to please God</u>!

NOT MERELY SAVING FAITH

"But as many as received Him, to them He gave the right to become children of God, to those who believe in His name" (John 1:12).

Every Christian possesses saving faith, but the gift of faith is different. It is a special type of faith. It is more than a general faith, it is specific faith. A person who possesses general faith can say, "God said it, I believe it, that settles it." The object of this faith is the Word (logos) of God. This general type of faith is simply taking God at His Word.

The Gift of Faith however is a <u>special impartation</u> of faith. This gift comes when God drops His faith into your spirit by the Holy Spirit on a specific occasion. Suddenly, you have a knowing that your prayer is answered. And this faith is a gift from God, neither earned nor merited.

Long ago, God told me, as audible as if it were you talking to me, "Ernie, never fight faith."

Teachers may say something a little extreme at times that sounds off-base to you, regarding faith. But, we all need more faith than we have. Just set aside a teaching if you cannot receive it. If someone's faith doesn't click with you, put that in the filing cabinet for consideration later. You don't have to worry about the accuracy of their teaching. Just realize that you need more faith.

God says we must believe that He is and that He will reward us when we diligently seek Him! Galatians 3:2-3 is a great passage,

> *"This only I want to learn from you: Did you receive the Spirit by the works of the law, or by the hearing of faith? Are you so foolish? Having begun in the Spirit, are you now being made perfect by the flesh?"*

Paul is saying, "Hey, you started your entire Christian life by faith. Are you so foolish, having begun in the spirit (with faith), are you going to be perfected by your flesh?" The answer is obviously no. Perfection can never be reached by the efforts of our flesh. It is a matter of faith. The spiritual life is a faith battle.

Let's consider Mark 11:22, *"So Jesus answered and said to them, 'Have faith in God...'"* In the original Greek New Testament, the word "in" is not actually present. Instead, we should see the word "of." (This is genitive case if you are an English teacher.) And this passage literally says, *"Have the faith of God."* It is about having God's faith. This is an entirely different thing from having faith in God. Jesus was telling us to have God's faith. It isn't your faith. It is a special faith imparted. It is a faith that is given to you.

I was praying for a lawyer's wife during a morning Bible Study. She had two growths on her back. She came forward and asked for prayer. When I laid my hand on her head, I simply knew that she was going to be healed. So, I just rebuked the sickness and those growths left instantly.

After the meeting she went home to her husband who had not been with her. So she said to her husband, "Give me a back rub." Astonished, he said, "Where did those lumps go?"

That was a gift of faith in action! It had nothing to do with me being spiritual or better than her or her husband. It was just faith that God dropped into me.

How to Grow in Faith

The way you begin to move in any gift is by praying in tongues. That gets you going into the flow of the Holy Spirit. It moves you out of the human realm. Praying in tongues is like the river of God flowing right into you. Praying in tongues is the way to have a word of faith released into your spirit. It opens you up to the flow of the Holy Spirit and makes your spirit more receptive to divine leadership.

I'm not creating a formula here, but with all miracles, the second step when moving in faith is usually hearing a specific word from God. <u>When you hear a word from God, faith always comes with it</u>. As you are praying and God gives you a specific word, you will not need a word from anyone else. One word from God is worth ten thousand words from a preacher!

When you hear a word of wisdom or a word of knowledge, faith is there as a natural byproduct. The key is to hear that word. The key to getting that word is praying in tongues and waiting on the Lord.

Getting a Word

"Then the LORD said to me, 'You have seen well, for I am watching over My word to perform it'" (Jeremiah 1:12, NAS)

As you are reading the written Scriptures, which are infallible in the original manuscripts and perfectly preserved by the Holy Spirit for use today, a verse often comes off the page suddenly, and in that instant, this verse begins to mean more to you. God is going to watch over that word that you received because His desire is to perform it.

"The centurion answered and said, 'Lord, I am not worthy that You should come under my roof. But only speak a word, and my servant will be healed'... When Jesus heard it, He marveled, and said to those who followed, 'Assuredly, I say to you, I have not found such great faith, not even in Israel!'" (Matthew 8:8 & 10).

Jesus said, *"I have not found so great a faith in all of Israel."* Can you see what He was saying? Jesus was looking for faith! Jesus marveled at this Centurion!

It astounds me that the Son of God, the Creator of the Universe, would marvel over anything. After all, He knows all things. But here we see this Roman soldier, a Gentile, and Jesus says, *"I have not found so great a faith in all of Israel."* He healed the soldier's servant without even going to his house. The soldier had said, *"Only speak a word."*

Jesus answers, "Whoa. I have not found so great faith among any of the Jews." Jesus was happy. That soldier must have really been a great blessing to Jesus.

Wouldn't it be great to bless Jesus where you are right now? What do you need to believe for today? What is lacking in your life? You don't need to believe for supper if you have it in the cupboard. If you are a gentle and sweet person, you don't need to believe for gentleness.

But if you are a "road rage" person who wants to run people off the road as you shake your fist, you are going to have to gain faith in that area. You need to pray, "Lord Jesus, cleanse me with Your blood of this anger and impatience. Help me to act like You Jesus. I need Your strength made perfect in my weakness." If you have a problem with anger, you must believe for love. If you have a problem with dirty thoughts, you must believe for good thoughts.

Did you know, the dirtiest thoughts you could ever have as far as God sees them, are thoughts of unbelief? Unbelief is nasty. It is ungodly. It displeases God. Impure sexual thoughts are horizontal, filthy, ungodly and simply wicked.

But doubting God is vertical! By doing this, you are basically telling God, *"I think You are a liar."* That goes way beyond nasty, dirty and is utterly corrupt in a different and much more damaging way.

Everyone has several areas in their life that need work. Some of us take great pride over the areas of our life where we have gained victory and thus become self-righteous. We might need some faith to get rid of that self-righteous attitude.

A man asked me one day, "Are you satisfied with your life, Ernie?"

I said, "I am satisfied, that I am not satisfied!" Rejoice in the victory you have, and exercise your faith to move on in, even closer to God.

"Then they were all amazed and spoke among themselves, saying, 'What a word this is! For with authority and power He commands the unclean spirits, and they come out'" (Luke 4:36).

These Jewish people were saying, "Man, there is a powerful word coming forth here."

How did God create the world? He spoke it into existence and in this passage we see demons coming out at Jesus' oral command.

Some of us need to have faith for deliverance. Anyone who has dabbled in the occult, psychic hot-line, seen fortune tellers, read tarot cards or consulted ouijua boards, has picked up a demonic influence and as a result will be depressed. Possibly even suicidal!

You have to confess that what you did was a sin and ask for the blood of Jesus to cleanse you of that sin and command it to leave you. We must despise the occult. We must never read a horoscope in the local newspaper. Faith will get rid of demons. That is what was going on in Luke 4.

"Jesus said to him, 'Go your way; your son lives.' So the man believed the word that Jesus spoke to him, and he went his way" (John 4:50). Jesus healed this nobleman's son right on the spot. Jesus didn't even go to his house. It just says the man believed the word. This is the principle: take hold of any scripture, believe it, and healing can come into your house.

"It is the Spirit who gives life; the flesh profits nothing. The words that I speak to you are spirit, and they are life" (John 6:63).

You see, God's Word is alive! And it brings life to the dying and hurting. Hebrews 4:12 tells us,

"For the word of God is <u>living</u> and powerful, and sharper than any two-edged sword, piercing even to the division of soul and spirit, and of joints and marrow, and is a discerner of the thoughts and intents of the heart"

When you feel that you don't know what is going on around you, get in the Word. Get alone with God. The Word will increase your discernment and bring light to your understanding.

In college I was exposed to the writings of Marx, Stalin and Lenin. I found that they are of a spirit, too – a demonic spirit! In some sense, all books are of a spirit. You must always ask yourself, "What spirit is underneath this writing?"

The Bible is like no other book. The Word of God is alive! It is not a combination of black and red letters on white paper. It is Holy Spirit and it is alive! When you read it, the Spirit comes into you. That life of God is transferred to your innermost being. The Word is sharper than any two-edged sword. This sword can cut two ways. It can bring great blessing, and it can cut off sin as you come under its discernment. It can separate between your soulish realm and your spirit realm. It can figure out what is merely human from what is the Holy Spirit. The Word will reveal the intentions of your heart.

PRAISE IS THE LANGUAGE OF FAITH

Praise IS the language of faith.

You must learn to praise God for the answer before you have received it. Praising flows from the belief that you have already received.

People often ask me, "Should I keep praying or stand on my previous prayers?" If you do not have the assurance of a complete answer, keep on asking, seeking and knocking as Jesus said. But once you have that blessed assurance, switch from petition to praise in your prayer life. You do continue to pray, but your prayer is now worship.

Instead of asking, "Should we continue to pray?" the better question would be, "Am I going to be petitioning God or praising Him?"

You are going to be doing one or the other, but regardless, keep going.

When you hear from God and you know your prayer has been answered, enter into a spirit of praise. If you do not have a complete answer, which does happen from time to time, just keep on. I have often felt like I received an answer, but sensed that it was just a piece in a larger puzzle. People are complex. In cases like this, there is always a mixture of praise when I see that part of the answer is on the way, while I am petitioning for the completion.

Go out on a limb with God. Anything can happen when you will step out in faith beyond your comfort zone.

A SPIRIT OF FAITH

"And since we have the same spirit of faith,
according to what is written, 'I believed and therefore

I spoke,' we also believe and therefore speak" (II Corinthians 4:13).

Faith is a spirit. It is one of the qualities of the Holy Spirit. If faith is a spirit, then unbelief is a spirit as well. Doubt and negativism are demon spirits as well. Paul says, "Because we have the same spirit of faith, we speak." If I listen to you talk for five minutes, I can tell you what kind of spirit you've got. I've only got to listen to your mouth.

I was thinking about Brother Copeland the other day. He has the spirit of faith. There is faith in him. We should all desire to have more faith. What kind of spirit do you have? Once you see that faith is a spirit, wherever you are, you can diagnose what kind of spirit is operating in an individual.

THE SEED

"And Jesus rebuked the demon, and it came out of him; and the child was cured from that very hour. Then the disciples came to Jesus privately and said, 'Why could we not cast it out?' So Jesus said to them, 'Because of your unbelief; for assuredly, I say to you, if you have faith as a mustard seed, you will say to this mountain, 'Move from here to there,' and it will move; and nothing will be impossible for you'" (Matthew 17:18-21).

Do you see what I see?

Jesus said if you have faith as a mustard seed – dynamite things would happen. Have you ever held a mustard seed in your hand? I held one while standing in the garden tomb where Jesus was raised from the dead. These seeds are no larger than the size of a grain of ground pepper. They are exceedingly tiny. It makes no difference how much faith you have. Just take however much faith you've got, and plant it in Him. If you have faith as a mustard seed, you will eventually see results.

We all have that much faith. You wouldn't be saved if you didn't have that much faith. Plant your faith, and throw in some prayer and fasting against your personal mountains. God says you can move your mountains with this faith.

I remember praying over a hippie kid once when God said to me, "He has a demon of cocaine."

I asked the hippie, "Are you on cocaine?" I had never seen him before.

He said, "Yes I am."

Demon of cocaine, you loose him." He was instantly set free and remained free. Those are the kinds of mountains I am interested in moving. How about you?

Let's think about that word "seed." You've got to plant a seed, but how do you plant it? Verse 21 says, *"By prayer and fasting."*

That must be how you plant it. The result is, *"...nothing will be impossible to you."*

This scripture says nothing is impossible to YOU! And this scripture applies to everyone.

So plant it, take the little faith you've got. Start praying. Start fasting. Expect your mountains to move!

EXPEL SIN

I want you to become ruthless about any sin operating in your life. Don't accommodate it. Don't ever adjust or concede to sin. "Well, everyone has a temper," or "everybody has wrong thoughts at times." Be ruthless today! Do not accept sin in your life. Just name the sin and be ruthless about repenting.

I like that word "ruthless." What does ruthless mean?

It means total, radical intensity without adjustment. You have to plant that tiny seed of faith. It may take you a few months, but one day you will get to the place where you can come to church on Sunday morning and say, "Jesus gave me the victory." His is the victory that overcomes the world! You can be at peace with yourself, your family and your God. But you must become ruthless!

Webster Defines "ruthless" as being without compassion or pity. We should have no sympathy for the sin in our lives. There should be no skeletons hidden in the closets of our hearts. We are to be ruthless, expelling the works of darkness to constantly make more room for the Holy Spirit and His work.

> *"Fight the good fight of faith, lay hold on eternal life, to which you were also called and have confessed the good confession in the presence of many witnesses,"* (I Timothy 6:12).

Our fight is the "good" faith fight. There are a lot of bad fights to distract us these days: controversy, hate, bitterness, revenge, getting even, unforgiveness, resentment, anger, hurts and wounds. But, Paul says, "fight the good fight." This battle is always over the issue of whether you are going to doubt or believe God and His Word for you.

He says, *"Fight the good fight, lay hold on eternal life."* Now, there's an awesome connection. By fighting the good fight of faith, you can take a hold of eternal life. He's not talking about initial salvation here. He's talking about having the "zoe" or life-force of God activated within you – active in you!

Let's focus on that word "life." It has to do with how you treat your wife and how well you get along with people. It means being a peacemaker when you see people misunderstanding one another. It also means that you stop drugs and alcohol. Drugs will kill you. Alcohol will kill you.

Fight the good fight of faith and lay hold of God's life – that would be righteousness, joy, peace and the Holy Spirit.

Examine what your attitudes and your habits are – that is all part of having God's life. Fight that good fight of faith! If you are defeated anywhere in your life, the only way to get out of that defeat is by trusting Jesus for the victory. Believe dear saint – is your destiny to both fight and win!

Holiness is where it is at, being like Jesus! Have you got anger towards your relatives? You need to fight that. Don't succumb to it. Don't give in to any cancer of the soul. Fight the good fight of faith and lay hold on eternal life, instead of eternal death.

PERSISTENT FAITH

Luke 18:8 is a very powerful verse on faith. This is the parable of the widow who refused to take "no" from an unjust judge. The parable starts out saying that this unjust judge did not respect God. He did not respect man either.

Jesus said, in effect, The Heavenly Father is a righteous judge. He is fair. Because this woman would not give up, she got her answer. Even from an unjust judge. He ends the parable saying, how much more will you receive your answer if you don't give up. God is just. He wants to say, "Yes!"

We are always to pray and not to faint. Verse 8 asks, *"Nevertheless, when the Son of Man comes, will He really find faith on the earth?"* This is the punch line of the parable.

The battle of the latter day Christian is going to be the faith battle. Jesus says, "Will I really find faith on the earth?"

What is your answer to that question? It should be, "Yes Lord, You will because I am here and I am going to be believing."

If you are going to fight a battle, you need to be fighting where it is significant. You want to be fighting on hill number 7 if that is where the real battle is, instead of sitting in the mess hall on hill number 9. Whether you win or lose the battle depends on faith. Jesus asks you, "Will there be faith when I come back?"

"For whatever is born of God overcomes the world. And this is the victory that has overcome the

world – our faith. Who is he who overcomes the world,
but he who believes that Jesus is the Son of God?"
(I John 5:4-5).

You are going to last if you are born of God. If you were born-again to doctrine and concepts, you cannot help but fail.

He that overcomes the world, is he who believes Jesus is the Son of God. Faith is the fight and the front lines are where the battle rages. We see that faith is the victory and that it overcomes the world.

Just a while back, I received an 8 page document from a Christian that I have known for 20 years. In his mind 1998 was the beginning of the last 7 years spoken of in the book of Revelation. He went through 6 pages of evidence demonstrating how everything will wrap up by the year 2005. Of course he admits that the Bible says nobody knows the day or the hour, but notice that it says nothing about the year. Then a couple days later, a friend that I know equally as well had a vision of worldwide nuclear destruction. In a dream he saw the Eiffel Tower coming down and the Statue of Liberty.

As we move towards that appointed time, we are going to have more essays like that, dreams and visions as well. You may say, "Well, what I want to know is, are they true?"

I cannot say!

I will tell you what most definitely is true, we need to repent and get on with God's program. Get holy and make ready because He is going to come at such an hour that you think not!

My point is that prophesies, dreams and visions abound today. Some of them are going to be way off, and others are going to be partially right. I cannot give you a day or an hour or year, but I am convinced that we are in the last of the last days. <u>The issue today is faith</u> and the good fight God has called us to. Today you need to be thinking about faith.

"For I am not ashamed of the gospel of Christ, for it is the power of God to salvation for everyone who believes, for the Jew first and also for the Greek. For in it the righteousness of God is revealed from faith to faith; as it is written, 'The just shall live by faith'" (Romans 1:16-17).

The first part of the verse says you are saved by faith but the last part of the verse says you live by faith as well. The end of this verse does not speak of salvation. It speaks of living by faith. Paul says, *"from faith to faith."* This could just as well be translated, "faith on top of faith." Our life in Christ starts with faith and continues with faith.

Everything in your Christian life is by faith. The older you get, the more you will realize that you do not have what it takes. You never did have what it takes. All of your promises and all of your commitments are worthless. Even your repentance needs to be repented of. Even the tears you shed need to be washed in the blood of Jesus.

You can not trust your commitments or promises. You must put your faith totally in Jesus. You must have zero faith in your flesh, and 100% of your faith in Jesus. You were saved by faith, healed by faith and baptized in the Holy Spirit by faith. Now God will give you the victory by faith, for God Who dwells inside of you will WIN!

"But thanks be to God, who gives us the victory through our Lord Jesus Christ" (I Corinthians 15:57).

"...everyone born of God overcomes the world. This is the victory that has overcome the world, even our faith!" (I John 5:4, NIV)

APPENDIX ONE

HEALING – NEW TESTAMENT

The word *iaomai* is a Greek word meaning to cure, heal or make whole. It also means to be free from error and sin, or to bring about one's salvation. This word is used 25 times in the New Testament. Of these, 23 instances are used to describe physical healing. The remaining 2 instances describe spiritual healing.

Matthew 8:8, 13, *"The centurion answered and said, 'Lord, I am not worthy that You should come under my roof. But only speak a word, and my servant will be <u>healed</u> . . . Then Jesus said to the centurion, 'Go your way; and as you have believed, so let it be done for you.' And his servant was <u>healed</u> that same hour."*

Matthew 13:15, *"For the hearts of this people have grown dull. Their ears are hard of hearing, and their eyes they have closed, lest they should see with their eyes and hear with their ears, lest they should understand with their hearts and turn, so that I should <u>heal</u> them."*

Matthew 15:28, *"Then Jesus answered and said to her, 'O woman, great is your faith! Let it be to you as you desire.' And her daughter was <u>healed</u> from that very hour."*

Mark 5:29, *"Immediately the fountain of her blood was dried up, and she felt in her body that she was <u>healed</u> of the affliction."*

Luke 5:17, *"Now it happened on a certain day, as He was teaching, that there were Pharisees and teachers of the law sitting by, who had come out of every town of Galilee, Judea, and Jerusalem. And the power of the Lord was present to <u>heal</u> them."*

Luke 6:17, 19, *"And He came down with them and stood on a level place with a crowd of His disciples and a great multitude of people from all Judea and Jerusalem, and from the seacoast of Tyre and Sidon, who came to hear Him and be <u>healed</u> of their* *diseases... And the whole multitude sought to touch Him, for power went out from Him and <u>healed</u> them all."*

Luke 7:7, *"Therefore I did not even think myself worthy to come to You. But say the word, and my servant will be <u>healed</u>."*

Luke 8:47, *"Now when the woman saw that she was not hidden, she came trembling; and falling down before Him, she declared to Him in the presence of all the people the reason she had touched Him and how she was <u>healed</u> immediately."*

Luke 9:2, *"He sent them to preach the kingdom of God and to <u>heal</u> the sick."*

Luke 9:11, *"But when the multitudes knew it, they followed Him; and He received them and spoke to them about the kingdom of God, and <u>healed</u> those who had need of <u>healing</u>."*

Luke 9:42, *"And as he was still coming, the demon threw him down and convulsed him. Then Jesus rebuked the unclean spirit, <u>healed</u> the child, and gave him back to his father."*

Luke 14:4, *"But they kept silent. And He took him and <u>healed</u> him, and let him go."*

Luke 17:15, *"And one of them, when he saw that he was <u>healed</u>, returned, and with a loud voice glorified God."*

Luke 22:51, *"But Jesus answered and said, 'Permit even this.' And He touched his ear and <u>healed</u> him."*

John 4:47, *"When he heard that Jesus had come out of Judea into Galilee, he went to Him and implored Him to come down and <u>heal</u> his son, for he was at the point of death."*

John 5:13, *"But the one who was <u>healed</u> did not know who it was, for Jesus had withdrawn, a multitude being in that place."*

John 12:40, *"He has blinded their eyes and hardened their hearts, Lest they should see with their eyes, Lest they should understand with their hearts and turn, So that I should <u>heal</u> them."*

Acts 9:34, *"And Peter said to him, 'Aeneas, Jesus the Christ <u>heals</u> you. Arise and make your bed.' Then he arose immediately."*

Acts 10:38, *"How God anointed Jesus of Nazareth with the Holy Spirit and with power, who went about doing good and <u>healing</u> all who were oppressed by the devil, for God was with Him."*

Acts 28:8, *"And it happened that the father of Publius lay sick of a fever and dysentery. Paul went in to him and prayed, and he laid his hands on him and <u>healed</u> him."*

Hebrews 12:12-13, *"Therefore strengthen the hands which hang down, and the feeble knees, and make straight paths for your feet, so that what is lame may not be dislocated, but rather be <u>healed</u>."*

James 5:16, *"Confess your trespasses to one another, and pray for one another, that you may be <u>healed</u>. The effective, fervent prayer of a righteous man avails much."*

I Peter 2:24, *"who Himself bore our sins in His own body on the tree, that we, having died to sins, might live for righteousness— by whose stripes you were <u>healed</u>."*

RAPHA

Rapha is a Hebrew word which means: to stitch, to sew up, to mend, to cure, to heal. What follows is an extensive listing of occurrences for this word in the Old Testament. God has always healed His people!

Genesis 20:17, *"So Abraham prayed to God; and God <u>healed</u> Abimelech, his wife, and his female servants. Then they bore children..."*

Genesis 50:2, *"And Joseph commanded his servants the physicians to <u>embalm</u> his father. So the physicians <u>embalmed</u> Israel."*

Exodus 15:26, *"...If you diligently heed the voice of the LORD your God and do what is right in His sight, give ear to His commandments and keep all His statutes, I will put none of the diseases on you which I have brought on the Egyptians. <u>For I am the LORD who heals you.</u>"*

Exodus 21:19, *"if he rises again and walks about outside with his staff, then he who struck him shall be acquitted. He shall only pay for the loss of his time, and shall provide for him to be thoroughly <u>healed</u>."*

Leviticus 13:18, 37, *"If the body develops a boil in the skin, and it is <u>healed</u> . . . But if the scale appears to be at a standstill,* *and there is black hair grown up in it, the scale has <u>healed</u>. He is clean, and the priest shall pronounce him clean."*

Leviticus 14:3, 48, *"And the priest shall go out of the camp, and the priest shall examine him; and indeed, if the leprosy is <u>healed</u> in the leper . . . But if the priest comes in and examines it, and indeed the plague has not spread in the house after the house was plastered, then the priest shall pronounce the house clean, because the plague is <u>healed</u>."*

Numbers 12:13, *"So Moses cried out to the LORD, saying, 'Please <u>heal</u> her, O God, I pray!'"*

Deuteronomy 28:27, 35, *"The LORD will strike you with the boils of Egypt, with tumors, with the scab, and with the itch, from which you cannot be <u>healed</u> . . .The LORD will strike you in the knees and on the legs with severe boils which cannot be <u>healed</u>, and from the sole of your foot to the top of your head."*

Deuteronomy 32:39, *"Now see that I, even I, am He, and there is no God besides Me; I kill and I make alive; I wound and I <u>heal</u>; nor is there any who can deliver from My hand."*

I Samuel 6:3, *"...if you send away the ark of the God of Israel, do not send it empty; but by all means return it to Him with a trespass offering. Then you will be <u>healed</u>, and it will be known to you why His hand is not removed from you."*

I Kings 18:30, *"Then Elijah said to all the people, 'Come near to me.' So all the people came near to him. And he repaired the altar of the LORD that was broken down."*

II Kings 2:21-22, *"Then he went out to the source of the water, and cast in the salt there, and said, 'Thus says the LORD: 'I have <u>healed</u> this water; from it there shall be no more death or barrenness.' So the water remains <u>healed</u> to this day, according to the word of Elisha which he spoke."*

II Kings 8:29, *"Then King Joram went back to Jezreel to recover from the wounds which the Syrians had inflicted on him at Ramah, when he fought against Hazael king of Syria. And Ahaziah the son of Jehoram, king of Judah, went down to see Joram the son of Ahab in Jezreel, because he was sick."*

II Kings 9:15, *"But King Joram had returned to Jezreel to recover from the wounds which the Syrians had inflicted on him when he fought with Hazael king of Syria. And Jehu said, 'If you are so minded, let no one leave or escape from the city to go and tell it in Jezreel.'"*

II Kings 20:5, *"Return and tell Hezekiah the leader of My people, 'Thus says the LORD, the God of David your father: 'I have heard your prayer, I have seen your tears; surely I will <u>heal</u> you. On the third day you shall go up to the house of the LORD.'"*

II Kings 20:8, *"And Hezekiah said to Isaiah, 'What is the sign that the LORD will <u>heal</u> me, and that I shall go up to the house of the LORD the third day?'"*

II Chronicles 7:14, *"if My people who are called by My name will humble themselves, and pray and seek My face, and turn from their wicked ways, then I will hear from heaven, and will forgive their sin and <u>heal</u> their land."*

II Chronicles 16:12, *"And in the thirty-ninth year of his reign, Asa became diseased in his feet, and his malady was severe; yet in his disease he did not seek the LORD, but the physicians."*

II Chronicles 22:6, *"Then he returned to Jezreel to recover from the wounds which he had received at Ramah, when he fought against Hazael king of Syria. And Azariah the son of Jehoram, king of Judah, went down to see Jehoram the son of Ahab in Jezreel, because he was sick."*

II Chronicles 30:20, *"And the LORD listened to Hezekiah and <u>healed</u> the people."*

Job 5:18, *"For He bruises, but He binds up; he wounds, but His hands make whole."*

Job 13:4, *"But you forgers of lies, you are all worthless physicians."*

Psalm 6:2, *"Have mercy on me, O LORD, for I am weak; O LORD, <u>heal</u> me, for my bones are troubled."*

Psalm 30:2, *"O LORD my God, I cried out to You, and You <u>healed</u> me."*

Psalm 41:4, *"LORD, be merciful to me; <u>heal</u> my soul, for I have sinned against You."*

Psalm 60:2, *"You have made the earth tremble; you have broken it; <u>heal</u> its breaches, for it is shaking."*

Psalm 103:3, *"Who forgives all your iniquities, who <u>heals</u> all your diseases."*

Psalm 107:20, *"He sent His word and <u>healed</u> them, and delivered them from their destruction's."*

Psalm 147:3, *"He <u>heals</u> the brokenhearted and binds up their wounds."*

Ecclesiastes 3:3, *"A time to kill, and a time to <u>heal</u>; a time to break down, and a time to build up."*

Isaiah 6:10, *"Make the heart of this people dull, And their ears heavy, And shut their eyes; Lest they see with their eyes, and hear with their ears, and understand with their heart, and return and be <u>healed</u>."*

Isaiah 19:22, *"And the LORD will strike Egypt, He will strike and <u>heal</u> it; they will return to the LORD, and He will be entreated by them and <u>heal</u> them."*

Isaiah 30:26, *"Moreover the light of the moon will be as the light of the sun, And the light of the sun will be sevenfold, As the light of seven days, In the day that the LORD binds up the bruise of His people and <u>heals</u> the stroke of their wound."*

Isaiah. 53:5, *"But He was wounded for our transgressions, He was bruised for our iniquities; The chastisement for our peace was upon Him, and by His stripes we are <u>healed</u>."*

Isaiah 57:18-19, *"I have seen his ways, and will heal him; I will also lead him, And restore comforts to him And to his mourners. 'I create the fruit of the lips: peace, peace to him who is far off and to him who is near,' says the LORD, 'And I will <u>heal</u> him.'"*

Jeremiah 3:22, *"Return, you backsliding children, and I will <u>heal</u> your backslidings. Indeed we do come to You, for You are the LORD our God."*

Jeremiah 6:14, *"They have also <u>healed</u> the hurt of My people slightly, saying, 'Peace, peace!' When there is no peace."*

Jeremiah 8:11, *"For they have <u>healed</u> the hurt of the daughter of My people slightly, saying, 'Peace, peace!' When there is no peace."*

Jeremiah 8:22, *"Is there no balm in Gilead, is there no physician there? Why then is there no recovery for the <u>health</u> of the daughter of my people?"*

Jeremiah 15:18, *"Why is my pain perpetual And my wound incurable, Which refuses to be <u>healed</u>? Will You surely be to me like an unreliable stream, As waters that fail?"*

Jeremiah 17:14, *"<u>Heal</u> me, O LORD, and I shall be <u>healed</u>; Save me, and I shall be saved, For You are my praise."*

Jeremiah 19:11, *"...thus says the LORD of hosts: 'Even so I will break this people and this city, as one breaks a potter's vessel, which cannot be made whole again; and they shall bury them in Tophet till there is no place to bury.'"*

Jeremiah 30:17, *"'For I will restore <u>health</u> to you and <u>heal</u> you of your wounds,' says the LORD, 'Because they called you an outcast saying: 'This is Zion; No one seeks her.'"*

Jeremiah 33:6, *"Behold, I will bring it <u>health</u> and <u>healing</u>; I will <u>heal</u> them and reveal to them the abundance of peace and truth."*

Jeremiah 51:8, *"Babylon has suddenly fallen and been destroyed. Wail for her! Take balm for her pain; Perhaps she may be <u>healed</u>."*

Jeremiah 51:9, *"We would have <u>healed</u> Babylon, But she is not <u>healed</u>. Forsake her, and let us go everyone to his own country; For her judgment reaches to heaven and is lifted up to the skies."*

Lamentations 2:13, *"How shall I console you? To what shall I liken you, O daughter of Jerusalem? What shall I compare with you, that I may comfort you, O virgin daughter of Zion? For your ruin is spread wide as the sea; who can <u>heal</u> you?"*

Ezekiel 34:4, *"The weak you have not strengthened, nor have you <u>healed</u> those who were sick, nor bound up the broken, nor brought back what was driven away, nor sought what was lost; but with force and cruelty you have ruled them."*

Ezekiel 47:8-9, *"Then he said to me: 'This water flows toward the eastern region, goes down into the valley, and enters the sea. When it reaches the sea, its waters are <u>healed</u>. 'And it shall be that every living thing that moves, wherever the rivers go, will live. There will be a very great multitude of fish, because these waters go there; for they will be <u>healed</u>, and everything will live wherever the river goes.'"*

Ezekiel 47:11, *"But its swamps and marshes will not be healed; they will be given over to salt."*

Hosea 5:13, *"When Ephraim saw his sickness, And Judah saw his wound, Then Ephraim went to Assyria and sent to King Jareb; Yet he cannot cure you, Nor heal you of your wound."*

Hosea 6:1, *"Come, and let us return to the LORD; For He has torn, but He will heal us; He has stricken, but He will bind us up."*

Hosea 7:1, *"When I would have healed Israel, Then the iniquity of Ephraim was uncovered, And the wickedness of Samaria. For they have committed fraud; A thief comes in; A band of robbers takes spoil outside."*

Hosea 11:3, *"I taught Ephraim to walk, Taking them by their arms; But they did not know that I healed them.*

Hosea 14:4, *"I will heal their backsliding, I will love them freely, For My anger has turned away from him."*

Zechariah 11:16, *"For indeed I will raise up a shepherd in the land who will not care for those who are cut off, nor seek the young, nor heal those that are broken, nor feed those that still stand. But he will eat the flesh of the fat and tear their hooves in pieces."*

STAY WELL BY MAINTAINING HARMONY

Principles dealing with spiritual warfare and divine health:

1. The number one blockage to healing or deliverance is unforgiveness!

2. If you don't correct someone, you will sooner or later reject them!

3. However, if you correct injudiciously and irresponsibly , you will be rejected.

4. Treat all parties with respect, as persons equal with you. Never be condescending.

5. Do not have a conclusion before the meeting (encounter) has occurred. This is pride! You cannot possibly know all the potentially excellent outcomes God may have for you.

6. Always assume by faith that a situation can be resolved. <u>Faith creates flexibility.</u>

7. Be "<u>solution orientated</u>," not authority orientated!

8. Have a "hearing ear," instead of an authoritative mouth.

9. Prayerfully find a "righteous resolution," <u>instead of imposing your predetermined solution.</u>

10. The temptation in relational problems is always "<u>to let things slide.</u>" Do not let the sun go down on your wrath. (Ephesians 4:26)

11. The power of agreement discussed by Christ in Matthew 18 has a purpose: it is to allow <u>ministry to happen</u> and <u>for breakthroughs to occur</u>! With disharmony, neither will take place consistently.

12. Spiritual warfare <u>primarily involves right relationships</u>. You can bind demons all you want, but if you have <u>unresolved conflicts</u> with real people, you have already set in motion some things that will be impossible to bind, until they are resolved.

APPENDIX TWO
BIBLICAL EXAMPLES OF THE GIFT OF MIRACLES:

Miracles of Deliverance	Miracles of Provision	Miracles of Judgment
Moses' rod and hand Exodus 4:1-8	Waters of sweeten Exodus 15:22-27	Quail Multiplied Numbers 11:31-35
Red Sea divided Exodus 14:21-31	Manna from heaven Exodus 16:14-35	Earth swallows Korah Numbers 16:1-32
Amalek defeated Exodus 17:8-16	Water out of rock Ex. 17:6; Num.20:11	Brazen Serpent Numbers 21:1-9
Jordan river parts Joshua 3:7-17	Clothes and sandals Deuteronomy 29:5	Walls of Jericho Joshua 6:1-21
Samson kills lion Judges 14:6	Meal and oil – Elijah I Kings 17:8-16	Altar at Bethel split I Kings 13:1-5
Aaron's rod blossoms Numbers 17:1-10	Jordan parts – Elijah II Kings 2:8	Three year drought I Kings 17:1-18:41
Fire from heaven I Kings 18:21-39	Jordan parts – Elisha II Kings 2:14	Fire falls from heaven II Kings 1:8-14
Delivered by ditches II Kings 3:11-25	Waters healed-Elisha II Kings 2:18-22	Bears destroy rebels II Kings 2:23-24
3 saved--fiery furnace Daniel 3:1-30	Oil multiplied-Elisha II Kings 4:1-7	Gehazi's leprosy II Kings 5:20-27
Daniel & lion's den Daniel 6:1-28	Pottage healed-Elisha II Kings 4:38-41	Syrian army blinded II Kings 6:15-18
Jonah and the whale Jonah 2:1-10	Food multiplied II Kings 4:42-44	**Miracles of Raising the Dead**
Apostles out of jail Acts 5:16-23	Iron ax swims—Elisha II Kings 6:1-7	Child by Elijah I Kings 17:21-22
Peter from death Acts 12:1-18	Feeding the 5,000 Matthew 14:15-21	Child by Elisha II Kings 4:32-37
Earthquake in jail Acts 16:22-28	Feeding the 4,000 Matthew 15:32-39	Man in Elisha's tomb II Kings 13:21
Paul from ship wreck Acts 27:21-44	Water turned to wine John 2:5-11	Widow of Nain's son Luke 7:11-16
Miracles of Healing	Great catch of fish Luke 5:4-9	Jairus' Daughter Luke 8:41-48
Jeroboam's hand I Kings 13:4-6	Coin in fish's mouth Matthew 17:24-27	Lazarus John 11:1-47
Naaman's leprosy II Kings 5:1-14	2nd great fish catch John 21:5-12	Jesus' resurrection Luke 24:1-6
King Hezekiah II Kings 20:1-11	**Miracles over Nature:**	Dorcas Acts 9:40-42
Not one feeble Psalm 105:37	Sun stopped Joshua 10:12-14	Eutychus Acts 20:9-12
	Tempest stilled Matthew 8:23-27	
	Walking on water Matthew 14:22-32	

BIBLICAL EXAMPLES OF THE GIFT OF MIRACLES (CONT.):

Numerous O.T. Victories not listed	New Testament Healings	Healing in the Book of Acts
Fig tree cursed Matthew 21:19-20	Leper Cleansed Matthew 8:1-5	Lame man healed Acts 3:1-16
Ananias and Sapphira Acts 5:1-10	Centurion's servant Matthew 8:5-13	Peter's shadow Acts 5:15-16
Elymas Acts 13:8-12	Peter's mother-in-law Matthew 8:14-15	Aeneas Acts 9:33-35
King Herod slain Acts 12:19-24	Paralytic Matthew 9:2-6	Lame man Acts 14:8-10
	Lady's issue of blood Matthew 9:20-22	Prayer clothes Acts 19:11-12
	Two blind men Matthew 9:27-31	Paul's viper bite Acts 28:1-6
	Man's withered hand Matthew 12:9-14	Father of Publius Acts 28:7-9
	Syro-Phoenician girl Matthew 15:22-28	
	Lunatic son Matthew 17:14-21	
	Deaf and mute man Mark 7:32-37	
	Blind man Mark 8:22-26	
	Back trouble Luke 13:11-17	
	Man with dropsy Luke 14:1-6	
	Ten lepers Luke 17:12-19	
	Noble man's son John 4:46-54	
	Invalid man John 5:1-9	
	Man born blind John 9:1-41	
	Malchus' ear John 18:10-11	

APPENDIX THREE

DEMONS IN THE NEW TESTAMENT

What follows are the some occasions in the New Testament where demons or unclean spirits are mentioned.

"And Jesus went about all Galilee, teaching in their synagogues, preaching the gospel of the kingdom, and healing all kinds of sickness and all kinds of disease among the people. Then His fame went throughout all Syria; and they brought to Him all sick people who were afflicted with various diseases and torments, and those who were demon-possessed, epileptics, and paralytics; and He healed them" (Matthew 4:23-24).

[δαιμονιζομενους] **dahee-mon-id'-zom-ahee** "daimonizomai:" The ones being demonized.

When we look at the public ministry of Jesus we see that casting out demons was as much a part of His public ministry as was healing. More accurately translated verse 24 says, *"They brought to him sick people afflicted with various diseases and torments and those who were demonized."*

The concept of demon possession we have today is the result of mistranslation. In the Greek, the word "possess" isn't there. We simply have the verb that means demonized. We need to reject the whole concept of demon possession because it ultimately denies personal responsibility and accountability.

Healing and casting out demons are closely linked in this passage. Sometimes in scripture and ministry, there is a direct link between sickness and demonic oppression. In the New Testament, casting out demons is placed under the overall umbrella of healing, by telling us Jesus healed the paralytics, the epileptics and the demonized without distinction.

"Many will say to Me in that day, 'Lord, Lord, have we not prophesied in Your name, <u>cast out</u> demons in Your name, and done many wonders in Your name?' *And then I will declare to them, 'I <u>never knew</u> you; depart from Me, you who practice <u>lawlessness!</u>'"* (Matthew 7:22-23).

[ἐξεβᾶλομεν] **ek-bal'-lo** "ekballo:" we expelled, cast out, demons.

[γινώσκω] **ghin-oce'-ko** "ginosko:" to know at the highest levels of intimacy. In marriage this level of "knowing" implies sexual intercourse.

This is an extremely interesting verse because Jesus did not say, "I once knew you," He said, "I <u>never</u> knew you."

These people were never saved, not even one day in their life. The Greek word for lawlessness is used here as well: [ὀνομίᾳ] **an-om-ee'-ah**, and it means no law, or against the law. These are people who say, "Bless God, I'm going to do what I want to do."

These will be people who, during their life, supposedly operated in the gifts of prophesy, deliverance, healing and so on without "knowing" Christ.

We must make up our minds to reject anything that is not founded on scripture. We cannot accept people's subjective experiences as authoritative. We cannot accept our Christian or charismatic culture as "norms" or as authoritative to justify unscriptural practices. All our doctrine and practice must line up with scripture.

I was in a particular evangelist's meeting, and he did something that was actually pretty dangerous. There were about 250 people in a particular meeting and he said, "I am doing this in Jesus name—I command every demon in this place to manifest itself right now." They did just that.

It was the most unorthodox way of ministering I have ever seen, period. It certainly cannot be found in scripture. For the next two hours, people were falling all over the floor, wriggling like snakes and screaming out. Ten or 20 of us who had been fasting, started going around and casting out demons. It looked like an emergency area after a train wreck— it was the most bizarre thing I have ever seen!

The key to understanding the above verse lies in what Jesus said, "I never knew you," the word translated knew actually means to know intimately. When I first got married, my wife knew me and I knew her – well sort of. 10 years later, I **knew** my wife, and she **knew** me."

That is what Jesus was saying here, "I was never intimate with you."

"When evening had come, they brought to Him many who were demon-possessed. And He cast out the spirits with a word, and healed all who were sick," (Matthew 8:16).

[δᾱιμονιζομενους] **dahee-mon-id'-zo-men-os** "daimonizomenos:" The ones being demonized.

[ἐξεΒᾱλομεν πνεῡμᾱ λαγος] **ek-bal'-lo-men** "ekballo," **pnyoo'-mah** "pneuma," **log'-os** "logos:" literally, He cast out the spirits with a word.

Again we see healing and deliverance from demons placed side by side. There is a connection. This passage says, He cast out the spirits with a "logos," or Word of God, *"In the beginning was the* (logos) *Word...with God...was God,"* (John 1:1-3). Getting into the Word will enable you to loose a lot of demons from their hold on people. We can cast out spirits with scripture.

One day the phone rang and a little tiny voice said, "Are you Ernie Gruen?"

I said, "Yes, I am."

"Did you write a book called, "Freedom to Choose?"

"Yes."

And then she started pouring out her life to me on the phone. This 19-year-old girl had cried night and day for the last year. She had been clinically diagnosed as a manic-depression case. As we were talking, I got to thinking about Isaiah 40:31,

> "But, they that wait upon the Lord shall renew their strength. They shall mount up with wings as eagles. They shall run and not be weary. They shall walk and not faint" (KJV).

I asked, "Have you been waiting on the Lord?"

"No I haven't," she said.

"Have you been looking at the scripture?" I asked.

"No," was her reply.

I said, "Well, no wonder you are weary. I am going to give you an assignment. Read Isaiah chapter 40 through 48, and when you finish these chapters, read the entire Gospel of John.

She thought she had committed the "unpardonable sin." A couple hours later in the evening she called me back and we talked again. She was in her right mind. All it took was a Word from God to end her depression.

Can you see the point I am making with this story? The Word of God will without human intervention, set people free from demons. You may not have to confront the person or the demon in some kind of dramatic situation. The person doesn't even have to realize what you are doing. In fact, it's often better they don't. Just give them the Word of God. The Word alone will often bring deliverance.

Getting in God's presence is always the first step towards permanent deliverance.

> "When He had come to the other side, to the country of the Gergesenes, there met Him two demon-

possessed men, coming out of the tombs, exceedingly fierce, so that no one could pass that way. And suddenly they cried out, saying, 'What have we to do with You, Jesus, You Son of God? Have You come here to torment us before the time?' Now a good way off from them there was a herd of many swine feeding. So the demons begged Him, saying, 'If You cast us out, permit us to go away into the herd of swine.' And He said to them, 'Go.' So when they had come out, they went into the herd of swine. And suddenly the whole herd of swine ran violently down the steep place into the sea, and perished in the water. Then those who kept them fled; and they went away into the city and told everything, including what had happened to the demon-possessed men. And behold, the whole city came out to meet Jesus. And when they saw Him, they begged Him to depart from their region" (Matthew 8:28-34).

[δύο δᾳμονιζομενους] **doo'-o** "duo," **dahee-mon-id'-zom-ahee** "daimonizomai:" literally, two demonized men.

As you read this scripture, there are some things which practically jump off the page. First of all, the demons knew that their end was a place of eternal torment. Also, the demons knew exactly who Jesus was. They recognized His deity. In their query, "*What have we to do with You, Jesus, You Son of God?*" we can tell right off that they were in direct opposition to Christ.

Notice their demented attitude toward the person of Jesus. They obviously saw God as a tormenter. What a distorted view of Jesus, our Savior! He has come to save and to help. He died on the cross to accomplish that. A demonized person often gets it all backwards.

I see people all the time who do not believe that God loves them, which is a primary sign of demonic activity. As we see in this verse, a demonized person also tends to be oppressed by more than one demon. Demons travel in packs or groups. If someone has a demon of lust, they will probably also have other sexual categories of demons.

Of notable importance is the fact that these demons had to ask permission of Jesus to leave the man and enter the pigs. They were under the Lord's sovereignty. They begged Jesus to permit them to go into the pigs. After getting permission, the demons left and immediately destroyed the hogs.

The heart of a demon is focused on how to steal, kill and destroy! (See John 10:10).

"As they went out, behold, they brought to Him a man, mute and demon-possessed. And when the demon was cast out, the mute spoke. And the multitudes marveled, saying, "It was never seen like this in Israel! But the Pharisees said, "He casts out demons by the ruler of the demons" (Matthew 9:32-34).

[ανθρωπος κωφας δᾳμονιζομενους] **anth'-ro-pos** "anthropos," **ko-fos** "kophos," **dahee-mon-id'-zo-men-os** "daimonizomeno:" a demonized deaf man.

THE DANGER OF DELIVERANCE

"When an unclean spirit goes out of a man, he goes through dry places, seeking rest, and finds none. Then he says, 'I will return to my house from which I came.' And when he comes, he finds it empty, swept, and put in order. Then he goes and takes with him seven other spirits more wicked than himself, and they enter and dwell there; and the last state of that man is worse than the first. So shall it also be with this wicked generation" (Matthew 12:43-45).

Key Words:

[ἀκάθαρτος πνεῦμᾳ] **ak-ath'-ar-tos** "akathartos," **pnyoo'-mah** "pneuma:" an unclean, lewd, impure spirit.

[σχολάζω] **skhol-ad'-zo** "scholazo:" to be unoccupied, empty, to take a holiday.

[σὅραω] **sar-o'-o** "saroo:" swept.

[κοσμέω] **kos-meh'-o** "kosmeo:" put in order

Here we see maintaining deliverance goes way beyond removing evil and getting one's life in order. It is important to replace the old occupant of "the house" with a real One who will keep it that way... the Spirit of God. It is noteworthy also that an entire "generation" can become "demonized."

"And behold, a woman of Canaan came from that region and cried out to Him, saying, 'Have mercy on me, O Lord, Son of David! My daughter is <u>severely</u> <u>demon-possessed</u>'" (Matthew 15:22).

[κακῶς δᾳμονιζομενους] **kak-oce'** "kakos," **dahee-mon-id'-zom-ahee** "daimonizomai:" badly demonized; The New American Standard Version says, *"my daughter is grievously vexed with a demon."*

"And when they had come to the multitude, a man came to Him, kneeling down to Him and saying, 'Lord, have mercy on my son, for he is an <u>epileptic</u> and <u>suffers</u> <u>severely</u>; for he often falls into the fire and often into the water. So I brought him to Your disciples, but they could not cure him.' Then Jesus answered and said, 'O faithless and perverse generation, how long shall I be with you? How long shall I bear with you? Bring him here to Me.' And Jesus rebuked the demon, and it came out of him; and the child was cured from that very hour" (Matthew 17:14-18).

Key Words:

[σελ ηνιάζομᾳι]   **sel-ay-nee-ad'-zom-ahee**
"seleniazomai:" to be moon-struck, crazy, or a lunatic

[κακῶς πάσχω] **kak-oce'** "kakos," **pas'-kho** "pascho:" sore or grievously vexed

"Now there was <u>a man</u> in their synagogue <u>with</u> <u>an unclean spirit</u>. And he cried out, saying, 'Let us

alone! What have we to do with You, Jesus of Nazareth? Did You come to destroy us? I know who You are; the Holy One of God!' But Jesus rebuked him, saying, 'Be quiet, and come out of him!' And when the unclean spirit had convulsed him and cried out with a loud voice, he came out of him. Then they were all amazed, so that they questioned among themselves, saying, 'What is this? What new doctrine is this? For with authority He commands even the unclean spirits, and they obey Him'" (Mark 1:23-27).

A man in the synagogue tells us that, this event happened during church! Don't be surprised if people start acting out "demonically" in any spiritual setting. It is to be expected, so be prepared.

[ανθρωπος εὐ ἀκάθαρτος πνεῦμᾳ] the unique construction of the Greek here indicates that the man was **in** an unclean spirit, not the reverse.

Points of Interest:

1. He cried out: disruptive, the personality of demons.
2. Note the plurals: demons travel in packs, i.e. groups.
3. Demons know their eternal destiny.
4. Demons know who Jesus is.
5. Jesus refused their testimony. Demons offer "flattery" or legitimate praise in an effort to hide, avoid expulsion, or lull others into toleration of their presence.
6. The man was "in" the evil spirit, rather than the evil spirit being "in" him. He was in an evil spirit as we are in a cloud.

Key Words of Note:

[φιμαω] **fee-mo'-o** "phimoo:" be muzzled, be quiet

[σπᾶρόσσω] **spar-as'-so** "sparasso:" = to convulse, to tear and the demons also cried out with a loud voice.

"At evening, when the sun had set, they brought to Him all who were sick and those who were demon-

possessed. And the whole city was gathered together at the door. Then He healed many who were sick with various diseases, and cast out many demons; and He did not allow the demons to speak, because they knew Him" (Mark 1:32-34).

[δἁιμονιζομενους]   **dahee-mon-id'-zom-ahee**
"daimonizomai:" demonized.

Points of interest:

1. "Whole city gathered:" deliverance will get a crowd.

2. "Many" went through deliverance that were from the city. In a crowd you can expect "many" to need ministry and deliverance not just one or two, but many.

3. Jesus did not allow the demons to speak. Because of their given ability to distract, demons will attempt to direct God's moving among us by acting out. We should not try and get them to "act out" just get rid of them.

"And He was preaching in their synagogues throughout all Galilee, and casting out demons" (Mark 1:39).

Casting out demons was a fundamental and constant part of the ministry of Jesus, to churches! Demonic activity is not a "rare" thing... people need deliverance.

"For He healed many, so that as many as had afflictions pressed about Him to touch Him. And the unclean spirits, whenever they saw Him, fell down before Him and cried out, saying, 'You are the Son of God.' But He sternly warned them that they should not make Him known" (Mark 3:10).

Some so called "slaying in the spirit" is actually a demon manifesting itself at the presence of Jesus. We should always see if a person's needs are met, after they fall under the power. It can be the power of God, a demonic manifestation, or a trained human fleshly happening. We need to carefully discern the difference.

"And He went up on the mountain and called to Him those He Himself wanted. And they came to Him. Then He appointed twelve, that they might be with Him and that He might send them out to preach, and to have <u>power</u> *to heal sicknesses and to cast out demons"* (Mark 3:13-15).

Not only did Jesus cast out demons, but as soon as He chose the twelve disciples, they did too. He appointed them to do three things: <u>to preach, to heal sickness and cast out demons</u>. A functional New Testament Church must do these three things to represent Christ's ministry in the earth.

The Greek word used here for power is "Ex-soo-si-a" and it means authority. We have been given authority to heal sickness. There are two Greek words which are commonly translated power. One is [ἐξονσίᾳ] "exousia" which means to have authority. The other is [δύνᾳμις] "dunamis" which is where we derive our word dynamite and dynamo. Dunamis means power, ability and strength. A policeman's gun has "dunamis" power, but his badge and commission "oath of office" is his exousia or authority.

When it comes to the spiritual world, the issue is never who has the Dunamis, but who has the Exousia. Jesus gave the 12 <u>authority</u> (Exousia) to cast out demons, and heal the sick.

He has given us that very same authority in His name. It is our responsibility to use that authority to cast out demons and heal the sick. That is our God-given commission, just as much as it is to preach the gospel!

"And the scribes who came down from Jerusalem said, 'He has Beelzebub,' and, 'By the ruler of the demons He casts out demons.' So He called them to Himself and said to them in parables: 'How can Satan cast out Satan? If a kingdom is divided against itself, that kingdom cannot stand. And if a house is divided against itself, that house cannot stand. And if Satan

has risen up against himself, and is divided, he cannot stand, but has an end. No one can enter a strong man's house and plunder his goods, unless he first binds the strong man. And then he will plunder his house. Assuredly, I say to you, all sins will be forgiven the sons of men, and whatever blasphemies they may utter; but he who blasphemes against the Holy Spirit never has forgiveness, but is subject to eternal condemnation' – because they said, 'He has an unclean spirit'" (Mark 3:22-30).

Here scribes from Jerusalem opposed Jesus and deliverance, by attributing His power to Beelzebub or the devil. Intellectuals always have a problem with deliverance.

First bind the strong man, the Greek word for strong is [ἰσχυρὰς] **is-khoo-ros'** "ischuros:" violent, boisterous.

"Then they came to the other side of the sea, to the country of the Gadarenes. And when He had come out of the boat, immediately there met Him out of the tombs a man with an unclean spirit, who had his dwelling among the tombs; and no one could bind him, not even with chains, because he had often been bound with shackles and chains. And the chains had been pulled apart by him, and the shackles broken in pieces; neither could anyone tame him. And always, night and day, he was in the mountains and in the tombs, crying out and cutting himself with stones. When he saw Jesus from afar, he ran and worshiped Him" (Mark 5:1-6).

[ἀκόθαρτος πνεῦμᾳ] **ak-ath'-ar-tos** "akathartos," **pnyoo'-mah** "pneuma:" a man **in** an unclean spirit.

This man was dwelling among the tombs (i.e. the dead). And he was extremely violent, completely untamed; possessing a supernatural strength. He was living in the mountains, withdrawn, a loner, isolated and asocial. His crying and cutting indicated his intense feelings of guilt and suicidal tendencies. He attempted a twisted form of self-atonement through self-mutilation.

When this man saw Jesus from afar, he ran to, and worshiped Him. Thus demonstrating that his free will was yet intact, and was still operating. He came to Jesus from afar, and he ran; he didn't walk. He worshipped Him.

[προσκυνέω] **pros-koo-neh'-o** "proskuneo" means to "kiss the hand."

In the New Testament this was done by kneeling or prostration to do homage to one, or in order to express respect and make supplication. This was the kind of homage shown only to men and beings of superior rank!

> *"And he cried out with a loud voice and said, 'What have I to do with You, Jesus, Son of the Most High God? I implore You by God that You do not torment me.' For He said to him, 'Come out of the man, unclean spirit!'"* (Mark 5:7-8).

This man's demon possessed an abnormal view of God as His tormentor.

A "legion" is a large body of soldiers. In the time of Augustus Caesar, a single legion would have consisted of 6,826 men (6,100 foot soldiers, and 726 horsemen).

> *"Also he begged Him earnestly that He would not send <u>them</u> out of the country. So all the demons begged Him, saying, 'Send us to the swine, that we may enter them.' And at once Jesus gave them permission. Then the unclean spirits went out and entered the swine (there were about two thousand); and the herd ran violently down the steep place into the sea, and drowned in the sea"* (Mark 5:10-13).

Demons desperately want to inhabit something in order to manifest their evil personality. Notice that demons have to ask permission of Jesus before doing anything! [ἐπιτρέπω]

ep-ee-trep'-o "epitrepo:" to allow, to permit, to give leave. By the way, Jews were not supposed to have pigs.

"And those who saw it told them how it happened to him who had been demon-possessed, and about the swine. Then they began to plead with Him to depart from their region. And when He got into the boat, he who had been demon-possessed begged Him that he might be with Him. However, Jesus did not permit him, but said to him, 'Go home to your friends, and tell them what great things the Lord has done for you, and how He has had compassion on you'" (Mark 5:16-19).

Verses 16-19 give us the <u>five-fold evidences of deliverance.</u> <u>The man was</u>:

1. sitting – founded in stability.

2. clothed.

3. apparently in his right mind, and thinking reasonably.

4. went home to live with his family.

5. called to be living witness in the community where he lived.

"He called the twelve to himself, and began to send them out two by two and gave them [Exousia, power or authority] *over <u>unclean spirits</u>"* (Mark 6:7).

"So they went out and preached that people should repent. And they cast out many demons, and anointed with oil many who were sick, and healed them" (Mark 6:12-13).

[ἐξουσίᾳ], **ex-oo-see'-ah** "exousia:" Authority.

[ἀκάθαρτος], **ak-ath'-ar-tos** "akathartos," [pneuma] **pnyoo'-mah** "pneuma:" Evil Spirits or demons.

It was a fundamental part of the ministry of the 12 disciples to both cast out demons and heal the sick.

[ἐξεβᾶλομεν πολύς δᾳμανιον] **ek-bal'-lo pol-oos' dahee-mon'-ee-on** "ekballo," "polus," "daimonion:" cast out many demons.

This passage also shows the apostles anointing with oil those who were sick and oppressed by demons. One day, I stepped out in front of a pulpit and was holding the communion elements in my hand. As I did, the Lord said to me, "If I could put My anointing in prayer cloths, don't you think I can put it in the communion?" In a split second my theology changed. I realized that communion was more than a symbol.

The Lord said, "Withdraw from those who take the form of godliness, but deny the power thereof," (see II Timothy 3:5). I would never deny the power of water baptism, or communion, or anointing with oil. God doesn't institute anything as an empty form.

We then have three specific acts of obedience by which to impart grace:

Baptism, Communion and Anointing with oil.

I remember a college student who came to the elders at my church. He had been given only six months to live. He said, "The Bible says to anoint the sick with oil. I want to be anointed for my healing from God."

He said, we did and so did God!

That boy did not die! He didn't "feel the power" or see any bright lights flashing, either. There was nothing dramatic or demonstrative. But the boy was healed by the power of God... through the grace of God transmitted in anointing him with oil.

He obeyed God's word, asking that the elders be assembled and that they would anoint him with oil. We did our part – the young man believed – and God did His part by healing him.

"From there He arose and went to the region of Tyre and Sidon. And He entered a house and wanted no one to know it, but He could not be hidden. For a woman whose young daughter had an unclean spirit heard about Him, and she came and fell at His feet. The woman was a Greek, a Syro-Phoenician by birth, and she kept asking Him to cast the demon out of her daughter. But Jesus said to her, 'Let the children be filled first, for it is not good to take the children's bread and throw it to the little dogs.' And she answered and said to Him, 'Yes, Lord, yet even the little dogs under the table eat from the children's crumbs.' Then He said to her, 'For this saying go your way; the demon has gone out of your daughter.' And when she had come to her house, she found the demon gone out, and her daughter lying on the bed" (Mark 7:24-30).

This amazing passage tells of Jesus casting a demon out of a girl, when the girl wasn't even present! This is a precedent setting event in scripture as far as deliverance is concerned. People will be delivered, even while sitting in a jail cell somewhere, just because you pray for them. Never give up on anyone because you can't get your hands on them!

"And He asked the scribes, 'What are you discussing with them?' Then one of the crowd answered and said, 'Teacher, I brought You my son, who has a mute spirit. And wherever it seizes him, it throws him down; he foams at the mouth, gnashes his teeth, and becomes rigid. So I spoke to Your disciples, that they should cast it out, but they could not.' He answered him and said, 'O faithless generation, how long shall I be with you? How long shall I bear with you? Bring him to Me.' Then they brought him to Him. And when he saw Him, immediately the spirit convulsed him, and he fell on the ground and wallowed, foaming at the mouth. So He asked his

father, 'How long has this been happening to him?'
And he said, 'From childhood. And often he has thrown
him both into the fire and into the water to destroy
him. But if You can do anything, have compassion on
us and help us.' Jesus said to him, 'If you can believe,
all things are possible to him who believes.'
Immediately the father of the child cried out and said
with tears, 'Lord, I believe; help my unbelief!' When
Jesus saw that the people came running together, He
rebuked the unclean spirit, saying to it, 'Deaf and
dumb spirit, I command you, come out of him and
enter him no more!' Then the spirit cried out, convulsed
him greatly, and came out of him. And he became as
one dead, so that many said, 'He is dead.' But Jesus
took him by the hand and lifted him up, and he arose.
And when He had come into the house, His disciples
asked Him privately, 'Why could we not cast it out?'
So He said to them, 'This kind can come out by nothing
but prayer and fasting" (Mark 9:16-29).

Key Words:

[αλαλος] **al'-al-os** "alalos:" a mute spirit, lacking the faculty of speech. Functioning much like an epileptic seizure:

[κατᾶλαμβάνω] **kat-al-am-ban'-o** "katalambano:" seizes, grasps, lays hold of

[ῥήγνυμι] **hrayg'-noo-mee** "rhegnumi:" to tear in pieces, to cause convulsions

[ὀφρίζω] **af-rid'-zo** "aphrizo:" to foam at the mouth

[τρίζω] **trid'-zo** "trizo:" to gnash (grind, grit) one's teeth

[ξηρᾷνω] **xay-rah'ee-no** "xeraino:" to waste away, to dry up, to wither

[σπλαγχνίζομᾷι] **splangkh-nid'-zom-ahee** splagchnizomai:" to have the bowels yearn, to be moved with compassion, to feel sympathy (the bowels were regarded to be the seat of love/pity).

"Now John answered Him, saying, 'Teacher, we saw someone who does not follow us casting out demons in Your name, and we forbade him because he does not follow us.' But Jesus said, 'Do not forbid him, for no one who works a miracle in My name can soon afterward speak evil of Me" (Mark 9:38-39).

John had become sectarian and narrow minded; the power is in the Name of Jesus! John thought the name of Jesus worked because of his special "calling" to ministry – not so. Jesus made it clear, "My name will work for anybody who uses it in faith."

"...in My name they will cast out demons..." (Mark 16:17). Casting out demons is a sign of being a believer.

"When the sun was setting, all those who had any that were sick with various diseases brought them to Him; and He laid His hands on every one of them and healed them. And demons also came out of many, crying out and saying, 'You are the Christ, the Son of God!' And He, rebuking them, did not allow them to speak, for they knew that He was the Christ," (Luke 4:40-41).

Demons often will come out crying, screaming, shouting aloud. Expect it and don't be shocked.

"And He came down with them and stood on a level place with a crowd of His disciples and a great multitude of people from all Judea and Jerusalem, and from the seacoast of Tyre and Sidon, who came to hear Him and be healed of their diseases, as well as those who were tormented with unclean spirits. And they were healed. And the whole multitude sought to touch Him, for power went out from Him and healed them all," (Luke 6:17-19).

Tormented, troubled, vexed by unclean spirits come from the Greek word [ὀχλέω] **okh-leh'-o** "ochleo:" which means to be mobbed, molested, vexed. This passage demonstrates the word oppression—oppressed or mobbed by the devil. Demons run in packs to increase their power and influence.

"And that very hour He cured many of infirmities, afflictions, and evil spirits; and to many blind He gave sight" (Luke 7:21).

[θεράπεύω πονηρᾳς πνεῦμα] **ther-ap-yoo'-o** "therapeuo," **pon-ay-ros'** "poneros," **pnyoo'-mah** "pneuma:" the phrase means Jesus cured many of unclean spirits. We derive the English words "therapy" and "therapeutic" from the Greek word "therapeuo." In English they mean an ongoing course of healing or restorative treatment.

"For John the Baptist came neither eating bread nor drinking wine, and you say, 'He has a demon,'" (Luke 7:33).

John the Baptist accused of having a demon (Matt 11:18). No matter the means of delivery. When you get involved in any level of ministry, you started the likelihood of being accused of demonic possession. Which in today's language, might mean they call you "insane."

"Now it came to pass, afterward, that He (Jesus) went through every city and village, preaching and bringing the glad tidings of the kingdom of God. And the twelve were with Him, and certain women who had been healed of evil spirits and infirmities – Mary called Magdalene, out of whom had come seven demons..." (Luke 8:1-2).

Deliverance is customary and ordinary: Mary Magdalene was restored to a normal productive life in serving Christ after her delivery. Her life was not a "stigma" socially, it was a testimony to the power and grace of a living Christ.

"Then they sailed to the country of the Gadarenes, which is opposite Galilee. And when He stepped out on the land, there met Him a certain man from the

city who had demons for a long time. And he wore no clothes, nor did he live in a house but in the tombs. When he saw Jesus, he cried out, fell down before Him, and with a loud voice said, 'What have I to do with You, Jesus, Son of the Most High God? I beg You, do not torment me!' For He had commanded the unclean spirit to come out of the man. For it had often seized him, and he was kept under guard, bound with chains and shackles; and he broke the bonds and was driven by the demon into the wilderness. Jesus asked him, saying, 'What is your name?' And he said, 'Legion,' because many demons had entered him. <u>And they begged Him that He would not command them to go out into the abyss.</u> Now a herd of many swine was feeding there on the mountain. So they begged Him that He would permit them to enter them. And He permitted them. Then the demons went out of the man and entered the swine, and the herd ran violently down the steep place into the lake and drowned. When those who fed them saw what had happened, they fled and told it in the city and in the country. Then they went out to see what had happened, and came to Jesus, and found the man from whom the demons had departed, sitting at the feet of Jesus, clothed and in his right mind. And they were afraid. They also who had seen it told them by what means he who had been demon-possessed was healed. Then the whole multitude of the surrounding region of the Gadarenes asked Him to depart from them, for they were seized with great fear. And He got into the boat and returned. Now the man from whom the demons had departed begged Him that he might be with Him. But Jesus sent him away, saying, 'Return to your own house, and tell what great things God has done for you.' And he went his way and proclaimed throughout the whole city what great things Jesus had done for him. So it was, when Jesus returned, that the *multitude welcomed Him, for they were all waiting for Him"* (Luke 8:26-40).

[αβυσσος] **ab'-us-sos** "abussos:" bottomless pit, abyss, a very deep gulf or chasm in the lowest parts of the earth used as the common receptacle of the dead and especially as the abode of demons.

This passage gives us the eight signs of demonic oppression:

- Wore no clothes.
- Homeless.
- A loner.
- Loud voice, interruptive.

- Abnormal fear of God.
- Violence.
- Supernatural strength.
- 'Driven' behaviors.

"Now it happened on the next day, when they had come down from the mountain, that a great multitude met Him. Suddenly a man from the multitude cried out, saying, 'Teacher, I implore You, look on my son, for he is my only child. And behold, a spirit seizes him, and he suddenly cries out; it convulses him so that he foams at the mouth, and it departs from him with great difficulty, bruising him. So I implored Your disciples to cast it out, but they could not.' Then Jesus answered and said, 'O faithless and perverse generation, how long shall I be with you and bear with you? Bring your son here.' And as he was still coming, the demon threw him down and convulsed him. Then Jesus rebuked the unclean spirit, healed the child, and gave him back to his father. And they were all amazed <u>at the majesty of God</u>. But while everyone marveled at all the things which Jesus did, He said to His disciples" (Luke 9:37-43).

[μεγαλειότης] **meg-al-i-ot'-ace** "megaleiotes:" means the magnificence of God; majesty of God; the visible splendor of the divine majesty. Destroying demonic influence brings a revelation to people regarding the glory of God! Deliverance glorifies God!

A spirit seizes upon a boy who suddenly cries out. The evil spirit convulses the boy who foams at the mouth. The spirit departs from him with great difficulty, bruising him. Jesus zeros in on the problem and chief obstacle to deliverance – unbelief!

Unbelief is a form of believing ideas that are contrary to the mind of God. It is not doubt per se, nor is it non belief or indifference – it represents a choice to not believe what one reasonably knows should be believed.

"Then the seventy returned with joy, saying, 'Lord, even the demons are subject to us in Your name.' And He said to them, 'I saw Satan fall like lightning from heaven. Behold, I give you the authority to trample on serpents and scorpions, and over all the power of the enemy, and nothing shall by any means hurt you. Nevertheless do not rejoice in this, that the spirits are subject to you, but rather rejoice because your names are written in heaven" (Luke 10:17-20).

The testimony of the Seventy is given here as they returned from a season of ministry, was one of great joy, not fear. They reported that the demons were subject to them in Jesus Name. True believers, with a "right spirit" will rejoice not cower at the prospect, promise or provision of deliverance from demonic influence in the world around them.

[οὐ μή] **oo may** "ou me:" Nothing shall by any means hurt you. A double negative in the Greek language always strengthens the denial, that is to say, "never, certainly not, not at all, and by no means shall anything hurt you!"

"And He was casting out a demon, and it was mute. So it was, when the demon had gone out, that the mute spoke; and the multitudes marveled. But some of them said, 'He casts out demons by Beelzebub, the ruler of the demons.' Others, testing Him, sought from Him a sign from heaven. But He, knowing their thoughts, said to them: 'Every kingdom divided

against itself is brought to desolation, and a house divided against a house falls. If Satan also is divided against himself, how will his kingdom stand? Because you say I cast out demons by Beelzebub. And if I cast out demons by Beelzebub, by whom do your sons cast them out? Therefore they will be your judges. But if I cast out demons with the finger of God, surely the kingdom of God has come upon you" (Luke 11:14-20).

They could not explain away the miracle, so they dangerously attributed it to be from the devil.

"But if I cast out demons <u>with the finger</u> of God, surely the kingdom of God has come upon you," an ominous statement that Jesus made! <u>When demons are expelled it is a manifestation of God's Kingdom coming upon us.</u>

"Now He was teaching in one of the synagogues on the Sabbath. And behold, there was a woman who had a spirit of infirmity eighteen years, and was bent over and could in no way raise herself up. But when Jesus saw her, He called her to Him and said to her, 'Woman, you are loosed from your infirmity.' And He laid His hands on her, and immediately she was made straight, and glorified God. But the ruler of the synagogue answered with indignation, because Jesus had healed on the Sabbath; and he said to the crowd, 'There are six days on which men ought to work; therefore come and be healed on them, and not on the Sabbath day.' The Lord then answered him and said, 'Hypocrite! Does not each one of you on the Sabbath loose his ox or donkey from the stall, and lead it away to water it? So ought not this woman, being a daughter of Abraham, whom Satan has bound; think of it; for eighteen years, be loosed from this bond on the Sabbath?' And when He said these things, all His adversaries were put to shame; and all the multitude

rejoiced for all the glorious things that were done by Him. Then He said, 'What is the kingdom of God like? And to what shall I compare it? It is like a mustard seed, which a man took and put in his garden; and it grew and became a large tree, and the birds of the air nested in its branches.' And again He said, 'To what shall I liken the kingdom of God? It is like leaven, which a woman took and hid in three measures of meal till it was all leavened'" (Luke 13:10-21).

[πνεῦμα ἀσθένεια] **pnyoo'-mah** "pneuma" **as-then'-i-ah** "astheneia:" Back trouble was caused by a spirit of sickness for 18 years, an amazing fact!

This incident happened in church a (synagogue) with an angry preacher and a shameful collection of supposed believers.

This woman was called by Jesus a "daughter of Abraham"—Interesting, she must have been a child of faith!

Notice the Kingdom connections to the parables in verses 18-21.

"On that very day some Pharisees came, saying to Him, 'Get out and depart from here, for Herod wants to kill You.' And He said to them, 'Go, tell that fox, 'Behold, I cast out demons and perform cures today and tomorrow, and the third day I shall be perfected'" (Luke 13:31-32).

Jesus here gave what turns out to be an amazing prophecy that healing and deliverance will continue for 2,000 years (the church age), until His day i.e. the millennium. Refer also to these verses: Hosea 6:1-2; II Peter 3:8-9. Study these passages together for a tremendous revelation—one day is as a thousand years.

"Therefore there was a division again among the Jews because of these sayings. And many of them said, 'He has a demon and is mad. Why do you listen to

Him?' Others said, 'These are not the words of one
who has a demon. Can a demon open the eyes of the
blind?'" (John 10:19-21).

Jesus causes a division among the people. This still
happens today. <u>Deliverance causes a division also.</u>

"'Did not Moses give you the law, yet none of you
keeps the law? Why do you seek to kill Me?' The people
answered and said, 'You have a demon. Who is seeking
to kill You?'" (John 7:19-20).

Jesus was accused of having a demon by the crowd.

"And believers were increasingly added to the
Lord, multitudes of both men and women, so that they
brought the sick out into the streets and laid them on
beds and couches, that at least the shadow of Peter
passing by might fall on some of them. Also a multitude
gathered from the surrounding cities to Jerusalem,
bringing sick people and those who were <u>tormented</u>
by unclean spirits, and they were all healed. Then the
high priest rose up, and all those who were with him
(which is the sect of the Sadducees), and they were
filled with indignation" (Acts 5:14-17).

[ὀχλέω πνεῦμα ἀκάθαρτος] **okh-leh'-o** "ochleo"
pnyoo'-mah "pneuma" **ak-ath'-ar-tos** "akathartos:" vexed
with unclean spirits. "Tormented with unclean spirits," here
literally means to be mobbed by unclean spirits.

"Then Philip went down to the city of Samaria
and preached Christ to them. And the multitudes with
one accord heeded the things spoken by Philip,
hearing and seeing the miracles which he did. For
unclean spirits, crying with a loud voice, came out of
many who were possessed; and many who were
paralyzed and lame were healed" (Acts 8:5-8).

In the Greek, the word "possessed" does not occur, it is
simply "having unclean spirits" they came out, crying with a

loud voice i.e. shrieking. <u>Here is a primary incident of post ascension, non-apostolic deliverance from physical maladies and demons.</u>

"...how God anointed Jesus of Nazareth with the Holy Spirit and with power, who went about doing good and healing all who were oppressed by the devil, for God was with Him." (Acts 10:38).

This verse summarizes Jesus' life and ministry.

Because God was with Him, He healed all who were oppressed by the devil. The devil makes people sick. If God is with us, we, through Christ should be in the healing and deliverance business.

[ἰὀομ̃α κατὰδυνὰστεύω πᾶς διὰβολος] **ee-ah'-om-ahee** "iaomai" **pas** "pas" **kat-ad-oo-nas-tyoo'-o** "katadunasteuo" **dee-ab'-ol-os** "diabolos:" <u>this Greek phrase literally means, curing or healing all those exploited tyrannized, dominated, oppressed by the devil.</u>

[κατὰδυνὰστεύω] **kat-ad-oo-nas-tyoo'-o** "katadunasteuo:" to exercise harsh control over another, to use one's power against another.

"Now it happened, as we went to prayer, that a certain slave girl possessed with a <u>spirit of divination</u> met us, who brought her masters much profit by fortune-telling. This girl followed Paul and us, and cried out, saying, 'These men are the servants of the Most High God, who <u>proclaim to us the (literally "a" — no definite article in the Greek) way of salvation.</u>' And this she did for many days. But Paul, greatly annoyed, turned and said to the spirit, 'I command you in the name of Jesus Christ to come out of her.' And he came out that very hour. But when her masters saw that their hope of profit was gone, they seized Paul and Silas and dragged them into the marketplace to the authorities. And they brought them to the

magistrates, and said, 'These men, being Jews, exceedingly trouble our city'" (Acts 16:16-20).

[Πύθων] **poo'-thone** "Puthon:" having a python spirit, a spirit of divination—very interesting. One famous American fortune teller testified in her writings of a vision where she "looked into the python's eyes and the saw the wisdom of the ages."

Literally, the demon was demeaning the message of Christ: "they announce unto us 'a' way of salvation. Jesus is not "a" way, He is <u>THE</u> way!

"Now God worked unusual miracles by the hands of Paul, so that even handkerchiefs or aprons were brought from his body to the sick, and the diseases left them and the evil spirits went out of them" (Acts 19:11-12).

This exceptional scripture tells of <u>miracles of healing and deliverance that came by means of prayer cloths</u>. We continue to see healing and deliverance from evil spirits mentioned side by side. These prayer cloths brought about both healing and deliverance. A truly interesting point to remember. Paul did not have to be present to cast out the demons and heal diseased bodies.

"Then some of the itinerant Jewish exorcists took it upon themselves to call the name of the Lord Jesus over those who had evil spirits, saying, 'We exorcise you by the Jesus whom Paul preaches.' Also there were seven sons of Sceva, a Jewish chief priest, who did so. And the evil spirit answered and said, 'Jesus I know, and Paul I know; but who are you?' Then the man in whom the evil spirit was leaped on them, overpowered them, and prevailed against them, so that they fled out of that house naked and wounded. This became known both to all Jews and Greeks dwelling in Ephesus; and fear fell on them all, and the name of the Lord Jesus was magnified. And many who had

believed came confessing and telling their deeds. Also,
many of those who had practiced magic brought their
books together and burned them in the sight of all.
And they counted up the value of them, and it totaled
fifty thousand pieces of silver. So the word of the Lord
grew mightily and prevailed" (Acts 19:13-20).
[περιέρχομα̣ι   ἐξορκιστής] **per-ee-er'-khom-ahee**
"perierchomai" **ex-or-kis-tace'** "exorkistes:" "wandering
exorcists," is a non-Christian word; and never used of Jesus
or the apostles. It is only found once in the New Testament.
These exorcists traveled from place to place like modern
"Gypsy fortune-tellers." People may recognize demonic
activity without being saved... only the saved should use that
name against demonic activity. The literal translation of
demonic dialogue, "Jesus I know, and I am acquainted with
Paul, but who are you?"

"Now we have received, not the spirit of the world,
but the Spirit who is from God, that we might know
the things that have been freely given to us by God"
(I Corinthians 2:12).

Literally, "Now we have not received the spirit of the
world, but <u>"the spirit out of God,"</u> in order that we may know
the things that have been freely given to us by God."

"Rather, that the things which the Gentiles
sacrifice they sacrifice to demons and not to God, and
I do not want you to have fellowship with demons.
You cannot drink the cup of the Lord and the cup of
demons; you cannot partake of the Lord's table and
of the table of demons" (I Corinthians 10:20-21).

Here all Gentile religions are said to be demonic;
fellowshipping with demons; drinking the cup of demons; or
partaking at the table of demons.

"Now the Spirit expressly says that in latter times
some will depart from the faith, giving heed to

deceiving spirits and doctrines of demons, speaking lies in hypocrisy, having their own conscience seared with a hot iron, forbidding to marry, and commanding to abstain from foods which God created to be received with thanksgiving by those who believe and know the truth. For every creature of God is good, and nothing is to be refused if it is received with thanksgiving; for it is sanctified by the word of God and prayer" (I Timothy 4:1-5).

The phrase "giving heed to deceiving spirits and doctrines of demons," tells us that demons work primarily in the realms of deceit and false doctrines. In some sense, every demon is religious. Demons love religion. All religion contrary to the Bible is demonic in origin.

"You believe that there is one God. You do well. Even the demons believe – and tremble!" (James 2:19).

Simply believing that God exists, is not saving faith. The demons know that God is real and they tremble because they know hell is real. We must receive Jesus as our Master and Savior in order to be saved.

"This wisdom does not descend from above, but is earthly, sensual, <u>demonic</u>" (James 3:15).

[δαιμονιώδης] **dahee-mon-ee-o'-dace** "daimoniodes:" demon-like wisdom; proceeding from an evil spirit. (This is the only occurrence of this Greek word in the New Testament.) Note the demonic wisdom is earth based... in the natural realm where the senses are in operation. We walk by faith not by sight!

"But the rest of mankind, who were not killed by these plagues, <u>did not repent of the works of their hands, that they should not worship demons</u>, and idols of gold, silver, brass, stone, and wood, which can neither see nor hear nor walk" (Revelation 9:20).

The principle here is that demons accept, indeed desire, to be worshipped.

"And I saw three <u>unclean spirits like frogs coming out of the mouth</u> of the dragon, out of the mouth of the beast, and out of the mouth of the false prophet. For they are <u>spirits of demons</u>, performing signs, which go out to the kings of the earth and of the whole world, to gather them to the battle of that great day of God Almighty" (Revelation 16:13-14).

Demonic spirits will engineer and bring about the battle of Armageddon.

"And he cried mightily with a loud voice, saying, 'Babylon the great is fallen, is fallen, and has become a dwelling place of demons, a prison for every foul spirit, and a cage for every unclean and hated bird!'" (Revelation 18:2).

Babylon represents a combination of a world wide religion and political machine – the dwelling place of demons and every foul spirit.

QUESTIONS RELATING TO DEMON POSSESSION

I have ministered all over the world and I have come across a number of questions repeatedly that believers ask. The most frequently asked questions are:

1. Is there really such a thing as demon possession?

No. Wherever you see that in your Bible, it is an incorrect translation. The word "possession" is never coupled with "demon" anywhere in the original Greek. The Greek simply says "demonized," which means affected or controlled by demons. Why the translators added the word possession, I do not know.

Unfortunately, using the word "possession" tends to deny or minimize personal responsibility and accountability. Every person has been "demonized" at some point in their life...

But nobody is possessed to the point of having no control. The issue is not whether a person has a demon, but how thoroughly they have been "demonized."

2. Why do demonized people tend to manifest symptoms of more than one demon?

Demons tend to travel in packs or herds. Throughout scripture you will notice that when demons speak of themselves, they speak of themselves using plural words. "What do _we_ have to do with you?" "Have you come to torment _us_?" As you take people through deliverance, you will see certain clusters, such as, depression, despondency, discouragement, disillusionment, dejection. All those are companion spirits. If you run into one, the others are probably hanging around in proximity. They flock together in sinister, wicked alliances.

3. Can demons attach themselves to property? Is there any way to protect our homes?

When you buy a house, you really need to go through it and cleanse it, literally to get the demons out of it! You need to command every demon that is in the air, on the property, under, around or over it to get out! But know that wherever you are living is the property of Jesus Christ since you are a child of God. Spirits can and do inhabit certain properties, places or things. Remember, angels are spirits too, sent to minister for the heirs of salvation.

4. Why is it that many people get more upset about losing property than people, especially when it comes to demon possession?

This Addendum on demonology contains numerous examples of this. In Matthew 8:28-34, Jesus casts hundreds of demons out of a man, sending them into a herd of pigs. The man was restored to his proper mind, but the pigs all ran off a cliff and died. This resulted in the city leaders coming out to Jesus and asking him to leave. Matthew records no gratitude from the city for restoring the man's life. They only cared about their possessions.

As demonic oppression seeps in, people always lose interest in their family, parents, children and work. These are the symptoms of demonic oppression.

It would be nice if scripture said: "Behold the whole city came out to meet Jesus. And when they saw Him, they said, 'Oh it's so wonderful that you set this man free! Please hold your next meeting here in our city.'"

But, that is not what they said. Instead, they said, "Depart from our region, your ministry costs us our pigs!"

Deliverance is not popular. If you have been given a deliverance ministry, people will fight it. And, they will fight it because they are affected by demonic influence – they probably need deliverance themselves.

5. Can a true Christian commit suicide?

Suicide is the result of demonic activity, plain and simple. There is only one unpardonable sin however, which is not suicide! People who commit suicide can go to heaven! It is wrong, but it is not tantamount to blaspheming the Holy Spirit. A person is saved by Jesus, not by their works. Furthermore, there are people who committed suicide in God's Word listed right along with the heroes of faith. Samson for example knowingly committed suicide and he is listed with the heroes found in Hebrews 11! Some people who commit suicide are obviously are lost. Some are obviously saved.

A demon spirit brings depression, despondency, rejection and self-condemnation, which can lead a person to take his own life. Like a dark storm cloud hanging overhead, they are under that spirit's shadow.

When somebody commits suicide, that killer demon will invariably try to inhabit someone else in the immediate family, without exception. So, if you know someone that has lost a family member through suicide, get some ministry to them.

There was a man we knew well who committed suicide and as my wife was counseling his widow, she asked, "Have you had any thoughts regarding suicide yourself?"

The woman gasped, "No never – at least – not until my husband died. But I've been thinking about taking my life ever since."

That demon went down the family tree looking for a person to inhabit. In such cases, efforts must rebuke it and stop this progression with the name of Jesus.

You have the tools to make sure that this particularly deadly spirit doesn't hop from place to place—the blood of Jesus and the Name of Jesus.

6. What role does anointing play in healing and deliverance from demons?

Deliverance can come through the anointing of oil. The Bible says that when the apostles anointed prayer cloths, demons departed. More importantly, it says that people were delivered.

I believe this form of New Testament deliverance has a lot to do with your faith in God's grace for you. Whenever you mix faith with something, power is released. Otherwise it is just a form of Godliness without power. Communion is just religious form if you do not believe it does anything. But when you receive and consume the elements, believing that the Holy Spirit is literally in the bread and the cup, you will see results.

"According to your faith, be it unto you," is the way it works! This principle applies to anointing with oil.

7. How does demonic activity relate to the unity and sense of brotherhood within a church?

The answer to this is found in Psalm 133. *"Behold, how good and how pleasant it is For brethren to <u>dwell together in unity</u>! It is like the <u>precious oil upon the head</u>, Running down on the beard, The beard of Aaron, Running down on the edge of his garments. It is like the dew of Hermon, Descending upon the mountains of Zion; For there the LORD commanded the blessing – Life forevermore."*

When there is unity in a church or a family, there is life. I love this verse because it says where there is unity, God the Father turns to God the Son and says, "Command the blessing right there Son!" If the Lord commands a blessing, you better get ready because it <u>will</u> come. My church doesn't have unity because I am a excellent pastor, we have unity because of the grace of God!

Life is too short to bicker and fight. When you see fighting in church, it is so sad. When people are fighting in their own home, that too is really sad. Unity brings precious anointing.

8. Where can I receive more information? Pastor Gruen has a detailed outline study of every New Testament passage on demons which can be obtained by contacting him by e-mail at: ejgruen@juno.com

REFERENCE BIBLIOGRAPHY

Hewett, James Allen, *"New Testament Greek – A Beginner and Intermediate Grammar,"* Hendrickson Publishers, Inc., Peabody, MA, 1989.

Green, Jay P. Sr., *"The Interlinear Greek-English New Testament,"* Trinitarian Bible Society, London, England, 1976.

"The Englishman's Greek New Testament," Zondervan Publishing House, Grand Rapids, MI, 1970.

W. E. Vine, M.A., *"Vine's Expository Dictionary of New Testament Words,"* Mac Donald Publishing Company, Mc Lean, VA.

Spiros Zodhiates, *"The Hebrew-Greek Key Study Bible,"* AMG Publishers, Chattanooga, TN, 1994.

"Strong's Exhaustive Concordance of the Bible," Mac Donald Publishing Company.

"Young's Analytical Concordance to the Bible," WM. B. Eerdmans Publishing Company, Grand Rapids, MI.

Rex electronics rm 111
Scottish Inn
on l on 49
post budget inn on l